THE STRING QUARTET, 1750–1797

The String Quartet, 1750–1797

Four types of musical conversation

MARA PARKER
Widener University, USA

ASHGATE

Published by
Ashgate Publishing Limited
Gower House
Croft Road
Aldershot
Hampshire GU11 3HR
England

Ashgate Publishing Company
131 Main Street
Burlington, VT 05401-5600 USA

Ashgate website: http://www.ashgate.com

British Library Cataloguing in Publication Data
Parker, Mara
     The string quartet, 1750 - 1797 : four types of musical
     conversation
     1. String quartet 2. Music - 18th century
     I.Title
     785.7'194

Library of Congress Cataloging-in-Publication Data
Parker, Mara, 1957-
     The string quartet, 1750-1797 : four types of musical conversation / Mara Parker.
       p. cm.
     Includes bibliographical references and index.
     ISBN 1-84014-682-6
     1. String quartet – 18th century. I. Title.

ML1160.P37 2002
785'.7194'09033–dc21

                 2002019634

ISBN 1 84014 682 6

Printed and bound in Great Britain by MPG Books Ltd, Bodmin, Cornwall

Contents

List of musical examples   vii

Preface   xi

1   The string quartet as chamber music   1

2   Social aspects: from private to public   25

3   String quartet types: toward a reconsideration   47

4   The lecture   75

5   The polite conversation   127

6   The debate   183

7   The conversation   235

8   The string quartet during the second half of the eighteenth century   279

Personalia   283

Bibliography   291

Index   309

List of musical examples

3.1	Johann Georg Distler, Book II, Quartet No. 5 in C Major, Menuetto.	57
3.2	Johann Baptist Vanhal, Op. 1, No. 4, Mvt. II, mm 1–18.	59
3.3	Johann Georg Distler, Book II, Quartet No. 5 in C Major, Trio.	61
3.4	Felice de Giardini, Op. 14, No. 1, Mvt. IV.	62
3.5	Paul Wranitzky, Op. 23, No. 5, Mvt. I, mm 1–101.	66
3.6	Franz Hoffmeister, Op. 9, No. 2, Mvt. I, mm 88–162, cello part.	73
4.1	Antonín Kammel, Op. 4, No. 6, Mvt. I, mm 1–56.	84
4.2	Ignace Pleyel, Ben 302, Mvt. I, mm 1–89.	89
4.3	Ignace Pleyel, Ben 302, Trio.	93
4.4	Franz Neubauer, Op. 7, No. 3, Mvt. II, mm 1–18.	95
4.5	Franz Neubauer, Op. 7, No. 3, Mvt. II, minore section.	95
4.6	Wolfgang Amadeus Mozart, K.155, Mvt. III, mm 1–32.	99
4.7	Placidus Cajetan von Camerloher, *Sinfonia a 4tro* [in C Major], Mvt. I, mm 1–70.	102
4.8	Luigi Boccherini, G220, Mvt. I.	106
4.9	Luigi Boccherini, G165, Mvt. I, mm 1–23.	111
4.10	Gaetano Brunetti, Quartet in A Major, Mvt. III, mm 1–34.	113
4.11	Gaetano Brunetti, Quartet in A Major, Mvt. III, mm 90–127.	115
4.12	Pierre Vachon, Op. 11, No. 6, Mvt. II, mm 47–64.	117
4.13	Franz Danzi, Op. 6, No. 2, Mvt. I, mm 57–84.	119
4.14	Ignace Pleyel, Ben 346, Mvt. II, mm 17–32.	122
4.15	Joseph Schmitt, Op. 5, No. 2, Trio.	125
5.1a	Antoine Laurent Baudron, *Sei Quartetti*, No. 2, Mvt. III, mm 5–12.	134
5.1b	Antoine Laurent Baudron, *Sei Quartetti*, No. 2, Mvt. III, mm 21–26.	135
5.2	Ignace Pleyel, Ben 314, Mvt. I, mm 19–45.	136
5.3	Jean-Baptiste Sébastien Bréval, Op. 1, No. 3. Mvt. III, mm 37–61.	140
5.4	Ignace Pleyel, Ben 347, Mvt. I, mm 36–73.	144

5.5   Jean-Baptiste Sébastien Bréval, Op. 18, No. 4, Mvt. III,
       mm 29–66.   146
5.6   Nicolas-Joseph Chartrain, Op. 4, No. 5, Mvt. III,
       mm 103–122.   149
5.7   Giuseppe Maria Cambini, T57, Mvt. II.   151
5.8   Giuseppe Maria Cambini, T28, Mvt. I, mm 1–75.   157
5.9   Franz Anton Hoffmeister, Op. 9, No. 1, Mvt. I, mm 1–94.   162
5.10   Ferdinand Fränzl, Op. 1, No. 4, Mvt. I, mm 150–174.   169
5.11   Václav Pichl, Op. 13, No. 1, Mvt. I, mm 50–57.   171
5.12   Nicolas-Marie Dalayrac, Op. 8, No. 5, Mvt. I, mm 1–66.   173
5.13   Nicolas-Marie Dalayrac, Op. 8, No. 5, Mvt. I, mm 84–97.   177
5.14a Franz Krommer, Op. 4, No. 2, Mvt. I, mm 68–82.   179
5.14b Franz Krommer, Op. 4, No. 2, Mvt. I, mm 118–132.   180
6.1   Joseph Haydn, Op. 33, No. 2, Mvt. I, mm 1–14.   190
6.2   Joseph Haydn, Op. 33, No. 2, Mvt. I, mm 42–48.   191
6.3   Franz Hoffmeister, Op. 14, No. 3, Mvt. II, mm 1–8.   192
6.4   Franz Hoffmeister, Op. 14, No. 3, Mvt. II, mm 28–54.   193
6.5   Pierre Vachon, Op. 11, No. 6, Mvt. I, mm 1–64.   196
6.6   Joseph Schmitt, "Quartetto" in G, Mvt. I, mm 1–22.   199
6.7   Hyacinthe Jadin, Op. 1, No. 1, Minuet.   202
6.8   Pierre Vachon, Op. 5, No. 2, Mvt. III, mm 1–16.   204
6.9   Carlo d'Ordonez, Op. 1, No. 1, Mvt. III, mm 9–18.   207
6.10   Carlo d'Ordonez, Op. 1, No. 1, Mvt. III, mm 26–34.   208
6.11   Anton Teyber, Op. 2, No. 3, Mvt. I, mm 1–24.   210
6.12   Gaetano Brunetti, Op. 4, No. 4, Mvt. III, mm 38–70.   213
6.13   Nicolas-Joseph Chartrain, Op. 4, No. 5, Mvt. I, mm 58–89.   216
6.14   Wolfgang Amadeus Mozart, K.458, Mvt. IV, mm 97–112.   220
6.15   Karl Ditters von Dittersdorf, *Sei Quartetti*, Quartetto IV,
       Mvt. I, mm 1–46.   222
6.16   Karl Ditters von Dittersdorf, *Sei Quartetti*, Quartetto IV,
       Mvt. I, mm 82–109.   225
6.17   Johann Baptist Vanhal, Quartet in A Major (A1), Mvt. IV,
       mm 1–8.   228
6.18   Johann Baptist Vanhal, Quartet in A Major (A1), Mvt. IV,
       mm 17–30.   228
6.19   Franz Krommer, Op. 5, No. 1, Mvt. I, mm 1–8.   230
6.20   Franz Krommer, Op. 5, No. 1, Mvt. I, mm 29–61.   231
7.1   Luigi Boccherini, G.168, Mvt. III, mm 17–24.   240
7.2a   Luigi Boccherini, G.168, Mvt. III, mm 29–30.   240
7.2b   Luigi Boccherini, G.168, Mvt. III, mm 33–34.   241
7.3   Carlo d'Ordonez, Op. 1, No. 1, Mvt. I, mm 1–6.   242

7.4	Joseph Haydn, Op. 50, No. 2, Mvt. IV, mm 30–50.	244
7.5	Joseph Haydn, Op. 50, No. 2, Mvt. IV, mm 94–140.	246
7.6	Florian Leopold Gassmann, H.478, Mvt. II, mm 1–60.	251
7.7	Wolfgang Amadeus Mozart, K.590, Mvt. II, mm 9–28.	254
7.8	Wolfgang Amadeus Mozart, K.590, Mvt. II, mm 63–77.	257
7.9	Joseph Haydn, Op. 71, No. 2, Trio.	259
7.10a	Gaetano Brunetti, Quartet in A Major, Mvt. I, mm 30–33.	260
7.10b	Gaetano Brunetti, Quartet in A Major, Mvt. I, mm 58–62.	261
7.10c	Gaetano Brunetti, Quartet in A Major, Mvt. I, mm 95–98.	261
7.10d	Gaetano Brunetti, Quartet in A Major, Mvt. I, mm 115–119.	262
7.10e	Gaetano Brunetti, Quartet in A Major, Mvt. I, mm 145–148.	262
7.11	Franz Krommer, Op. 5, No. 2, Mvt. III, mm 1–32.	265
7.12	Ignaz von Beecke, Quartet in C Major (M1), Mvt. I, mm 33–41.	267
7.13	Giuseppe Maria Cambini, Op. 11, No. 3 (T45), Mvt. II.	270
7.14	Luigi Boccherini, G.222, Trio.	274
7.15	Joseph Haydn, Op. 55, No. 2, Minuet.	276

Preface

The string quartet of the second half of the eighteenth century is often presented as a medium which underwent a logical progression from first-violin dominated homophony to the conversation among four equal participants. To a certain extent, this holds true if one restricts oneself to the works of Haydn and Mozart, and some of their contemporaries. My own research initially led to me believe this be to a provable and convincing argument. Once I began examining the actual works, however, I realized my assumptions were continuously being challenged, and that things were not nearly as nice and tidy as I had expected. Increasingly, I found numerous exceptions to my model and it was not long before I realized that my hypothesis was simply wrong.

It then became incumbent upon me to create an alternate means of examining these works. Although structural analysis was helpful in understanding each composition, it did little to help solve the problem of how to treat the string quartet as a unique genre. Similarly, a simple treatment of the genre on a chronological basis was not helpful as each decade produced too many exceptions to be convincing.

As a performer of string quartets, I knew that the most important aspect was the intimate communication I experienced with the other members of the ensemble. Although musicologists pay homage to the idea that the medium is a conversation among equals, few go beyond that statement. Once I decided to work from that angle, everything fell into place. Since not all works were truly conversations among equals, the model required refinement. The compositions themselves suggested the solution. If one accepted the notion that the quartet was a form of communication, or discourse, between four players, then one could derive certain categories from this construct: lecture, polite conversation, debate, and conversation. Although these types might seem somewhat artificial and imply rigid boundaries, they served as a useful means of organizing the huge number of works written during the second half of the eighteenth century. They eliminated the danger of imposing a chronological arrangement where there really was not one, and they forced me to view the string quartet, first and foremost, as chamber music.

It should be stressed that these categories are in no way derived from contemporary eighteenth-century sources. Nor do I mean to imply that composers consciously thought in these terms. Rather, these artificial divisions merely provide a useful means with which to study the medium. There is precedent for imposing terminology retroactively. One need only consider Goethe's famous remark linking the quartet to four intelligent people engaged in conversation. Although the remark came from the first part of the 1800s, musicologists have accepted it as fully appropriate to the eighteenth-century form of the genre. Thus my approach is simply a refined and tangible application of an accepted analogy. I make no claim for historical legitimacy; rather I have merely constructed a means by which one can examine and assess the vast string quartet repertoire of the second half of the eighteenth century.

In the process of writing this book, I imposed certain restrictions upon myself. The first was a time frame. I intentionally chose to look at works written between 1750 and 1797. The former is easy enough to understand. It is the logical place to start the second half of the eighteenth century. But why 1797? Why not 1799 or 1800? Here the answer was more complex.

1797 marks the date of Joseph Haydn's Op. 76 – his last complete set of quartets. It is also the year prior to the start of Beethoven's first essay into the genre, and I deliberately chose to exclude that composer. As so much scholarship is devoted to Mozart and Haydn at the expense of other composers, I wanted to avoid this pitfall as much as possible. The inclusion of Beethoven would only further compound the problem. Moreover, in the hands of this last named composer, the string quartet became a different animal, and it was important not to add confusion to an already new way of examining the genre.

What I strove to do was present a balanced picture of the quartet. As so many of the works existed only in either eighteenth-century prints or in manuscript, I concluded that numerous musical examples would not only provide visual assistance, but would also introduce readers to the wealth of works that were written during this time period; hence, the inclusion of approximately seventy examples, some of which are rather lengthy. When, as in the case of Haydn, Mozart, Ordonez, Vanhal, and others, quartets have been published in authoritative or critical editions, I have relied on these. But in the majority of situations, I worked from eighteenth-century prints and manuscripts.

No attempt has been made to edit, amend, or alter the works. Instead, I have transcribed them as they existed so that the reader can get a sense of what the eighteenth-century performer would have worked from. Therefore original articulations, even when they conflict between the instrumental parts, are reproduced. Moreover, the cello part, if originally labeled as basso, is indicated in this book. Only on rare occasions, when an accidental was obviously missing, did I editorially add such a marking.

The choice of composers and compositions was purely my own. After fully analyzing over 650 quartets and briefly surveying many others, I developed a list of characteristics for each work (number of movements, structure, harmonic activity, motivic work, textural considerations, etc). As my primary goal was to categorize the compositions by discourse type, I noted which ones were the best and most representative examples of each (lecture, polite conversation, debate, and conversation). It was these that I incorporated into the tables and text. Since my goal was to put forward a different method of examination, its acceptance would be achieved only if the illustrations were clear. While I did not deliberately exclude the many examples of hybrids (mixed discourse types), I kept these to a minimum in order to avoid confusion. These works would certainly make an interesting and separate study. One might even argue that certain types of discourse were more likely to occur in certain places than others. A secondary consideration was the need to offer a balanced perspective of the genre; hence my intentional inclusion of compositions which span the entire second half of the eighteenth century by a wide variety of composers of diverse nationalities. If I found myself in a position of illustrating a point with two compositions, either by the same composer or by different ones, I always chose the latter option.

No preface is complete without thanks, and this one is no exception. To the many libraries around the world which graciously provided me with microfilms and photocopies, I can only express my sincere appreciation. Many of these were procured with financial assistance from a Provost's Grant provided by my home institution, Widener University, for which I am very grateful. Special thanks go to the staff at the Library of Congress in Washington D. C. who answered my many questions and were so helpful in providing me with access to hundreds of quartets. To Rachel Lynch and the staff at Ashgate, please accept my thanks for the opportunity to explore this topic which has fascinated me for so long. And finally, to my family members, who were extraordinarily patient with me during these last four years, and especially to Ilene Lieberman, whose unwavering support and encouragement helped me every step of the way, I cannot begin to say how much I appreciate them. It made it all worthwhile.

Mara Parker

Widener University
November 2001

Chapter 1

The string quartet as chamber music

There is a long history of studying the eighteenth-century string quartet from a structural or formal perspective. In general, musicologists have emphasized its evolution as a four-movement genre which employs a particular sequence of forms. Many have singled out the development of "motivische Arbeit" and its central role within the sonata allegro movement as the most important aspect; for these scholars, only in the presence of these aspects can one truly have a real string quartet. The relationship between the instruments, and especially the conversational aspect, is given only minimal attention. Thus, the eighteenth-century string quartet is viewed as a metaphor for *musical classicism*, rather than as a form of chamber music.

Early studies, such as those by Adolf Sandberger (1900), Friedrich Blume (1932), Hugo Rothweiler (1934), and Ursala Lehmann (1939) formed the basis for many a later researcher.[1] Their examinations differed from contemporary ones by Edward Dent, Marc Pincherle, and Arthur Eaglefield Hull in that they no longer attempted to identify the very first quartet,[2] but rather concerned themselves with the origins of the genre and the point at which the classical string quartet reached its zenith.

Common to all is an examination of the string quartet's "evolution" from its earliest stage to its perfection in the works of Joseph Haydn. Sandberger, for example, reaches back to the seventeenth-century dance suite as the forerunner of the quartet, and classical chamber music in general. Moving forward, he traces the development of the string quartet from its immediate predecessors – the cassatio, the notturno, the quadro, and the divertimento[3] – up through Haydn's Op. 33.

---

[1]   Adolf Sandberger, "Zur Geschichte des Haydnschen Streichquartetts", *Altbayerische Monatsschrift* 2 (1900): 41–64; expanded in *Ausgewählte Aufsätze zur Musikgeschichte* (Munich: Drei Masken Verlag, 1921), pp. 224–65; Friedrich Blume, "Josef Haydns künstlerische Persönlichkeit in seinen Streichquartetten", in *Jahrbuch der Musikbiblitohek Peters* (1932): 24–48; Hugo Rothweiler, "Zur Entwicklung des Streichquartetts in Rahmen der Kammermusik des 18. Jahrhunderts" (PhD diss., University of Tübingen, 1934); and Ursula Lehmann, "Deutsches und italienisches Wesen in der Vorgeschichte des klassischen Streichquartetts" (Würzburg: Druckerei und Verlag Wissenschaftlicher Werke Konrad Triltsch, 1939).

[2]   See for example Edward J. Dent ("The Earliest String Quartets", *The Monthly Musical Record* 33 [1903]: 202–4) and Marc Pincherle ("On the Origins of the String Quartet", *The Musical Quarterly* 15 [1929]: 77–87) who argued for Alessandro Scarlatti and Arthur Eaglefield Hull ("The Earliest Known String Quartet", *The Musical Quarterly* 15 [1929]: 72–6) who found Gregorio Allegri as the most convincing originator.

[3]   Sandberger, "Zur Geschichte", pp. 44–52.

With early attempts by Christian Cannabich, Johann Christian Bach, and Pierre Vachon, and then especially with each new set coming from Haydn, the quartet logically evolves to its state of perfection: the *basso continuo* disappears, the movement type and sequence become regularized, and most importantly, the principle of thematic or motivic work ("motivische Arbeit") is established.[4] Sandberger identifies Haydn's Op. 33 as pivotal, for it contains all the necessary ingredients of a true quartet; the fact that it appears after a long pause of ten years and is written in a "new and special way" is doubly significant.

Blume's own study relies heavily on Sandberger's, but gives Haydn a near-Schoenbergian mystique. Blume sees the composer as working towards an immutable target: Op. 33.[5] In the process, he establishes all the requirements of a quartet: the regularization of a four-movement cycle, each unit with its own identity and function, and the required employment of motivic work, especially in the sonata form movements.[6]

Rothweiler also relies on Sandberger but extends his observations to include the influence of Italian composers such as Giuseppe Tartini, Giuseppe Sammartini, Antonio Sacchini, and Gaetano Pugnani. In doing so, he provides a context within which to examine the melodic style of Haydn's quartets, which are, in his view, the best examples of the genre's evolution.[7] Rothweiler concludes that the history of the string quartet lies with the way composers have reconciled the Italian melodic style with the polyphonic fugal style. He suggests that the two merge in sonata form, and the best illustration of this reconciliation appears with the works of Joseph Haydn.

Like Rothweiler, Lehmann points to Italy's importance.[8] Acknowledging the impact of Blume's writing on the formulation of her own views, Lehmann traces the quartet back to the four-part Renaissance settings and then moves forward until she reaches Haydn, whose Op. 33 represents the culmination of the "classical" string quartet.[9] Lehmann views the string quartet as a "schema", a

---

[4] Ibid., p. 62.

[5] Blume, "Josef Haydns künstlerische Persönlichkeit", p. 26.

[6] Ibid., pp. 32–5.

[7] Rothweiler, *Zur Entwicklung des Streichquartetts*, pp. 26–9, 43–4. Rothweiler, like Blume and Sandberger, focuses on the importance of Op. 33, but in his case, it is the incorporation of folk and popular elements rather than the thematic work that is of prime importance.

[8] This emphasis on Italy's importance culminates with the work of Fausto Torrefranca, "Avviamento alla Storia del Quartetto Italiano, con Introduzione e Note a Cura di A. Bonaccorsi", *L'Approdo Musicale* 12 (1966): 6–181. It continues to be present in later texts as well including Sylvette Milliot's *Que Sais-Je? Le quatuor* (Paris: Presses Universitaires de France, 1986). In contrast to a vast majority of musicologists, Milliot makes no mention of the divertimento at all; rather he sees a direct line from the Italian *concerto a quattro* to the French *quatuor concertant*, which in turn leads to the works of the Mannheim symphonists, and finally to Haydn and Mozart.

[9] Lehmann, "Deutsches und italienisches Wesen", pp. 57, 71.

structural idea which can be used as a representation of the classical style and as the embodiment of sonata form. Thus the development of the string quartet is strongly connected with the development of sonata form.

This persistence in both linking the string quartet and sonata form, and the centralizing of Haydn's Op. 33 culminates in Ludwig Finscher's *Studien zur Geschichte des Streichquartetts,*[10] which, to this day, remains one of the most influential texts on the eighteenth-century quartet. Finscher discusses in minute detail the pre-history of the quartet, problems of terminology, and those early forms which are crucial to our understanding of the genre. In particular, he eliminates the ensemble pieces of the sixteenth and seventeenth centuries as forerunners to the string quartet, and refutes earlier suggestions that works such as Gregorio Allegri's four-part *Sinfonia*, the English viol consort pieces, and Alessandro Scarlatti's *Sonate a quattro* comprise early examples of the genre. He turns instead to the quartet symphony, the church sonata, the *concerto a quattro*, the *sonata a quattro*, the quartet divertimento, the string partita, and the *quadro*. From these he isolates the divertimento as the most important. By doing so, he strengthens his case that the string quartet is an Austro-Bohemian contribution, and not an Italian one. This allows him to dismiss the works of Luigi Boccherini, as well as the French *quatuor concertant* and *quatuor brilliant*, as mere episodes.[11] The divertimento quartet thus becomes the direct predecessor of the Viennese quartet, which is synonymous with the eighteenth-century string quartet in its classic form.[12]

Without going into great detail here, Finscher traces the evolution of Haydn's quartets up through Op. 33. For him, each set builds upon the advances of the previous one in a process that is inescapable. The significance of Op. 33 lies in its embodiment of all the characteristics typically associated with "musical classicism": its new popular tone, its simplicity and clarity, and its thematic development. It is the culmination of a whole evolutionary process.[13] For the first time, we can speak of a distinct genre. Only after this set do we see a virtual explosion in the production of quartets by a host of other composers. The reason, according to Finscher, is that for the first time, there is a style to be imitated, one which meshes the popular and learned styles, and one which presents a

---

[10]   Ludwig Finscher, *Studien zur Geschichte des Streichquartetts: Die Enstehung des klassischen Streichquartetts von den Vorformen zur Grundlegung durch Joseph Haydn* (Kassel: Bärenreiter, 1974).

[11]   Finscher's view (Ibid., pp. 13–14) holds that Boccherini's first set of quartets (composed 1761, published 1767/68) paved the way for the *quatuor concertant* as represented in the works of Cambini. By the time of Haydn's Op. 33, however, this French form was replaced by the *quatuor brillant*, which was little more than a solo violin with accompanying instruments. Both types were completely overshadowed by the Viennese quartet.

[12]   Ibid.

[13]   Ibid., pp. 14–15, 18, 238–75.

schematized sonata form with established rules. Thus Haydn is credited with the creation of the classical string quartet both in tone and manner.[14]

Even though Finscher's book appeared over a quarter century ago, no other research has focused effectively on the eighteenth-century form of the genre.[15] Paul Griffiths' *The String Quartet*,[16] which covers the medium up to the present day, provides only a cursory examination of the eighteenth-century contributions.[17] We have, however, seen a burgeoning of research on various aspects of the string quartet, and classical chamber music in general. Studies such as Warren Kirkendale's *Fugue and Fugato in Rococo and Classical Chamber Music*[18] and Reginald Barrett-Ayres's *Joseph Haydn and the String Quartet*[19] look at the divertimento but then focus solely on the Viennese tradition. Specialized studies devoted to the French *quatuor concertant*,[20] the relationship between the divertimento and quartet,[21] and works of one composer or a group of

---

[14]   Despite criticism and further studies by others, Finscher has maintained this position. As late as 1988, in his "Corelli, Haydn und die klassischen Gattungen der Kammermusik", in *Gattungen der Musik und ihre Klassiker* (ed. by Hermann Danuser; Laaber: Laaber-Verlag, 1988), pp. 185–95, Finscher still assigns a monumental place to Haydn's Op. 33. As the long-awaited resolution of the Op. 20 crisis, Op. 33 establishes the differentiation of movement characters, the special use of the minuet, the importance of thematic work, and the ideal of the four-voice conversation.

[15]   Wulf Konold's *The String Quartet From its Beginnings to Franz Schubert* (trans. by Susan Hellauer; New York: Heinrichshofen, 1983) relies heavily on Finscher and offers little that is new.

[16]   New York: Thames and Hudson, Inc., 1983.

[17]   See also John Herschel Baron, *Intimate Music: A History of the Idea of Chamber Music* (Stuyvesant, New York: Pendragon Press, 1998) for another brief survey.

[18]   2nd edition, Durham, North Carolina: Duke University Press, 1979.

[19]   London: Barrie and Jenkins, 1974.

[20]   The two classic studies are those by Dieter Lutz Trimpert, *Die Quatuors concertants von Giuseppe Cambini* (Tutzing: Hans Schneider, 1967) and Janet Muriel Levy, "The Quatuor Concertant in Paris in the latter Half of the Eighteenth Century" (PhD diss., Stanford University, 1971).

[21]   See Eve R. Meyer, "Florian Gassmann and the Viennese Divertimento" (PhD diss., University of Pennsylvania, 1963); Gayle Alen Henrotte, "The Ensemble Divertimento in Pre-Classic Vienna" (PhD diss., University of North Carolina, Chapel Hill, 1967); James Carson Webster, "The Bass Part in Haydn's Early String Quartets and in Austrian Chamber Music 1750–1780" (PhD diss., Princeton University, 1973); and Roger Charles Hickman, "Six Bohemian Masters of the String Quartet in the Late Eighteenth Century" (PhD diss., University of California, Berkeley, 1979).

closely related ones,[22] are particularly welcomed, but still leave us without an understanding of how everything fits together.

In spite of these recent efforts, Finscher's history has remained the standard and has strongly influenced all successive studies. Common to nearly every one of them is a concentration on the structural aspects of the string quartet. Musicologists have focused on the genre as a cycle of four movements, each with a particular function, the use of thematic development, and a delight in harmonic experimentation; thus individual pieces are analyzed in light of musical theory of the second half of the eighteenth century. Since the string quartet is seen as one of the main achievements of the classical period, evaluations are based on the inclusion of those characteristics normally viewed as key to this time period: use of sonata form, motivic development, and the appearance of folk and popular elements. It is not unusual to read an overview of the string quartet which emphasizes Haydn as its creator, the evolution from the five-movement divertimento to the four-movement unified cycle, the overshadowing of the Viennese quartet above all other types, and the isolation of the early 1780s as the peak of the classical string quartet.[23]

There are of course exceptions to the evolutionary approach; most notable are the writings of Roger Hickman and James Webster. Hickman criticizes the developmental approach, stating that the idea that Haydn invented the string quartet and single-handedly advanced the genre is based on only a vague notion of the true history of the eighteenth-century genre.[24] In a number of articles, Hickman argues for the recognition of various types of quartet, each of which can be related to and distinguished from each other, and whose popularity and prominence rises and falls.[25] Similarly, Webster cautions against viewing the quartet as a unified genre. He contends that the whole concept of a classical string quartet was really a creation of the 1790s and early 1800s, due to the glorification of Mozart (after his death) and late Haydn: "Haydn did not synthesize the

---

[22]   See for example, A. Peter Brown's series of publications on Carlo d'Ordoñez, Klaus Fischer's work on G. B. Viotti, Orin Moe's work on Haydn's quartets, Fiona Little's excellent *The String Quartet at the Oettingen-Wallerstein Court: Ignaz von Beecke and his Contemporaries* (New York: Garland Publishing, Inc., 1989), and my own "Soloistic Chamber Music at the Court of Friedrich Wilhelm II: 1786–1797" (PhD diss., University of Indiana, Bloomington, 1995).

[23]   See Hubert Unverricht, *Die Kammermusik* (Köln: Arno Volk Verlag, 1972), pp. 11–13, and Ulrich Mazurowicz, *Das Streichduett in Wien von 1760 bis zum Tode Joseph Haydns* (Tutzing: Schneider, 1982), pp. 180–83.

[24]   Roger Hickman, "Joseph Haydn and the String Quartet", *Notes* 32 (Dec. 1975): 292.

[25]   See "The Nascent Viennese String Quartet", *The Musical Quarterly* 67 (1981): 193–212; "Haydn and the 'Symphony in Miniature'", *Music Review* 43 (1982): 15–23; "Kozeluch and the Viennese '*Quatuor Concertant*'", *College Music Symposium* 26 (1986): 42–52; and "The Flowering of the Viennese String Quartet in the late Eighteenth Century", *Music Review* 50 (1989): 157–80.

elements of preclassical chamber music to create the quartet; rather his individual solution to a local problem later became the central element in a historical aesthetic model of the rise of the genre".[26]

Regardless of whether or not one takes an evolutionary stance, inherent in nearly every approach has been the desire to equate the eighteenth-century string quartet with musical classicism. Thus one can make a persuasive argument for the highlighting of Haydn's Op. 33 if the criteria is based solely on the musical style of the second half of the eighteenth century. Each quartet of the set is a four-movement cycle, and each portion fulfills a particular function. The sonata form movements exhibit a polarity between two closely related keys and motivic development. The entire collection features four soloistic string instruments, none of which can be dispensed with. But these characteristics do not automatically transform Op. 33 into the epitome of the eighteenth-century string quartet. What is needed is an evaluation of the work, and the many others written during this time period, *as chamber music*.

To do this, it is necessary to set aside our expectations as to what a piece written during this time period should contain. If we approach a composition looking for a particular structure, melodic construction, or harmonic progression, we immediately examine it from a theoretical and formal perspective. Our expectations may or may not be met. Nonetheless, we have looked at such quartet in terms of musical style of the second half of the eighteenth century. We have not examined it as chamber music. In order to take this second approach (the piece *as* chamber music), it is important to consider the actual meaning of the term "chamber music" and the conventions in place at the end of the eighteenth century.

Toward a contemporary definition of chamber music

Several musicological studies draw extensively on the writings of such eighteenth- and early nineteenth-century theorists as Meinrad Spiess, Johann Mattheson, Heinrich Koch, and Johann Daube to form the basis for a discussion of chamber music. Among the more notable ones are those by Warren Kirkendale, Leonard

---

[26] Webster, "The Bass Part", p. 12. This thesis is central in many of Webster's contributions. See also "Towards a History of Viennese Chamber music in the Early Classical Period", *Journal of the American Musicological Society* (hereafter referred to as *JAMS*) 27 (1974): 212–47; and "Violoncello and Double Bass in the Chamber Music of Haydn and his Viennese Contemporaries, 1750–1780", *The Musical Quarterly* 29 (1976): 413–38. For Webster's most strongly worded objection to the myth of a unified classical style, see his *Haydn's "Farewell" Symphony and the Idea of Classical Style* (Cambridge: Cambridge University Press, 1991), pp. 335–73.

Ratner, and Ruth Rowen.[27] A summation of the eighteenth-century conception of chamber music is given below.

In its original sense, "chamber music" simply meant music which belonged to the nobility at court as opposed to music of the church or theater. This is confirmed in the contemporary writings of Johann Walter (*Musicalisches Lexikon*, 1732), Meinrado Spiess (*Tractatus Musicus Compositorio-Practicus*, 1745), and Heinrich Koch (*Musikalisches Lexikon*, 1802). By the mid-eighteenth century, it also was heard in the common household and served as a form of relatively inexpensive private entertainment.[28] Although our current convention is to use the term to designate a medium which requires but one person to a part, during the 1700s, "chamber music" denoted something different.

Eighteenth-century musicians and theorists recognized three functions of music: to enhance worship in church (*ecclesiasticus*), to heighten the drama in the theater (*theatralis*), and to provide entertainment in the court or chamber (*cubicularis*). This distinction was maintained well into the last quarter of the eighteenth-century, not only amongst theorists but by the general public as well.[29] Daube himself made this differentiation throughout his *Der Musikalische Dilettant*, identifying those compositional styles appropriate for church, chamber, and theater. Although scholars stressed that the real difference between these three lay in the location of performance, others argued that the actual character of the music had to agree with the site. Johann Mattheson wrote that in practice, the classification of music into church, chamber, and theater styles applied only to the work itself and not to the place of performance.

> One has the wrong idea if one thinks that the word church, etc. would only be used here for the classification of the styles merely as regards the place and time; for it is very different, namely it relates to the worship service itself, to the sacred performances and to the actual prayers or devotions, not the building or the walls of the temple; for, wherever God's word is taught and heard, be it sung or spoken, there incontestably is God's house. When Paul preached in Athens, the theater was his church.

---

[27] See Kirkendale, *Fugue and Fugato*; Leonard Ratner, *Classic Music: Expression, Form and Style* (New York: Schirmer Books, 1980); Ruth Rowen, *Early Chamber Music* (with a new preface and supplementary bibliography by the author; New York: Da Capo Press, 1949; reprinted, 1974), and Rowen, "Some Eighteenth-Century Classifications of Musical Style", *The Musical Quarterly* 33 (1947): 90–101.

[28] Rowen, "Some Eighteenth-Century Classifications", pp. 90–92.

[29] See von Trattner's announcement of Daube's *Der Musikalische Dilettant* in the April 1773 issue of the *Wienerisches Diarium* cited in Susan P. Snook-Luther, trans., *The Musical Dilettante: A Treatise on Composition by J. F. Daube* (Cambridge: Cambridge University Press, 1992), p. 12. This distinction was still being made as late as 1799 by the Viennese publisher Traeg in his catalogue. See Unverricht, *Die Kammermusik*, p. 8.

> It is precisely the same with the theater and the chamber: neither place nor time are of special consideration here. In a hall, a sacred piece can just as well be performed as a dinner concert; hence it is well if we describe the chamber style through the adjective domestic, in the event consideration is directed toward moral things and matters, just as the morals teacher Ecclesiasticus is likewise called a domestic tutor; not because of the dwellings or the time and place, but on account of his special or private instruction in good manners and morals.[30]

The true meaning of the music should emerge regardless of setting.[31] Location did not always determine the style. Rather, each type of music had its own specific requirements; chamber music evolved its individual set of "technical procedures, tonal and emotional textures, and patterns of design characteristically different from those [obtained] in church or theater music".[32]

Eighteenth-century practice allowed most instrumental genres to be included under the title "chamber music": sonata, concerto, symphony, etc. Thus it was not necessarily soloistic; concert music of many types could be subsumed under the designation. The term "sonata" has been a source of puzzlement, for we find it employed in church music as well.[33] Therefore, any discussion of the three functions of music requires us to address the confusion between those sonatas labeled "sonata da chiesa" and "sonata da camera". Although works for the church are most frequently associated with performance within that institution, by 1700, there were many *da chiesa* works performed as secular domestic music as well; terminological clarification can be obtained only with an examination of the period prior to this time.

By the 1630s, the sonata was defined as a serious, abstract sectional work; it served as a replacement for the term "canzona", which earlier had designated instrumental ensemble works. By the 1650s, publishers began to attach the modifiers *da chiesa* or *da camera* to the title pages of their editions; this occurred at precisely the time that instrumental music played less of a role in publications containing sacred or secular vocal music. Specific affixations to individual works were rare. In this sense, the *da camera/da chiesa* dichotomy was one established

---

[30] Johann Mattheson, *Der vollkommene Capellmeister* (Hamburg, 1739; facsimile reprint, Kassel: Bärenreiter, 1954), p. 69, sec. 7–8. English translation in Ernest C. Harriss, *Johann Mattheson's "Der vollkommene Capellmeister": A Revised Translation with Critical Commentary* (Ann Arbor: UMI Research Press, 1981), pp. 190–91.

[31] For further discussion of Mattheson's views, see Rowen, "Some Eighteenth-Century Classifications", p. 94; and Kirkendale, *Fugue and Fugato*, p. 35.

[32] Rowen, *Early Chamber Music*, p. 14.

[33] This statement also applies to the term "symphony".

by commercial demands rather than by composer specifications.[34] These words were descriptive, not restrictive.

The traditional view of the *sonata da chiesa* as seen with Arcangelo Corelli's Op. 1 (1681) and Op. 3 (1689) holds that it is a four-movement work with the tempo sequence slow-fast-slow-fast. It is a serious composition with one movement, often the second slow one, outside the home key. While the first, third, and final movements are homophonic, the second – the weightiest – is fugal in texture.[35]

Originally *da camera* simply meant "for use at court". This definition was soon widened to include non-church, secular and diversional, and chamber music.[36] The *da camera* modifier, most often used in conjunction with dance music publications, was really quite versatile. Up to the 1680s, it also designated the single, often stylized dance piece. John Daverio's examination of seventeenth-century sources led him to conclude that the term "sonata da camera" referred mainly to the single dance and not to an entire dance group. A single dance was a sonata by virtue of the fact that it was an individual instrumental piece.

> There is no connection between the *da camera* modifier and the appearance of dance groups. Most . . . publications mix grouped and ungrouped dances indiscriminately. In collections like Bononcini's of 1667 and 1669, and Polaroli's of 1673, which consist entirely or largely of ungrouped dances, *sonata da camera* must refer to the individual dance, not the dance group. Even in publications which contain a sufficient number of dance groups, there is no indication that *sonata da camera* is to be equated with *suite*.[37]

The meaning of the term changed only with Corelli's Op. 2 of 1685. In this collection, each dance group was labeled "sonata" in the print itself, a departure from previous practice in which only the title page bore such a designation.[38] This set marked the first time *sonata da camera* was used to designate an entire dance group. From this point on, that term became synonymous with "dance group". By way of illustration, Sebastian de Brossard, in his *Dictionaire de Musique*

---

[34] John J. Daverio, "Formal Design and Terminology in the Pre-Corellian 'Sonata' and Related Instrumental Forms in the Printed Sources" (PhD diss., Boston University, 1983), pp. v, 17, 31–2.

[35] A summation of the traditional conception of the "sonata da chiesa" is given in William S. Newman, *The Sonata in the Baroque Era* (4th ed.; New York: W. W. Norton and Co., 1983), p. 34.

[36] For an overview of "da camera" see Newman, *Sonata in the Baroque Era*, p. 35.

[37] Daverio, "Formal Design", p. 45.

[38] Ibid., p. 202.

(1705), described the *sonata da camera* as the equivalent of a suite of dance pieces.[39]

Although writers and publishers continued to differentiate between *da camera* and *da chiesa* sonatas, the styles and types soon overlapped. Once again, Corelli's sonatas were pivotal. Church sonatas invariably concluded with a disguised dance movement, most often a gigue; *da camera* works incorporated abstract elements. Eventually the two were virtually indistinguishable on a stylistic basis. The determining factor between the church and chamber sonata was the first *Allegro* movement, for only the second movement of the former was always polyphonic in *all* parts and conceived without reference to dance types.[40]

By 1700, the *da camera/da chiesa* distinction disappeared. Works for dancing were designated as *balletto da camera* or some related term, while the *da chiesa* modifier was dropped from the church sonatas. The term "sonata" became more inclusive and implied diversional chamber music that could be used in either the church or chamber. For composers, the location of performance and the function of music was no longer of consequence in the determination of musical style, which became paramount. This concentration on a "chamber style" was also reflected in the musical treatises of the eighteenth century.

Theorists such as Meinrad Spiess specifically identified the chamber style as fluent, delicate, charming and balanced. It was equated with the galant style:

> Chamber music, also called *galanterie-music*, takes its name from the rooms and salons of the nobility, where it is usually performed. Whoever looks for delight, artifice, invention, art taste, affection (tendresse) will find them all in the so-called Concerti Grossi, Sonatas da Camera, etc. in which one cannot fail entirely to be pleased to hear all the high, middle, and low voices concert with each other, imitate each other, and compete for attention, all with neatness and zest.[41]

Chamber music carried with it certain restrictions due to the size of the room in which it was played. But this provided the composer with the chance to experiment and work with subtle nuances not possible in music for the larger church or theater setting. It also required greater care on the part of the performer:

> This style in the chamber also requires far more diligence and perfection than elsewhere, and must have pleasant, clear interior parts which as it were continually contend for precedence with the upper parts in an

---

[39]   Sebastian de Brossard, *Dictionaire de Musique* (Paris: Ballard, 1705), pp. 118–19. See also Newman's description of the third edition to Brossard's work in which he further elaborates on the *da camera/da chiesa* distinction in *Sonata in the Baroque Era*, pp. 24–5.

[40]   Newman, *Sonata in the Baroque Era*, pp. 67–94; Rowen, *Early Chamber Music*, pp. 92–6.

[41]   Meinrad Spiess, *Tractatus Musicus compositorio-practicus* (Augsburg, 1746), p. 162. For an English translation, see Ratner, *Classic Music*, p. 7.

agreeable manner. Slurs, syncopations, arpeggios, alternations between *tutti* and *solo*, between *adagio* and *allegro*, etc., are such essential and characteristic things that one for the most part seeks them in vain in churches and on the stage; because there is more reliance upon the prominence of the human voices, and the instrumental style is only used there to improve and to accompany or strengthen; whereas it clearly asserts superiority in the chamber; indeed, even if the melody should occasionally suffer a little thereby, it is still embellished, ornamented and effervescent. That is its distinctiveness.[42]

In its original sense, the word "camera" denoted the "administration of the princely residence". Chamber music of the seventeenth and eighteenth centuries was for the nobility, and the term signified music performed in a salon or private chamber, or in the concert room of a noble establishment. Daube equated it with music for connoisseurs and amateurs; the concerting voices reflected the polite dialogues of elegant society.[43]

Most instrumental genres could be included under the heading "chamber music" – sonata, concerto, symphony, etc. The number of players in a given group or per individual part was unspecified. Initially the term simply denoted music which was to be played in a chamber (small room) as opposed to either a church or theater. This music could, and did, include orchestral as well as soloistic music, as well as non-staged secular vocal music. Thus the term referred to the location, not the genre.[44] It was only toward the end of the century that a sharper distinction was drawn between soloistic chamber music – one to a part – and orchestral music.[45] The term "chamber style" was coined to designate this

---

[42] Mattheson, *Der vollkommene Capellmeister*, p. 91, sec. 106. English translation in Harriss, *Johann Mattheson*, p. 222.

[43] Snook-Luther, *The Musical Dilettante*, p. 19.

[44] James Webster, "The Scoring of Mozart's Chamber Music for Strings", in *Music in the Classic Period: Essays in Honor of Barry S. Brook* (ed. by Allan Atlas, New York: Pendragon Press, 1985), p. 263.

[45] Thus the present custom of assuming a soloistic performance took hold only later. Unverricht (*Die Kammermusik*, pp. 8–9) argues that the eighteenth century is a grey area with regard to instrumentation and that an insistence on chamber music as solely soloistic is an imposition of nineteenth-century ideals on an earlier period. He cautions that it is easy to confuse *Hausmusik* with chamber music, the former of which had only minimal demands and was not designed for a specific situation or function. Unverricht argues that soloistic chamber music does not really appear until 1830. See "Das Divertimento für Streicher", in *Zur Entwicklung der Kammermusik in der zweiten Hälfte des 18. Jahrhunderts* (Blankenburg: Michaelstein, 1986), pp. 68–9. See also Roger Hickman, "The Nascent Viennese String Quartet", p. 194, who argues for "orchestral" chamber music prior to the late 1760s based on stylistic grounds. For a contrasting view, see Webster's numerous writings on mid-eighteenth century chamber music (bibliography).

genre and this definition has held to the present day.[46] Mattheson also noted this soloistic vs. orchestral distinction, for in both his *Das neu-eröffnete Orchestre* (Hamburg, 1713) and *Das beschützte Orchestre* (Hamburg, 1717) he referred to the *Stylus Phantasticus*, a subdivision of the *Stylus Symphoniacus*, which included the idea of chamber music with one instrument per part.[47]

Writers of the late-eighteenth century still distinguished between the three uses of music – theater, church, and court – but only court society actively cultivated music as a function.[48] As late as 1802, chamber music was still closely associated with the nobility as illustrated by Koch's description:

> Chamber music is in the real sense of the word, such music as is only customary in courts, and to which, since it is merely arranged for the private entertainment of the reigning princes, no one without special permission is allowed entrance as an auditor. But at various courts they still tend to designate by this expression the so-called court-concerts, which indeed are meant really only for the court and what is connected to it, but where also other persons may take part as listeners in the concert-salon isolated from the court.[49]

He differentiated the chamber style from that of the church, which expressed religious ideas, and the theater, which expressed moral emotions. Chamber music was intended solely to be performed in the room, with few instruments, for the pleasure of the princes. Due to these requirements, Koch wrote, chamber music placed more requirements on the performers with regard to nuance and technique.[50] This corresponds to Mattheson's own description as noted above.

Although chamber music was initially the domain of the aristocracy, it was soon available to many. It was an inexpensive form of entertainment accessible to the general public in coffee houses, homes, or open rooms.[51] Amateur chamber music organizations such as the Friday Academy, established in Berlin during Frederick the Great's reign, became commonplace.[52] Participation in instrumental chamber music blossomed, particularly during the last half of the eighteenth century. The university collegium musicum flourished in Germany as did literary and artistic academies in Italy. We also know of the existence of

---

[46]   Heinrich Christoph Koch, *Musikalisches Lexikon* (Frankfurt am Main: August Hermann den Jüngern, 1802), col. 1454.

[47]   See in particular Mattheson, *Das beschützte Orchestre*, p. 137.

[48]   William S. Newman, *The Sonata in the Classic Era* (3rd ed., New York: W. W. Norton and Co., 1983), p. 43.

[49]   Koch, *Lexikon*, cols 820–21. English translation in Rowen, "Some Early-Eighteenth Century Classifications", p. 91.

[50]   Koch, *Lexikon,* cols 820–21.

[51]   Kirkendale, *Fugue and Fugato*, p. 43.

[52]   Snook-Luther, *The Musical Dilettante*, p. 2.

musical clubs in England such as those at Oxford or that of Thomas Britton in London.[53]

The divertimento

Chamber music of the mid-eighteenth century was known under a variety of names: divertimento, concerto, quartet, symphony, cassatio, notturno, serenade, and partita. Idioms were undefined. Aspects such as mode of performance, number of people per part, and style of writing were not clearly established; they were often interchangeable.[54] A *sonata a quattro* or *quadro*, for example, might be performed either one to a part or as a chamber symphony simply by doubling the parts.

Nomenclature during the period ca.1740–ca.1780 was particularly vague. Various terms were used with few specifications. Initially ensemble works, most of which were trio sonatas, were labeled partita, sonata, trio, divertimento, or sinfonia. There was great flexibility with regard to terminology during this period, although partita was the most common title until 1760 when it was superseded by divertimento as the term of choice. For the next two decades, divertimento was the main designation for all non-orchestral music, including not only the classical string quartet and quintet, but the cassation, the partita, the sonata for melodic instrument and basso, and those pieces with obligato scoring for wind instruments.[55] It was not until after 1780 that "string quartet" supplanted the divertimento. Webster credits this change to the move from private to public musical culture and to the rise of native publishing firms around 1780.[56]

[53] See especially, Stanley Sadie, "British Chamber Music, 1720–90" (PhD diss., University of Cambridge, 1958), and Simon McVeigh, *Concert Life in London from Mozart to Haydn* (Cambridge: Cambridge University Press, 1993).

[54] The differences between the terms are murky and confusing. Webster, in "The Bass Part", PhD diss., pp. 35–6, relates this to eighteenth-century practices where theoretical works prior to 1780 almost ignore the terms. For further elaboration, see the discussions by Sandberger, Rowen, Engel, Henrotte, Seidel, Hausswald, Finscher, Meyer, and Webster (bibliography).

[55] See Webster, "Towards a History", pp. 218–19, 244–7. Although Webster's comments focus on Viennese composers and practices, his conclusions allow us to draw comparisons with other contemporary approaches. Webster's series of articles on Viennese chamber music and the bass part (see bibliography) as well as Finscher's *Studien zur Geschichte des Streichquartetts*, Kirkendale's *Fugue and Fugato*, and Hickman's "Six Bohemian Masters" provided the basis for the following discussion.

[56] Webster, "Towards a History", pp. 246–7. Finscher (*Studien zur Geschichte*, p. 105) notes that once Viennese publishers had established themselves, they also used the Parisian designation (*quatuor*).

Just as the terminology is confusing, so too is the relationship between the divertimento and the string quartet. While some view the former as the forerunner to the latter,[57] or as closely related but known under different titles,[58] others argue strongly in favor of two distinct entities.[59] Eve Meyer, for example, warns against viewing the divertimento as a "stepping stone" to the quartet and symphony, noting that it was an entirely independent form of music.[60] Gayle Henrotte cautions against the evolutionary approach, for in viewing the divertimento as a transition to the string quartet, one loses sight of that genre's own individuality and uniqueness:

> The majority of scholarly discussions about the divertimento tend to regard Haydn's works in this genre as the pivotal point. From this point they tend to look backward and try to determine what could have led to the divertimento as it existed in Haydn's time. As a group, the scholars also tend to forget that one may also look forward, and by constantly looking backward, they disregard the fact that the divertimento has continued its own humble course into the twentieth century.[61]

Meyer notes that while the divertimento is usually described as chamber music with one or two people per part, it can also be realized by a small orchestra of fifteen to twenty-five players. This is in keeping with the loose distinction between chamber and orchestra at the time. Thus the term tells us little about instrumentation. Haydn, for example, used the word for a variety of works: string quartets, trios, duos, solos, baryton trios, clavier sonatas, concerto-like works, and small orchestral pieces.[62] Instrumentation should not be viewed as a divertimento's primary trait. Rather it is characterized by a homophonic texture with melody in the top voice; the bass voice, which rarely has thematic material, supplies the harmonic foundation, often through the use of repeated eighth notes (*Trommelbass*) or long-held pedal points. The inner voices are blended and may move in parallel thirds, sixths, or tenths, with each other or with the melody.

---

[57] For a discussion of the primary supporters of this theory see the beginning of this chapter; see especially Finscher's *Studien zur Geschichte* for the most convincing and complete argument. See also Hubert Unverricht, "Das Divertimento für Streicher", in *Zur Entwicklung der Kammermusik in der zweiten Hälfte des 18. Jahrhunderts* (Blankenburg: Michaelstein, 1986), pp. 66, 70–71, who notes that the "change" occurs when the textural problems are worked out.

[58] See the various writings of James Webster, noted in footnotes and in bibliography.

[59] See Meyer, "Florian Gassmann", and the various articles and dissertation by Roger Hickman (bibliography).

[60] Meyer, "Florian Gassmann", pp. 11–12.

[61] Henrotte, "The Ensemble Divertimento", pp. 17–18.

[62] Ibid., pp. 167–9.

Sometimes melodic motives are shared between the upper parts;[63] the emphasis is on simplicity and clarity. Divertimenti often contain a balanced, symmetrical movement scheme, and are filled with diatonic harmonies, restricted keys, and uncomplicated binary and ternary structures.[64]

Meyer distinguishes between two types of divertimento: a larger one for winds, strings or mixed ensemble, and a smaller one for string trio or quartet, possibly with flute or oboe, piano-violin duos, or solo keyboard. While the former, intended for festive occasions and possibly for outdoor use, comprises four to nine movements, the latter, designed for indoor performance, at small garden parties, or possibly on the streets of Vienna, consists of two to four movements. Sound quality further differentiates the two types. The larger divertimento reveals a connection to orchestral music with its use of scale passages, horn-call style themes, arpeggiation, energetic crescendi, dynamic contrast, antiphonal effects, themes which derive from rhythmic and harmonic figuration, and popular themes. The smaller type exhibits a more intimate and charming character. It is often indistinguishable from other types of chamber music and leans toward a greater equalization of parts. Meyer suggests that the divertimento, both large and small, peaked during the period 1755–1780; once the string quartet was fully established, there was less need for the chamber divertimento. The larger type remained in use for various social occasions, although by the 1780s, it had become too unwieldy and decreased in popularity.[65]

A separation between divertimento and string quartet may also be argued on the basis of movement types and sequence, and mode of performance. While the string quartet usually consists of three to four movements in a symphonic plan, with the outer ones nearly always fast, the divertimento has many possible combinations and may contain anywhere from three to five (or more) movements.

> Regardless of its format, the divertimento reflects a unity of conception which clearly separates it from the string quartet. Like the other "pre-quartet" genres . . . the divertimento does not embody the three defining criteria of a "true" string quartet – obligatory solo performance, freedom from the basso continuo, and scoring for two violins, viola, and cello. Rather, the divertimento is essentially orchestral and could be played by either a large ensemble or soloists.[66]

Realization of parts is also useful as a point of distinction. Meyer, who cautions against reading too much into the chamber concept, especially when regarding a divertimento, suggests that the word "chamber" merely refers to

---

63 Eve Meyer, "The Viennese Divertimento", *The Music Review* 28 (1967): 168.
64 Orin Moe, Jr., "Texture in Haydn's Early Quartets", *The Music Review* 35 (1975): 4.
65 Ibid., pp. 169–70. See also Meyer, "Florian Gassmann", pp. 13–14, 16, 128.
66 Hickman, "Six Bohemian Masters", p. 13.

private music-making – music which can be played in the chamber or private apartment of a sovereign or ruling prince. It tells us nothing about the number of performers per part.[67] While the divertimento may be realized by an orchestra, the string quartet must be executed by four individuals. This orchestral/quartet performance option for the divertimento becomes central when one examines the stylistic approach to the string instruments.

The mid-century orchestral conception includes such characteristics as homophony, repetitive rhythms, abrupt dynamic changes, simple harmonies, disjunct thematic material, use of tremelos, doubling of viola and bass, and a limited range for the instruments. Roger Hickman argues that these same features appear in the mid-century divertimento, making that genre amenable to large ensemble performance. In contrast, the solo string quartet style is filled with subtle dynamic nuances, independent lines, lyric, conjunct melodies, difficult figuration, and inclusion of long, sustained notes. These features are not found in divertimenti, nor can they be successfully rendered by several performers on each part.[68]

Hickman concluded that the string quartet proper appeared in Vienna only in the late 1760s, distinct from the divertimento which remained an independent genre. The divertimento did not succumb completely to the dominance of the quartet but maintained an independent existence, especially in the hands of a master such as Florian Gassmann. It was not merely a step in the evolution of the string quartet; it was a "related but independent genre conceived in an entirely different spirit".[69]

A contrasting view is presented by James Webster who argues against viewing the divertimento as a separate genre and in favor of soloistic realization.[70] Webster stresses that during the period 1750–1780, there was a great flexibility with regard to titles and terminology. Divertimento was the most commonly used, especially after 1760. By adding the modifier *a quattro* after divertimento, one has a piece which "in no way implies that the work which bears it is anything other than a full-fledged string quartet".[71] Thus for Webster, the word divertimento means nothing more than "composition" or "ensemble music" and implies no specific sequence or number of movements. It is not a genre, nor does it suggest stylistic or functional limitations; neither is it a transition between the Baroque suite and the classical symphony, between older types of chamber music and the string quartet. Instead, the term simply means multi-movement ensemble music of an informal character.[72]

---

[67] Meyer, "Florian Gassmann", p. 47.
[68] Ibid., p. 21. See also Hickman, "The Nascent Viennese String Quartet", pp. 195–200.
[69] Hickman, "Six Bohemian Masters", p. 23; "The Nascent Viennese String Quartet", p. 211.
[70] For a similar view, see Henrotte, "The Ensemble Divertimento."
[71] Webster, "The Bass Part" (PhD diss.), p. 55.
[72] Webster, "Towards a History", pp. 215–16, 225–6.

Dismissing the Baroque suite-symphony connection, Webster argues that the divertimento was performed soloistically, and in fact could only have been transmitted in this fashion. "The theoretically tenable position that the single title *Divertimento* might have transmitted both soloistic and informal orchestral music founders on the lack of evidence for the latter's existence."[73] The case for soloistic scoring can be made with reports in letters, diaries, autobiographies, and anecdotes such as Dittersdorf's regarding the performance of Richter's Op. 5, Haydn's for the party at Baron Fürnberg's, and Dr. Burney's which describes a performance which took place in Vienna on 4 September 1772.[74] Furthermore, if one assumes that the title "divertimento" implies orchestral scoring, one would have to conclude that Haydn, who did not use titles such as "quartet" until the 1780s, did not write soloistic music until that time.

Webster concluded that there was no difference between the string quartet and the *divertimento a quattro*. The *a quattro* affixation merely specified four distinct parts. Chamber music with this title was a string quartet in everything but name. Even by 1781, the term *divertimento a quadro* was used in lieu of string quartet on the title page of published chamber works as for example, with Haydn's Op. 33. The two terms were used interchangeably until the 1780s.[75] At this point the terminology changed for a variety of reasons: as a reflection of the rise of music printing in Vienna, of French practices, and the more public focus and performance mode. Only then did the divertimento assume an identity as a separate genre, used for different purposes, performed in different settings, and disseminated by different methods.[76]

Both views offer cogent arguments but neither is totally convincing. There is much to be said for viewing the string quartet as a "divertimento with a name change", especially as it provides a sense of continuity and explanation of relationship between the two. Likewise, the stylistic differences between orchestral and chamber styles allow us to regard the divertimento as distinct from the string quartet, thereby presenting the divertimento as a separate and equally worthy medium for study. Perhaps the answer lies somewhere in between. If we accept the notion that initially the word divertimento was used as a catch-all

---

[73] Ibid., p. 235.

[74] Ibid. See also Webster's discussion in "The Bass Part" (PhD diss.), pp. 391–3.

[75] James Webster, "The Bass Part in Haydn's Early String Quartets," *The Musical Quarterly* 63 (1977): 394–5. Webster contends that prior to 1770, the string quartet was simply called divertimento. It is only in the 1780s that the usage of the former overrode that of the latter. This nomenclature change (from divertimento to string quartet) occurs simultaneously with the gradual specificity of the bass line (from basso to violoncello), which did not indicate a change in scoring, but rather a move toward terminological precision (see below). See Webster, "The Bass Part" (PhD diss.), pp. 303–4, 310–11; "Towards a History", pp. 229–30; and "Violoncello and Double Bass in the Chamber Music of Haydn and his Viennese Contemporaries, 1750–1780", *The Musical Quarterly* 29 (1976): 425–6.

[76] Webster, "The Bass Part" (PhD diss.), pp. 41, 73–4.

category for all types of chamber music, then not only would the as yet unnamed string quartet come under this terminology, but so would a host of other types of chamber music. As terminology became more specific, many of the vaguely specified chamber works assumed a particular identity, and developed a history and set of characteristics unique to them. Such is the case with the string quartet. What is important though, is to understand that the term divertimento and works designated as such did not die out. As the divertimento "membership" diminished, the term came to refer more specifically to those types of works which remained. The weeding out of different genres allowed the divertimento to achieve its own specificity because fewer and fewer different forms of chamber music were subsumed under that heading. Thus the divertimento did not die out once designation of certain types of works as string quartet became commonplace. It simply relinquished its ability to be connected to those works for two violins, viola, and cello.

Lacking in the above, however, is a consideration of the role of the one ingredient central to chamber music: interaction between the participants. If we accept the view that a string quartet represents a form of interaction between four participants, we are forced to look beyond the traditionally presented arguments. This, coupled with the difficulties in pinpointing the emergence of the quartet, require us to turn to the eighteenth-century string quartet and view it, not as the embodiment of musical classicism, but as chamber music.

The string quartet as chamber music

The historical roots of the string quartet are difficult to pinpoint as there is neither a single specific event or idea which stands out as central, nor is the terminology clear. There is a history of four-part writing for strings in the *sonata a quattro*, the *concerto* and *concertino a quattro*, the Italian sinfonia, the French *sonate en quatuor*, the *symphonie en quatuor*, and the *ouverture à quatre*, the divertimento, the cassation, the notturno, the serenade, the *quartettsymphonie*, and the *quartettdivertimento*.[77] However, Finscher argues that none of these scorings or genres proved stable, nor did any one unite all the features that we typically associate with the string quartet of the second half of the eighteenth century: the obligatory soloistic scoring with cello, the four-movement cyclic pattern featuring

---

[77] See Finscher, *Studien zur Geschichte des Streichquartetts*, pp. 44–89 and Kirkendale, *Fugue and Fugato*, pp. 15–17, for a discussion of these roots. Webster suggests five genres as the most likely precursors of the string quartet: *symphony a 4* in Italy, France, Austria, and Southern Germany; the *concerto a 4* in France and Italy; the *sonata a 4* in Italy and *concertino a 4* in France; the *quadro* in Northern Germany; and the various soloistic ensemble genres in Austria. See Webster's review of Finscher's *Studien zur Geschichte des Streichquartetts* in *Journal of the American Musicological Society* 28 (1975): 544.

sonata form, the synthesis of the popular and learned styles, and thematic development.[78] While generally accurate, these features as laid out most commonly apply to the works of Haydn and his Viennese contemporaries. Once one includes quartets by others outside this circle in the mix, modifications become necessary to reflect not a single standard but rather a fluid genre. Thus the string quartet is characterized by the following: obligatory soloistic scoring for two violins, viola, and cello; multiple movements, one or more of which may be in sonata form; and emphasis on interaction between the four members of the ensemble. Actual usage of the word "quartet" was minimal in the 1740s and the following decade. Although it made a modest appearance in the 1760s and increased its presence in the 1770s, the term only became standard throughout Europe in the 1780s. The increased usage corresponded to a decrease in the designation "divertimento".[79]

The rise of the string quartet is generally credited to the emancipation of the cello from the *basso continuo*, obligatory solo performance, the union of a new standard ensemble of four members of the violin family, and the belief in the special perfection of four-part texture.[80] Inherent in these characteristics is the problem of scoring the bass part. Traditionally, historical performance practice has allowed for numerous possibilities when the lowest line was indicated as "basso" – cello alone, string bass alone, cello and bass together, and even inclusion of the *basso continuo*. Up to the late 1760s, the *basso* line was often doubled by the viola and there was limited use of the pitches below F. When the double bass was used, it was up to the performer to deal with those passages that went below his range, that is, to transpose them up an octave.[81]

James Webster dispelled these notions with his 1973 dissertation, "The Bass Part in Haydn's Early String Quartets and in Austrian Chamber Music, 1750–1780". He argued against conventional theory for the simple reason that no one had proved that this variability applied to Haydn's works, and concluded that "*Basso* meant 'the bass part' in all scorings, soloistic and orchestral; it was entirely compatible with performance by solo cello (as well as solo double-bass); and it was used routinely in Austrian chamber music before 1780 and occasionally thereafter".[82] In chamber music, the term "basso" meant the bass part, not the double bass specifically, and could be used in soloistic music without implying

---

[78] Ibid., p. 545. Webster gives for a succinct summation of the main points of the text.

[79] Webster, "Towards a History", p. 227.

[80] Finscher, *Studien zur Geschichte des Streichquartetts*, pp. 134–63.

[81] See Jens Peter Larsen, Howard Serwer, and James Webster, ed., *Haydn Studies: Proceedings of the International Haydn Conference, Washington D.C. 1975* (New York: W. W. Norton and Co., 1981), pp. 238–9, for a summation of Hubert Unverrich's views. Hickman argues that basso parts up to the late 1760s were entirely compatible with double bass performance. See "The Nascent Viennese String Quartet", p. 201.

[82] Webster, "Towards a History", p. 242.

orchestral scoring.[83]   Webster also disputed the notion that a continuo could be used even if no figures were provided and no keyboard part was specified. The keyboard continuo was not used in Viennese secular ensemble music after 1750; its occasional appearance as indicated by the inclusion of figures in some prints such as those by Hummel derives from a tradition undertaken by publishers to satisfy the demands for this type of scoring.[84]

After the later 1760s and up to the mid-1780s, one finds a greater exploitation of the lower register. Following this, from the late 1780s and into the 1790s, one again finds a change in the now consistently designated cello line: the part is more technically demanding and it truly becomes a partner in the ensemble. It is at this point that we can speak of a four-part conversation.

The string quartet is thus defined by the use of solo cello for the bass part, a complete severing of ties with the basso continuo concept, a four-voice texture, and exploitation of soloistic capabilities. This last characteristic does not necessarily imply technical virtuosity; instead it relies on the composer's ability to include independent lines, each of which must be rendered by a single player. An individual can ably execute subtle inflections, lyric melodies, sigh figures reflecting a flexible bow control, a variety of rhythmic patterns, frequent use of outer registers, difficult figuration, and complicated ornamentation than multiple players per part.[85]   Thus the elimination of the orchestral style, coupled with an equality amongst the instruments, are both needed for a string quartet.

With this new medium comes a unique form of interaction, one which differs from previous chamber textures. Initially, theorists wrote about the string quartet in a idealistic manner, attempting to define what constituted the medium. Of particular interest is the fact that comments such as those by Koch, as provided below, focus on the equality of voices and conversational aspects, not the structural and stylistic components that appear uniformly in twentieth-century assessments.

In volume three of his *Versuch einer Anleitung zur Composition* (1793), Koch notes that a strict string quartet would have to be fugal, since all four instruments are equal. But because modern quartets are in the galant style, the predominant voice must be rotated among all four instruments:

> The quartet, currently the favorite piece of small musical societies, is cultivated very assiduously by the more modern composers.
>
> If it really is to consist of four obbligato voices of which none has priority over the others, then it must be treated according to fugal method.

---

83   Ibid., pp. 238–40; see also Webster, "The Bass Part" (PhD diss.), pp. 100–115.
84   Ibid., pp. 243–6.
85   Hickman, "Six Bohemian Masters", p. 21.

But because the modern quartets are composed in the galant style, there are four main voices which alternately predominate and sometimes this one, sometimes that one forms the customary bass.

While one of these parts concerns itself with the delivery of the main melody, the other two [melodic voices] must in connected melodies which promote the expression without obscuring the main melody.[86]

By 1802, when reassessing the medium, Koch still maintains that a strict quartet must be in the fugal style to allow for equality among the voices. Acknowledging that most quartets were not, Koch notes the use of the *galant* style. Again, as with the comments made nearly ten years earlier, the theorist mentions one voice taking the melody, two others with complementing melodic material, and the bass line supporting. But the entry implies that the bass line is not restricted to the cello; rather, any voice can assume that role:

> This instrumental composition for four instruments, which has been such a favorite for many years, is a special category of sonata, and in the strict sense, consists of four concerting instruments, none of which can claim exclusively the role of leading voice [*Hauptstimme*]. If this is to be accomplished without confusion and without overloading the melodic material, the quartet, in the strict sense, must be composed as a fugue, or entirely in the strict style. In the modern quartets the free style is generally used; the four voices alternate in taking the lead; of these, now one, now another will provide the kind of bass which is usual in galant compositions. While one voice takes the leading melody, the two others [aside from the voice serving as a bass] must continue with complementary melodic material that will reinforce the expression without beclouding the leading melody.[87]

Common to both entries is the emphasis on the "concerting" aspects of the medium and the equality of voices. This concentration on the *textural* and *conversational* components is in stark contrast to modern day analyses of the genre which examine the harmonic and formal motivic aspects. For example, while Finscher describes the quartet as a presentation of four voices having a "private, animated, reasonable conversation", he notes that this is not enough;

---

[86] Heinrich Christoph Koch, *Versuch einer Anleitung zur Composition*, Part 3 (Leipzig: Adam Friedrich Böhme, 1793), pp. 325–6. English translation in Nancy Kovaleff Baker, *Heinrich Christoph Koch: Introductory Essay on Composition: The Mechanical Rules of Melody Sections 3 and 4* (New Haven: Yale University Press, 1983), p. 207.

[87] Heinrich Christoph Koch, *Musikalisches Lexikon* (Frankfurt, 1802; facsimile ed., Hildesheim: Georg Olms Verlagsbuchhandlung, 1964), cols. 1209–10. Translation in Leonard G. Ratner, *Classic Music: Expression, Form, and Style* (New York: Schirmer, 1980), p. 125.

rather it should be viewed primarily as a representation of the entire classical period. In essence it becomes a metaphor for the second half of the eighteenth century.[88] Only with studies of the *quatuor concertant* do we find modern scholars willing to view the medium from some other viewpoint as the following comments of Janet Levy illustrate:

> The concern with part writing, the interaction or interplay of parts in a concertante string quartet, the role given one line or instrument in such a quartet, the attention to the fact that a true concertante quartet had one and only one instrument to a part, attention to a sonority created by certain textural arrangements and the differences in harmony allowed by these – all of these, which refer to texture, emerge as the primary focus of eighteenth-century theorists' thinking regarding the meaning of "Quatuor concertant". Texture, then, commands first place as a criterion for stylistic analyses of the literature of the quatuor concertant.[89]

While Levy's concern remains centered on the French quartet, her comments can, and should, be applied to the string quartet in general. For if we are to view the eighteenth-century quartet in its historical context, we must examine it in a manner similar to eighteenth-century theorists: as a form of discourse among four participants.

The traditional conception of the eighteenth-century string quartet argues for a path of logical growth and development, one which takes us from a first-violin dominated texture of the third quarter of the century up to a four-voice conversation among equal participants of the 1790s. The ideal of conversation as discussed by contemporary theorists has been viewed as a goal which composers strove for and only succeeded in attaining toward the end of the century. The concept of conversation was not restricted solely to the string quartet – it was a basic characteristic of chamber music. This is evidenced in the titles of many compositions of the time as in Guillemain's *Six Sonates en Quatuors ou Conversations galantes et amusantes entre Flûte traversière, un violon, une Basse de Viole et la Basse*, Op. 12, Haydn's early quartets/divertimenti which were

---

[88] Finscher, *Studien zur Geschichte des Streichquartetts*, pp. 10–11, 280. See also Barrett-Ayres, *Joseph Haydn*, p. 20 and Walther Siegmund-Schultze, "Die Entwicklung der Kammermusik in der zweiten Hälfte des 18. Jahrhunderts", in *Zur Entwicklung der Kammermusik in der zweiten Hälfte des 18. Jahrhunderts* (Blankenburg: Michaelstein, 1986), p. 9. Both characterize chamber music of the second half of the eighteenth century as a conversation among equals, then turn specifically to the harmonic, motivic, and structural aspects.

[89] Levy, "The Quatuor Concertant", p. 59.

published in France as *Six Simphonies ou Quatuors dialoguées*, and Toeschi's Op. 5, which was advertised in *Mercure de France* as *Il Dialogo musicale*.[90]

A musical conversation is not just strict imitation as in a fugue or canon, but describes a condition where an idea, which turns and changes, can be passed from voice to voice.[91] In a true musical conversation, each voice is differentiated by contrasting melodic shapes, phrase lengths, and rhythms. The ability to distinguish individual lines in itself does not guarantee an ensemble with four equal parts. A truly democratic quartet is only possible once the voices have achieved an interchangeability of function. At this point, specific roles and stratified pitch layers are pushed aside, thus allowing the composer to assign to any of the four instruments any of the roles discussed by Koch: the leading voice, the bass, or one of the inner voices.

In essence, a progression from the first-violin dominated works of the third quarter of the century, to the more integrated style of the 1780s, and finally to the nearly equal conversation of the 1790s seems to be a viable and accurate portrayal of the period 1750–1799, especially if one considers just the works of Haydn and Mozart. But if, as David Wyn Jones points out, we use these composers as our benchmarks, we end up with a "blinkered and misleading view" of the genre.[92] In reality, the progression was not so smooth, nor was there one type of quartet which overtook and supplanted another. All of the above-mentioned types as well as the French *quatuor concertant* were written concurrently and throughout the second half of the eighteenth century. Recognition of this fact forces us to discard the notion of the string quartet as a monolithic medium which followed a single line of development. Rather, each work must be viewed as a product of an individual composer's stylistic choices, location, intended performers and listeners. Once one leaves the sphere of Viennese composers, one finds a wide variety of quartets. As it fails to take these works into consideration except as parenthetical diversions, the evolutionary model provides an inaccurate picture of the string quartet. A reliance on either a linear approach or one which focuses on structural components leaves little room for a consideration of the most unique and important aspect of the string quartet – the relationship between the four voices. It is the task of the following chapters to correct this omission.

---

[90] Hans Engel, "Die Quellen des klassischen Stiles", in *Report of the Eighth IMS Conference: New York 1961* (Kassel: Bärenreiter, 1961), pp. 288–9.

[91] Karl Geiringer, "The Rise of Chamber Music", in *New Oxford History of Music*, vol. 8: *The Age of Enlightenment: 1745–1790* (London: Oxford University Press, 1973), p. 22.

[92] David Wyn Jones, "The String Quartets of Vanhal" (PhD diss., University of Wales, 1978), p. 234.

Chapter 2

Social aspects: from private to public

By the mid-eighteenth century, Europe's death rate was falling, the population was growing, and agricultural output was improving. The onset of the industrial revolution produced new forms of employment and increased the number of people in urban areas. While the nobility still maintained great wealth and power, it was challenged by a rising middle class. Royalty was no longer the chief patron and commissioner of music. Increasingly, the bourgeoisie achieved importance as a consumer both at the public concert, which became more common as the century progressed, and through the purchase of publications or subscriptions.[1] Thus, while music of the late-eighteenth century still functioned as an aspect of court life, it was also part of middle class existence.

For the musician, the old-fashioned employment by royal patron was no longer a guaranteed means of earning a living. The transformation from a patron-based system to that of free agency took place at different times in different locations, but by the 1770s it had reached a climax. The possibilities for earning a livelihood were as varied as they were numerous: one could be a part-time Kapellmeister; one could present individual works to royalty (that is, sets of trios or quartets) for which one would hope to receive some jewelled snuff box, gold coins or jewelry;[2] one could self-publish; one could give private lessons or play for special events such as weddings and funerals; one could perform in concert; or one could arrange popular operatic airs for alternative settings.[3] The options were many; none was wholly secure.

The rise of the public concert, the growing market for cheap sheet music and self-tutors, and the gradual replacement of small concert halls and court-

---

[1]   Levy, "The Quatuor Concertant", pp. 23–4. For a fine overview of the period, see Neal Zaslaw, "Music and Society in the Classical Era", in *The Classical Era: From the 1740s to the end of the 18th Century* (ed. by Neal Zaslaw; Englewood Cliffs, New Jersey: Prentice Hall, 1989), pp. 1–14.

[2]   Friedrich Wilhelm II, for example, was well-known for his gifts to those musicians not affilliated with his court. In appreciation for his Op. 5 sonatas for cello and piano, Ludwig van Beethoven was presented with a gold snuff box filled with louis d'ors. For his Quartet, K.575, Mozart received one hundred *Friedrichs d'or* in a gold snuff box. Peter Ritter, after performing two concerti for this same patron, received a gold watch and chain as well as a cello worth one hundred Dukats. After sending his six "Paris" symphonies to the King, Joseph Haydn was rewarded with a diamond ring worth three hundred Dukats.

[3]   Barry S. Brook, "Piracy and Panacea in the Dissemination of Music in the Late Eighteenth Century", *Proceedings of the Royal Musical Association* 102 (1975–76): 14.

sponsored opera houses with larger forums funded by ticket sales and public support changed the established patterns of patronage.[4] At the same time, home music-making increased as did the ever-growing number of small concerts in private domiciles; these provided entertainment for the middle class.[5] Chamber music, which was long perceived as a symbol of court culture, became increasingly attractive to the bourgeoisie.[6]

With these social changes came a new class of amateurs who needed accessible music. Aristocratic-court chamber music initially stood in sharp contrast to that associated with the general public. The latter was most often connected with *Hausmusik*; the style was simpler since this music was designed for everyday use and performance by all who wished to partake.[7] Some composers such as Ignaz Joseph Pleyel, Ferdinand Fränzl, Adalbert Gyrowetz, Paul Wranitzky, Leopold Kozeluch, and Franz Krommer remained dedicated to satisfying the needs of the dilettante. From the outset, their works were considered lighter and more comprehensible. These composers strove toward higher levels, but at the same time, remained accessible to the non-professional musician. Stylistically their compositions were predominantly homophonic, contained familiar thematic material, were unassuming in layout, and had a minimal two- or three-part interplay between voices.[8] These were the popular compositions of the day, and commercially, the most successful.

Amateurs had varying degrees of technical facility and musical comprehension. String quartets written for them were light, facile, pleasing to the ear, and intended for home use as opposed to professional public performance. The domestic setting was the favorite of smaller music societies for it allowed each person to participate on his own level.

> The ensemble for four solo string players was ideal entertainment [for the home] . . . ; not only were its subtle, intimate qualities pleasant for the listener, but the dominance of the first violin part also allowed musicians of unequal calibre to join together and display

---

[4]   Zaslaw, "Music and Society in the Classical Era", p. 9.

[5]   See Levy, "The Quatuor Concertant", pp. 23–4, for a summation of the basic research on the social history of music for the eighteenth century.

[6]   This is discussed in detail in Ludwig Finscher, "Hausmusik und Kammermusik", *Musica* 22 (1968): 320 and Wolfgang Ruf, "Die Kammermusik in der Musiklehre des 18. Jahrhunderts", in *Zur Entwicklung der instrumentalen Kammermusik in der 1. Hälfte des 18. Jahrhunderts* (Blankenburg/Harz: Rat des Bezirkes Magdeburg, 1984), p. 17.

[7]   Finscher, "Hausmusik und Kammermusik", p. 326.

[8]   Finscher, "Zur Socialgeschichte des klassischen Streichquartetts", in *Bericht über den Internationalsen Musikwissenschaftlichen Kongress Kassel 1962* (ed. by Georg Reichert and Martin Just; Kassel: Bärenreiter, 1963), p. 38.

their respective talents while performing works composed by the most eminent masters.[9]

Domination by the first violin served two purposes: a homophonic texture could be maintained and the other parts, which were significantly less difficult and prominent, could be allotted to weaker players. Pleyel's works were typical of this popularizing approach. The standard setting required a concertante first violin which had ample opportunity for virtuosic display at the expense of the other instruments. The repertoire was not restricted to actual or original string quartets. Home music-making sessions often included arrangements of opera arias, folk songs, oratorios, and as well as symphonies.

Between 1780 and 1810, even some of this music had become more difficult, so that by the later works of Haydn and Mozart, the amateur was effectively excluded. By the end of the eighteenth century, quartet (and ensemble) playing required those technical skills possessed primarily by the professional musician. More and more, the dilettante had to be content with the passive role of listener.[10] The growing separation between the amateur and professional musician became more and more noticeable by the end of the eighteenth century, at which time the two types of musicians ceased playing together in orchestral and chamber groups.[11] This was due mainly to the fact that the dilettante simply could not keep up with the technical demands of the composer. Consequently, by the end of the century, public performance of what we now consider standard repertoire became the domain of the expert music maker.[12]

The rise of the professional string quartet was one of the most important developments of the second half of the eighteenth century. Up to the 1790s, such a group, in the modern sense, was a rarity. Until that time, established quartets were staffed by the private servants of the nobility. Alternatively, these groups could be mixtures of professionals and wealthy patrons.[13] Whatever the case, public performance was rare. As music became more demanding, both technically and musically, the dilettante found he could not meet the challenges. As emphasis was placed on both execution and interpretation, successful performance of quartets became the province of the skilled professional.[14]

---

[9] Hickman, "Six Bohemian Masters", p. 76. See also the entry "Amateur" in Framery and Ginguene, ed., *Encyclopedie Méthodique* (Paris: Chez Panckoncke, 1791–1818), pp. 77–8.

[10] Finscher, "Zur Socialgeschichte", pp. 37–8.

[11] Zaslaw, "Music and Society", p. 9.

[12] Finscher, "Zur Socialgeschichte", p. 37.

[13] Baron, *Intimate Music*, p. 24.

[14] Unverricht, *Die Kammermusik*, p. 14.

What little evidence exists about quartet playing indicates that for most of the second half of the eighteenth century, it was a private affair, often for the pleasure of the musicians themselves or for a limited number of listeners. Most quartet parties or performances took place at court for private occasions or in the homes of the nobility. Participants were usually professionals, such as members of a Kapelle or visiting soloists, or skilled members of a royal family. For example, an anecdote in Karl Ditters von Dittersdorf's autobiography describes the time the violinist, his two brothers, and the cellist Schweitzer played "six new quartets by Richter" while "on the command" of the Imperial army during 1758.[15] A letter from Dittersdorf to Artaria dated 18 August 1788, in which he discusses the playing of quartets in the summer home of Breslau Fürstbischof Philipp Gotthard Graf Schaffgotsch, shows that quartet playing was still closely connected to the private domicile.[16] The Breslau choir director, Ignatz Lukas also wrote about private quartet parties which took place during the 1780s.[17]

Charles Burney's travel diary from the year 1772 is similarly instructive as we can learn something about not only the listeners and performers, but the intimacy of the setting as well. Many of Burney's entries detail the association of chamber music with royalty and small, private gatherings. In both Nymphenberg and Munich, the documenter was treated to concerts in the homes of nobility; his hosts often took part in the actual playing.[18] While in Vienna in September, Burney became acquainted with M. L'Augier, and through this association had the opportunity to hear "some of Haydn's quartettos, performed with the utmost precision and perfection".[19] He described the music parties he attended, the knowledgeable aristocrats who appreciated the music, and the various people of "great rank" that he met – Princess Piccolomini, Duke of Braganza, Lord Stormoht, General Valmoden and his lady, and Count Brühl, Duke of Bressciano – some of whom took part

---

[15]   [Karl Ditters von Dittersdorf], *The Autobiography of Karl von Dittersdorf Dictated to His Son* (trans. by A. D. Coleridge; London: Richard Bentley and Son, 1896; reprint edition, New York: Da Capo Press, 1970), p. 90.

[16]   Dittersdorf's letter is quoted in full in Hubert Unverricht, "Privates Quartettspiel in Schlesien von 1780 bis 1850", in *Musica Privata: Die Rolle der Musik im privaten Leben: Festschrift zum 65. Geburtstag von Walter Salmen* (ed. by Monika Fink, Rainer Gstrein, and Günter Mössmer; Innsbruck: Helbling, 1991), pp. 104–7. This was not an isolated event for Dittersdorf. Four years prior to this event, Michael Kelly noted that he heard Haydn, Mozart, Vanhal and Dittersdorf playing in a similar situation in Vienna.

[17]   Ibid., p. 107.

[18]   Charles Burney, *The Present State of Music in Germany, the Netherlands, and United Provinces* (London: 1775; facsimile ed., 2 vols; New York: Broude Brothers, 1969), pp. 131, 163–4, 174–7.

[19]   Ibid., pp. 258–74.

in the actual performances.[20] In particular, Burney documented a specific Viennese "musical party" which took place on a Friday. As with other occasions, those in attendance were members of the aristocracy and/or professional musicians: Duke of Braganza, the Portuguese minister, Count and Countess Thun, M. L'Augier, Madame and Mademoiselle Gluck, Abate Costa, and others. The dinner was followed by chamber music which included "some exquisite quartets by Haydn, executed in the utmost perfection; the first violin by M. Startzler, who played the *Adagios* with uncommon feeling and expression; the second violin by M. Ordonetz; Count Brühl played the tenor; and M. Weigl, an excellent performer on the violoncello, the base".[21]

Performance of quartets in private settings was still common during the following decade. A passing reference in Cramer's *Magazin der Musik* mentioned a winter 1782 private concert which included a "Quadro". A more formal report noted a private concert on 17 November 1783, which included two quartets from Haydn's Op. 19.[22] And in 1789, Mozart, upon reaching Dresden was known to have given a private concert at the Hôtel de Pologne in which he took part in the performance of quartets.[23] Similar recollections by Eduard Hanslick and Ludwig Spohr confirm the continued practice of performance in intimate setting as well as the participation by skilled players – either professionals or the aristocracy.[24]

The earliest professional string quartet was staffed by Pietro Nardini and Filippo Manfredi (violins), Giovanni Giuseppe Cambini (viola), and Luigi Boccherini (cello). These four musicians gave public performances in Milan in 1765, but only for a six-month period. The brevity of the group's existence suggests not so much a professional quartet as a group with professional musicians that simply came together for a limited period. The next known group of professionals was the Font family (a father and his three sons), in the service of Dom Luis in Madrid. Boccherini later joined this group as second cellist in 1770. At the same time, there was a quartet-in-residence at Esterháza: Luigi Tomasini served continuously as first violin; the remaining members varied depending upon whom was in the court orchestra.[25]

Thus the history of the string quartet during the second half of the eighteenth century reveals a continuous state of change, where the staffing of

20 Ibid., pp. 282–5.
21 Ibid., p. 290.
22 Carl Friedrich Cramer, ed., *Magazin der Musik*, (Hamburg: Hildesheim, 1783; reprint ed., New York: Georg Olms Verlag, 1971), vol. 1, pp. 153, 185.
23 Otto Erich Deutsch, *Mozart: A Documentary Biography* (trans. by Eric Blom, Peter Branscombe, and Jeremy Noble; London: Simon and Schuster, 1965), p. 339.
24 Cited in Ulrich Mazurowcz, *Das Streichduett in Wien von 1760 bis zum Tode Joseph Haydns* (Tutzing: Schneider, 1982), pp. 160–72.
25 Baron, *Intimate Music*, pp. 240–1.

the medium moved from the court circle of dilettantes to the *Kenner und Liebhaber* and then finally to the professional performer.[26] This shift corresponds to the general move in Western music by which the end of the eighteenth century sees a "culmination of a long process in which music was transformed from a semi-feudal craft serving church, town, and court into a free-enterprise profession supplying predominantly bourgeois markets".[27]

With this transformation came the development of the string quartet concert as well as growth in music distribution (copying, engraving, and printing). By the end of the century, composers could and did think in terms of public performance as opposed to the personal tastes of a single patron. While earlier works were written for the professional or skilled amateur to be played in the aristocratic home, by the end of the century, it was not uncommon to hear them in public concerts before audiences of various classes.[28]

As chamber music moved from the courts to the home, and with its establishment as viable concert fare, its definition became increasingly constricted: a soloistic instrumental ensemble music for two to nine players. In contrast, *Hausmusik* was less complicated and became the outlet for those still wishing to make music but now unable to keep up with the professional performer.[29] By the end of the eighteenth century, string quartets became the domain of the professional musician. Amateurs had to content themselves with listening to them, rather than playing them.[30]

Finscher has suggested that the distinction between *Hausmusik* and concert chamber music was in essence publisher created.[31] By 1770, with the exception of England, France and the low countries, music was disseminated in manuscript copies. Nowhere is this more true than if one compares the situation in Germany and the Austro-Hungarian empire with that in London and Paris. Burney complained that he was plagued by copyists just before he left Vienna in 1772. Moreover, his ability to purchase music was hampered because "everything is very dear in Vienna, and nothing more so than music, of which none is printed".[32] There was no regular tradition of printing music of any type either in Vienna or anywhere else in the Austrian-Bohemian domain before Artaria's establishment just prior to 1780. The main form of

---

[26]   Konold, *The String Quartet*, p. 12.

[27]   Brook, "Piracy and Panacea", pp. 13–14.

[28]   William Weber, "The Muddle of the Middle Classes", *19th-Century Music* 3 (1979–80): 183.

[29]   Finscher, "Hausmusik und Kammermusik", p. 326.

[30]   Paul Henry Lang, Review of *Studien zur Geschichte des Streichquartetts*, by Ludwig Finscher, *The Musical Quarterly* 63 (1977): 20.

[31]   Finscher, "Hausmusik und Kammermusik", p. 325.

[32]   Burney, *The Present State of Music*, pp. 367–8. Burney also writes, with pleasure, about the great number of manuscript copies given to him by Gassmann (p. 366).

dissemination was the manuscript copy; in effect, this restricted one's access to chamber music as only the more wealthy would have the funds needed to arrange for copies of various works.[33] Only gradually did music publishing take hold in Vienna, Bonn, Berlin and previously "non-printing" places.[34]

In contrast, printed music in Paris and London was the norm. Those cities were in fact the major centers of chamber music publication by the mid-eighteenth century. Brook suggests this difference was due to the economic and political climate – London and Paris had more people than Vienna, Rome and Berlin, which meant a greater demand for music. Furthermore, London and Paris had a large "music-hungry" middle class that wanted the latest in sonatas, quartets, and operatic airs.[35]

The above discussion suggests that the string quartet was received and cultivated differently depending on the city. While it is not possible here to look at quartet reception throughout Europe, an examination of how that medium functioned in Paris, London, and Vienna will shed some light on its place in European society.

Paris

Paris was the musical mecca of Europe, particularly during the third quarter of the eighteenth century. Between 1760 and 1789, Paris boasted more instrumental composers, performers, and publishers than any other city in the world.[36] Musicians from Bohemia and Germany stopped there as part of their western migration, as did Italians moving north. Even a cursory listing of visitors to that city reveals an impressive roster: Felice Bambini, Franz Beck, Luigi Boccherini, J. G. Burkhöffer, Giuseppe Maria Cambini, Joseph-Baptiste Canavas, Heinrich Domnich, Christoph Willibald Gluck, Carlo Graziani, Pierre Miroglio, Wolfgang Amadeus Mozart, Gaspard Proksch, Franz Xaver Richter, Henri-Jean and Henri-Joseph Rigel, Georg Wenzel Ritter, Valentin Roeser, Antonio Rosetti, Filippo Ruge, Mlle. Schenker, Johann Schobert, Anton, Carl, and Johann Stamitz, JohannWenzel Stich (Giovanni Punto), and Johann Baptist Wendling.[37]

Musical life during the second half of the century reflected the bourgeoisie's intellectual ambition along with its increased prosperity. More and more, artists worked not for the King but for those who set themselves up

---

33 Webster, "The Bass Part" (PhD diss.), pp. 18–19.
34 Brook, "Piracy and Panacea", p. 16.
35 Ibid., p. 15.
36 Levy, "The Quatuor Concertant", p. 3.
37 Brook, "Piracy and Panacea", p. 17.

in comfortable Parisian townhouses. This form of patronage lasted until the end of the eighteenth century.[38] Non-professionals formed the core of French musical society. The word "amateur" itself had multiple meanings and implied a wide range of musical abilities: those who enjoyed the art but did not have time to cultivate it; those who studied the art with success and performed in concerts; and those who studied and performed with great skill. Members of this last group might also compose as well.[39]

The growth of instrumental music in Paris was due to music publishing and the proliferation of concerts, both private and public. Music publishing thrived in Paris long before it was established anywhere else in Europe. The city remained in the forefront until the 1780s when the rest of Europe began to understand the potential benefits of music engraving. With the establishment of such firms as Artaria in Vienna, Joseph Schmitt in Amsterdam, and Hummel in the Hague, Amsterdam, and Berlin, Paris lost its near monopoly. Brook attributed this Parisian dominance directly to the public demand for music, especially during the period 1750–70.[40] Publishers presented works by both native as well as foreign composers and frequently served as conduits between the composer and the public; for example, Louis-Balthazar de La Chevardière supplied music for fifteen years to people in fashionable society. Often a composer's introduction to the public came with a publisher's catalogue. Thus this producer of sheet music served a social function as well as a commercial one: he discovered musical talent and presented it to the public or individual patrons.[41]

Paris was also a thriving concert center, enjoyed by both the bourgeoise (in the public arena) and the aristocracy (in the salon). There were a tremendous number of concerts – public and private – staffed by both professionals and amateurs particularly after 1750. Published records reveal a variety of venues for public performance: *Concert spirituel, Concert des Amateurs,*[42] *Concert*

---

[38] Jean Mongrédien, "Paris: the End of the Ancien Régime", in *The Classical Era: From the 1740s to the End of the 18th Century* (ed. by Neal Zaslaw; Englewood Cliffs, New Jersey: Prentice Hall, 1989), pp. 61–2.

[39] Richard J. Viano, "Jean-Baptiste Bréval (1753–1823): Life, Milieu, and Chamber Works with Editions of Ten Compositions and Thematic Catalogue" (PhD diss., City University of New York, 1983), pp. 31–4. For a discussion of the term "amateur", see the entry in Jean-Jacques Rousseau, *Dictionnaire de Musique* (Paris: Duchesne, 1768) and N. E. Framery and P. L. Ginguené, *Encyclopédie méthodique Musique*, vol. 1 (Paris: Panckovcke, 1791).

[40] Brook, *La Symphonie française*, p. 36; Brook, "Piracy and Panacea", p. 19.

[41] Mongrédien, "Paris: the End of the Ancien Régime", p. 65.

[42] Performances of the *Concert des Amateurs*, staffed by amateurs and in existence between ca. 1770 and 1781, were held at the Hôtel de Soubise.

d'Amis, Concert des Associés,[43] *Société de la Loge Olympique,*[44] *Société académique des Enfants d'Apollon,*[45] *Concerts de la Rue Grenelle, Concerts de la Rue de Cléry,* and *Théâtre Feydeau.* In addition, music could be heard at benefit concerts given by celebrities; benefit concerts given for schools, orphanages or other institutions; and at festival concerts at Colisée, Casino, Vauxhall Saint-Germain, Vauxhall (in the summer), and at the annual garden concert at Tuileries.[46]

Of the various concerts listed above, the most important was the *Concert spirituel.* Founded in 1725 by Anne-Danican Philidor, the *Concert spirituel* offered public performances to a paying audience. Concerts were held at the *Salle des Suisses* in the *Palais des Tuileries* until 1784; after this, they moved to the *Salle des Machenes,* where they continued on a regular basis up to 1790. Initially operas and works with non-French texts were forbidden, as were performances on opera days. Throughout the *Concert spirituel*'s existence, the focus was on large ensemble works (symphonic and choral) and virtuosic solo works. It was here that young composers, both native and foreign, had the chance to be heard.[47]

Programming of string quartets at the *Concert spirituel* and other public venues was not a consideration. There were no public string quartet performances before the nineteenth century; the medium did not become a viable professional form until well into the 1800s.[48] The few groups that did exist were oddities. The most common place to hear a string quartet performance was in the salon. Chamber music – either to listen to or to engage in – was for the amateur, and was best suited for the intimate concerts held in the privacy of one's home.[49]

---

[43] This was a trial ground for young artists who were not yet strong enough for public scrutiny.

[44] This *Société* was designed as a replacement for the *Concert des Amateurs.* Performances, held in the hall in the *Palais des Tuileries,* were led by Giovanni Battista Viotti.

[45] Between 1741 and 1789, one concert of solemn music was given each year.

[46] Brook, *La Symphonie française,* p. 28. See Mongrédien, "Paris: the End of the Ancien Régime", pp. 68–9, and Michel Brenet, *Les Concerts en France sous L'ancien Régime* (Paris: Librairie Fischbacher, 1900), especially pp. 363–6 for information about some of the organizations listed above.

[47] The most comprehensive study of the *Concert Spirituel,* both its history and the concert programs, is Constant Pierre's *Historie du Concert Spirituel, 1725-1790* (Paris: Heugel et Cie, 1975). See also Brenet, *Les Concerts en France.*

[48] A perusal of all the *Concert Spirituel* programs listed in Pierre's *Histoire du Concert Sprituel* reveals that not a single string quartet was performed during that organization's entire existence. Performances by four players did occur but the instrumentation was varied and was never the traditional string quartet: 10 April 1773 (no instrumentation listed), 2 February 1781 (keyboard, horn, clarinet, harp; repeated 4,15, and 22 April), and 2 February 1786 (keyboard, clarinet, horn, and *bon obl.*).

[49] Levy, "The Quatuor Concertant", pp. 37–8.

Unfortunately, our information about such settings is meager and incomplete. We know that Parisians had a huge appetite for quartet playing in the home. Circumstantial confirmation for this comes from the fact that after the first set of six French quartets were published in 1768 by Antoine Baudron (now lost), approximately one thousand other quartets appeared in print, including works by non-French musicians who correctly gauged the value of the Parisian market during the period 1770–1800. Since there were no public chamber concerts, there must have been widespread private performances.[50] Repertoire included not only the traditional quartets but arrangements of favorite opera tunes as well.[51] Private concerts were organized in the homes of both royalty and nobility alike. The queen, Madame de Pompadour (the king's mistress), the dauphin, dauphine Marie-Josephe of Saxony, the royal princesses, and Louis XV's daughters were well-known sponsors; royalty played as well as listened. Concerts could also be heard in the salons of the nobility such as the Prince of Conti, the Prince of Guéménée, the Duke of Aiguillon, Louis XV's minister, and the Prince of Condé at Chantilly.[52]

The Parisian salon was the meeting place for eighteenth-century society. It served as a stepping stone to a musical reputation and was an important performing venue; it was *the* place to meet culturally powerful people. Richard Viano has suggested that prior to the Revolution, the salon represented the decline of court influence and the rise of the bourgeoisie.[53] But even after the Revolution, Parisian salons remained for the cultured. Lofty conversation was a requirement as was refinement.

Music-making in the salon was more important than some scholars initially thought. Some salons, such as those of Antoine Crozat, Alexandre La Pouplinière, Baron de Bagge (which met on Fridays), and Prince de Conti (which met on Mondays), specialized in music. Other patrons, such as Mme Vigée-Lebrun, Mme de Genlis, and Mme d'Epinay, were known for their "mixed" salons. Rainer Gstrein argues that these were mainly literary gatherings which provided poets with a forum to present ideas and gave the nobility a place to engage in political as well as philosophical debate.[54] In either case, the main purpose of such gatherings was to discuss, hear, and experience the latest in French culture. Regardless of the size and motive, private concerts were expected and featured some of the leading musicians of

---

50   Mongrédien, "Paris: the End of the Ancien Régime", p. 78.
51   Levy, "The Quatuor Concertant", p. 35.
52   Mongrédien, "Paris: the End of the Ancien Régime", pp. 69–71.
53   Viano, "Jean-Baptiste Bréval", pp. 35–6.
54   Rainer Gstrein, "Musik in der *intimité* du salon: Pariser Salons des früher 19. Jahrhunderts als Stätten privaten Musizierens", in *Musica Privata: Die Rolle der Musik im privaten Leben* (ed. by Monika Fink, Rainer Gstrein, and Günter Mössmer; Innsbruck: Helbling, 1991), p. 113.

the day. Access was by invitation only. The patron decided who would come, who would play, and what would be listened to. Once admitted to a salon, one would not be surprised to see aristocrats, middle class writers, artists, and musicians mingling freely. Discussions ranged from the political to the financial and cultural interests of the day.[55] Music-making was present in all situations; the difference lay in its degree of emphasis. In all salons, whether they were musical or literary, one found an emphasis on stimulating conversation ("dialogué"), the spoken equivalent of chamber music. Musically, small chamber pieces – trios, quartets, etc. – were the norm, although the instrumentation was varied.

One may distinguish two types of "musical" salons: those with large resident performing ensembles; and those which featured chamber music performed by visiting and native professionals, and amateurs. The first mentioned is associated with the elite and the nobility: La Pouplinière, La Haye, Prince de Conti, Baron D'Ogny, Baron de Bagge, Prince de Guéménée, Duke d'Aiguillon, Maréchal de Noailles, Count d'Albaret, and Marquis de Seignelai. The number of private concerts in the homes of these aristocrats peaked in 1780. On these occasions, music was often regarded as but one form of entertainment; other activities might be planned. In the second type, found in the homes of such patrons as Madame de Genlis, M. de Rochechouart, and also Baron de Bagge, there was no need for dinner, conversation, or card games, for these were "truly private concerts, given by musicians for the pleasure and enlightenment of both musicians and musically literate *auditeurs*".[56]

Private concerts were often the only practical outlet for performance of small chamber pieces. Rehearsals were rare unless large forces were involved. Most often one expected to hear a solo voice accompanied by one or just a few instruments, but one might also hear operatic productions. Professional musicians mingled and played with the the noble-aristocratic amateur, whose skills were varied. As the century aged, the Parisian bourgeoisie became increasingly involved in actual performance. The middle class loved to perform, but actual records such as Burney's travel diaries are rare. Such conclusions are based on secondary sources and circumstantial evidence.

Baron de Bagge was one of the most renowned hosts of his day. Originally from Courland (Latvia), Bagge settled in Paris in 1751. His Friday evening concerts, although lacking in the "exclusivity" of those sponsored by royalty and nobility, were in a class by themselves. Bagge was connected to some of

[55] Richard J. Viano, "By Invitation Only: Private Concerts in France during the Second Half of the Eighteenth Century", *Recherches sur la Musique française classique* 27 (1991–92): 132–4.

[56] Ibid., p. 141.

the finest musicians of the day. The Mozarts visited in 1763 and 1778, and beginning in 1767, Luigi Boccherini remained with Bagge for two years. It was not unusual for a musician to debut at Bagge's *Hôtel* prior to a *Concert spirituel* performance. Among those musicians who passed through his door were Gaetano Besozzi, Nicholas Capron, François Devienne, Jean-Louis Duport, August Durand, Giovanni Giornovichi, Pierre Gaviniès, François-Joseph Gossec, Carlo Graziani, Rodolphe Kreutzer, Filippo Manfredi, Gertrud Mara, Etienne Ozy, Pierre Rode, Johann Wenzel Stich (Giovanni Punto), and Luiza Todi.[57] All played in his salon; some lived in his home for varying amounts of time.

Like Bagge, Alexandre-Jean-Joseph le Riche de la Pouplinière (d. 1762) sponsored many fine musicians.[58] A wealthy financier, la Pouplinière maintained an entire orchestra which was conducted, at different times, by Jean-Philippe Rameau, Johann Stamitz, and Gossec. He served as "protector" of young musicians and those making their debut. Concerts, which Georges Cucuel dubbed a "laboratoire musical", were held at his home in Passy and served as a testing ground prior to a musician's first public appearance.[59]

The Parisian salon offered the composer/performer the chance to obtain commissions and students, and served as a marketplace for manuscripts and published works. It was also a "dress rehearsal" before the public concert. Works could be previewed before being presented to the public at large.[60] Even during the Reign of Terror, when many fled Paris, patrons established salons in their residences-in-exile, then resumed activities once they returned to Paris. Such is the case with Madame de Staël in Coppett, Madame Necker in Geneva, Madame de Genlis in Berlin and Italy, Madame Vigée-Lebrun in London, and Madame de la Tour du Pin in Bordeaux.[61] Once the salon culture resumed, middle class salons[62] appeared beside those of the aristocracy.[63]

---

[57] For biographical information about Bagge, see especially Charles Michael Carroll, "A Beneficient Poseur: Charles Ernest, Baron de Bagge", *"Recherches" sur la Musique française classique* 16 (1976): 24–36 and Georges Cucuel, "Un mélomane au XVIIIᵉ siècle: La Baron de Bagge et son temps (1718-1791)", *L'Année Musicale* 1 (1911): 145–86.

[58] For biographical information about la Pouplinière, see Georges Cucuel, *La Pouplinière et la musique de chambre au XVIIIᵉ siècle* (Paris: Librairie, 1913; reprint ed., New York: Da Capo Press, 1971) and Brenet, *Les Concerts en France*, pp. 218–31.

[59] Cucuel, *La Pouplinière*, p. 228.

[60] Viano, "By Invitation Only", pp. 155–7.

[61] Ibid., p. 135.

[62] Such as those hosted by Madames de Lancy, Reccamier, Sophie Gay; journalist Emile de Girardin; writer Charles Nodier; and painter François Gerard.

[63] Among the more notable ones were those sponsored by Comte Chabral, governor of Paris, Vicomte d'Arlincourt, Marquise de Custine, Duchesse of Duros, Comtesse Baraguay d'Hilheis, and Ducesse d'Arantés. For a discussion of these salons, both in and out of France, see Gstrein, "Musik in der *intimité* du salon", p. 113.

London

In contrast to musical life in Paris, that in London grew out of entrepreneurship. Although the nobility and wealthy sponsored their own quartet parties and the like, home music-making among the middle class was a common occurrence. The general public had easy access to printed music, musical instruments, concert tickets, and music lessons. Music in late eighteenth-century London reflected the consumers' capabilities: simple enough for the amateur with pleasing tunes and standard harmonizations, yet at the same time, not so mundane as to be outside the "musically fashionable".[64]

Public concerts had existed in London since the 1670s; vocal selections were the standard fare. In the beginning, these concerts, mainly club meetings held in taverns, were informal, impromptu events. By the 1740s, programs still focused on larger vocal works. Only during the second half of the century did instrumental works become part of the regular concert fare. Even then however, there was no such thing as a harpsichord, chamber music, or solo song recital. The expected program consisted of a diverse group of of pieces with a wide variety of instrumentation.

By the second half of the eighteenth century, many concerts had moved out of the taverns and into larger halls with annual subscription series. An evening's entertainment was not limited solely to the concert hall; musical events were also held in theaters, city company halls, pleasure gardens,[65] dancing schools, as well as the taverns.[66] These last-mentioned venues were multi-functional, elegant spacious buildings. They were useful for banquets and social purposes as well as musical concerts.[67] In addition, they served as meeting places for musical societies. These gatherings of "serious amateurs" existed for the sole purpose of allowing a diverse group of people – leading businessmen, members of the gentry, and lower-middle-class artisans – to engage in music-making.[68] Most societies were private, but they did open their doors to the general public several times a year. According to C. F. Pohl, by the 1764–65 concert season, there were at least seven established groups: St. Cecilian Society, The Academy of Ancient Music, Castle-Society of Music,

---

[64]   William Weber, "London: a City of Unrivalled Riches", in *The Classical Era: From the 1740s to the end of the 18th Century* (ed. by Neal Zaslaw; Englewood Cliffs, New Jersey: Prentice Hall, 1989), pp. 295–7.

[65]   Among the better known ones were Vauxhall Gardens, Ranelagh Gardens, and Mary-le-bone Gardens.

[66]   Two of the better known ones were the London Tavern, and the Crown and Anchor Tavern

[67]   See Alec Hyatt King, "The London Tavern: a Forgotten Concert Hall", *Musical Times* 127 (1986): 382–5 for an interesting overview of the role of the tavern.

[68]   Hugh Arthur Scott, "London Concerts from 1700-1750", *The Musical Quarterly* 24 (1938): 197.

The Madrigal Society, The Noblemen and Gentlemen Catch Club, The Society of Musicians (Musical Fund Society), and The Corporation of the Sons of the Clergy.[69] All this confirms that in London, concert giving was a commercial activity.

Public concerts were initially small and poorly organized. Locations often seated a mere two hundred people. By the end of the century however, it was not uncommon for concerts to be held in larger rooms such as the Pantheon Hall, which could accommodate over two thousand. Such events rivaled opera performances and were important cultural affairs. Public concerts were as varied as there were many. Programs were a potpourri: symphonies alternated with vocal selections and other smaller ensembles. Pohl, for example listed the following types of compositions one might hear during the third quarter of the eighteenth century: sonatas, duos, trios, violin concerti, keyboard pieces, overtures, operas, and oratorios.[70] Noticeably missing was any mention of the string quartet. It was not until the 1790s that the string quartet became a regular part of the concert repertoire, and then, only in certain settings.

Most public concerts (excluding those connected to the theater) were centered in the fashionable West End of London. Market demand kept the personalities and repertoire in a state of constant change.[71] Performances were divided into several "Acts", each of which featured works for orchestra and smaller ensemble. The concert-going public had many choices: opera and oratorio, subscription and benefits concerts, or summer concerts in one of many gardens. All events were advertised. Leading performers usually gave an annual benefit concert which would be heavily advertised in such papers as the *Public Advertiser*. These same performers also played at concerts of the elite, although these were neither announced nor available for general admission. Whatever the case, Londoners enjoyed an active concert life, but one that focused primarily on the larger forces. The chamber concert on its own did not exist.

London's first public string quartet performance took place in 1769, and featured Antonín Kammel's Op. 4. From 1774 on and in contrast to Paris and Vienna, chamber works (although not necessarily string quartets) were a regular part of London's public concert programs. The repertoire was not simple; from the start it required professional level players.[72] By 1788,

---

[69]   C. F. Pohl, *Mozart und Haydn in London* (Vienna: Carl Gerold's Sohn, 1867), pp. 12–33. By 1791, the number of societies had increased to eleven: Academy of Ancient Music, Madrigal Society, Noblemen and Gentlemen Catch-Club, Concerts of Ancient Music, Professional Concerts, Glee Clubs, Corporation of the Sons of the Clergy, Royal Society of Musicians of Great Britain, New Musical Fund, and Choral Fund.

[70]   Ibid., pp. 10–11.

[71]   McVeigh, *Concert Life in London*, pp. 4–6.

[72]   Ibid., p. 105.

evidence suggests that a performing professional string quartet existed. Pohl mentions that Johann Peter Salomon worked on a regular basis with Borghi, Blake, and Smith.[73] Some quartets became strongly linked with particular performers; thus in 1788, Cramer was warned not to play a certain Pleyel quartet because of its recognized connection to Salomon.[74]

It was not until the 1790s that the string quartet entered the public concert repertoire with any frequency. By then, one could expect to see quartets programmed on concerts sponsored by either the Anacreonic Society or the New Musical Fund.[75] This more regular performance coincided with the establishment of the professional ensemble. For example, when Salomon organized his concert series, he routinely scheduled string quartet performances by his own group. Thus a quartet from Haydn's Op. 64 was premiered on 24 February 1791, by Salomon (violin 1), Mountain (violin 2), Hindmarsch (viola), and Menell (cello). During the next few years, this same group, with one personnel change, premiered the rest of Op. 64, Opp. 71/74, and works by others such as Pleyel. This group was different from previously "established" ones such as the Font family or the Esterháza Quartet in that it was a publicly recognized entity performing in a professional capacity. We also know that those concerts organized by Wilhelm Cramer featured performances of string quartets. In February 1791, a Haydn string quartet was played by Cramer, Borghi, Blake, and Smith. The program itself was a varied one and included a *sinfonie*, some songs, a piano sonata, a concerto, and an overture.[76]

Quartets could be heard both publicly and in private parties. The public aspect can be documented; the private one is much harder to determine except by anecdote. We know through an examination of programs that quartets were often heard in the Hanover Square Rooms during the 1791–92 season as part of the Salomon Concerts.[77] A similar perusal for the 1794–95 season reveals the continued frequency of quartet performance.[78] Quartets were also standard fare

---

[73] Pohl, *Mozart und Haydn*, p. 81.

[74] McVeigh, *Concert Life in London*, p. 97.

[75] See Pohl's comments in *Mozart und Haydn*, vol. 2, pp. 10, 23.

[76] Ibid., vol. 1, p. 116; vol. 2, pp. 3–5. See also vol. 1, p. 113, where Pohl mentions a Pleyel quartet performed at a 20 February 1791 subscription concert for the nobility.

[77] Landon, *Haydn: Chronicle and Works*, vol. 3, pp. 60–149, 155, lists the following concert dates for string quartet performance (composers are given in parentheses): 1 April 1791 (Kozeluch), 15 April 1791(Haydn), 6 May 1791 (Haydn), 13 May 1791 (Haydn), 20 February 1792 (Pleyel), 24 February 1792 (Gyrowetz), 5 March 1791 (Pleyel), 12 March 1792 (Rawlings Jr.), 16 March 1792 (Haydn), 20 March 1792 (Raimondi, Haydn), 23 March 1791 (Cambini or Haydn?), and 13 April 1792 (Gyrowetz).

[78] Noting just the performances of Haydn's quartets for the 1794–95 season, Landon, ibid., pp. 235–97, lists the following dates: 17 February 1794, 10 March 1794, 24 March 1794, 31 March 1794, and 24 March 1795.

for benefit concerts as seen at the 28 May 1792 event organized by Barthelemon and Haelser, and at a 1 June 1792 concert for Madame Mara.[79]

Although chamber music had entered the public repertoire, it was still, even in the 1790s, most closely associated with the private home. During the 1770s and 1780s, in particular, quartets were a featured part of private settings ("quartet parties"). These morning activities gave amateurs the chance to show off; professional string players added sophistication. For example, at the home of the surgeon William Sharp, one routinely expected to find a professional-level string quartet performance.[80]   Fanny Burney, in describing a private concert from March of 1778, mentioned the performance of several "quartettos".[81]   Over two decades later, these private parties were still part of the London musical scene, as evidenced in a letter from Rev. Thomas Twinning to Charles Burney dated 4 May 1791.[82]

In addition to these private parties, we also know, through anecdotal accounts, of quartet parties held by royalty. Members of George III's family were enthusiastic supporters and some were participants. In a diary entry of 3 November 1761, the Duchess of Northumberland wrote that Queen Charlotte had a chamber concert every Wednesday at which the Princess of Wales and all her children were present.[83] A similar setting is noted by Charlotte Papendiek who wrote that quartet parties were held at court twice a week during the year 1774.[84] And during the 1780s, the Prince of Wales often joined in the regularly held evening "quartett parties", many of which were led by the violin virtuoso, Felice de Giardini.[85] For the Prince, a skilled cellist, the string quartet was a favorite medium. He insisted on morning concerts, with no extraneous talking. These concerts continued up until his marriage in 1795.[86]

[79]   Pohl, *Mozart und Haydn*, p. 204.   Pohl lists the performers – Salomon, Barthelemon, Hindmarsch and Chr. Schram for the first, Salomon, Damen, Hindmarsch, and Menell for the second – but not the actual piece.

[80]   McVeigh, *Concert Life in London*, p. 46.

[81]   Ibid., pp. 45–6.

[82]   Landon, *Haydn Chronicles*, vol. 3, p. 155.

[83]   James Grieg, ed., *The Diaries of a Duchess: Extracts from The Diaries of the First Duchess of Northumberland (1716–1776)* (London: Hodden and Stoughton, 1926), p. 41.

[84]   Charlotte Papendiek, *Court and Private Life in the Time of Queen Charlotte* (2 vols; London: Bentley and Son, 1887), vol. 1, p. 65.

[85]   Ibid., vol. 1, p. 133. Giardini, who often adapted music for these gatherings, was also known to hold his own quartet parties.

[86]   McVeigh, *Concert Life in London*, pp. 51–2, 68.

Vienna

The old system of musical patronage lasted longer in Vienna than in either London or Paris. Vienna, seemingly dearth of public concerts, was much slower to develop an appropriate forum. There were individual concerts and series, but no long-lasting institutional sets. The small amount of non-private performance that did exist was dominated by theater and opera.[87] Such events did not occur until the last part of the century. Performances sponsored by the Tonkünstler-Societät or the Associiierten Cavaliers (under the direction of Gottfried van Swieten), or those at the summer palace of Prince Liechtenstein often programmed large works such as oratorios.[88]

Prior to 1800, solo instrumental sonatas and chamber music were not considered concert material. Performance of chamber music outside the noble domicile was almost unknown. Mary Sue Morrow noted that the period 1761–1810 saw not a single public performance of a string quartet,[89] no less an entire concert of such music. Audiences expected variety in their concerts; single-genre events were considered monotonous. Presentation of the string quartet in public was not supported by the music societies until the establishment of the series organized by Ignaz Schuppanzigh as part of the Gesellschaft der Musikfreunde concerts in 1812.[90]

For much of the second half of the eighteenth century, chamber music in Vienna was a nobility-supported endeavor. Finscher suggested that the Viennese nobility remained part of the music-making scene longer than in other cities because it had greater technical skill. Members of the upper class rarely lowered themselves to playing anything but that which required great competence and facility. Their disdain of the lighter works aimed at the

---

[87] For the most complete coverage of concert life in Vienna during this time period, see Mary Sue Morrow, *Concert Life in Haydn's Vienna: Aspects of a Developing Musical and Social Institution* (Steyvesant, New York: Pendragon Press, 1989). A brief overview can be found in Bruce Alan Brown, "Maria Theresa's Vienna," and John A. Rice, "Vienna under Joseph II and Leopold II", both of which appear in *The Classical Era: From the 1740s to the end of the Eighteenth Century* (ed. by Neal Zaslaw; Englewood Cliffs, New Jersey: Prentice Hall, 1989), pp. 99–125 and 126–165 respectively.

[88] Otto Biba, "Concert Life in Beethoven's Vienna", in *Beethoven, Performers, and Critics: Detroit 1977* (ed. by Robert Winter and Bruce Carr; Detroit: Wayne State University Press, 1980), pp. 80–1.

[89] Morrow, *Concert Life in Haydn's Vienna*, p. 161. A perusal of Appendix One ("Public Concert Calendar") however reveals two string quartet performances: 1 September 1783 (p. 254) and 21 December 1784 (p. 257). Both concerts were organized by Christoph Torricella and featured six quartets by a single composer. The former highlighted works by Hoffmeister, the latter featured those of Pleyel. Morrow lists these concerts as "Other" possibly indicating that these concerts took place at an otherwise unknown location.

[90] Biba, "Concert Life in Beethoven's Vienna", p. 81.

amateur may possibly stem from the desire to distance themselves from the bourgeoisie.[91]

The string quartet in Vienna was a connoisseur's genre. It was written for the skilled musician's amusement and required careful practice. What few descriptions we have of private Viennese concerts mention intimate gatherings in private salons, filled with knowledgeable musicians. According to Morrow, such evenings might start with a string quartet; this signaled the concert's beginning.[92]   Such concerts could be one of six different types: spontaneous social events, more formalized after-dinner entertainments, special parties and celebrations which included musical performances, participatory chamber music, gala occasions with elaborate productions, and regular formal concerts (musical salons). Not all were conducive to string quartet performance, but in at least the participatory and formal types, one could expect to hear quartets, especially toward the end of the century.[93]   In the former, music lovers – both professional and amateur – gathered for the express purpose of playing music. Of these daytime sessions, the most famous ones were held in the early 1780s by Baron Gottfried van Swieten, who presided over weekly music-making sessions in the imperial library. Similar gatherings took place in the salons of the Schmierer's and at the Hofrath Schubb's.[94]   The latter type – the private concert – was common amongst the nobility. Emperor Joseph held private quartet concerts every afternoon. A report of 1790 comments that this was a long-standing practice. Joseph either played piano or cello, or sang. He was joined by Johann Kilian Strack, Franz Kreibich, and Thomas Woborzill. In special circumstances Leopold Hoffmann, Bonnheimer,[95] Ignaz Umlauff, or Joseph Krottendorfer also participated. The concert took place after dinner and lasted until theater-time. One routinely expected to hear works by Gassmann and Ordoñez; works by Haydn and Mozart were programmed less frequently.[96]

Some patrons maintained whole musical establishments in their homes as was the case with Prince Joseph Friedrich of Saxe-Hildeburghausen[97] and Prince Paul Anton Esterházy. Archdukes and duchesses were musically accomplished enough that they could take part in private musical productions. The favored repertoire of the eighteenth-century salon was the lighter fare, including works by Kozeluch and Pleyel.

---

[91]   Finscher, "Zur Sozialgeschichte", p. 37.
[92]   Morrow, *Concert Life in Haydn's Vienna*, p. 142.
[93]   Ibid., pp. 3–9.
[94]   Ibid., p. 31. Morrow refers to the entry in Rosenbaum's diary in which he discusses the complete performance of a string quartet at the Schubb's place.
[95]   First name unknown. Kirkendale describes him as a "musician in Vienna".
[96]   Kirkendale, *Fugue and Fugato*, pp. 38–9.
[97]   Only when he left Vienna for his estates in 1761, did the Prince dismiss his musical establishment.

As the century wore on, it became common for a nobleperson to support a single concert or piece, rather than house and fund a permanent performing ensemble. This new type of patron might invite local musicians to his home to perform in weekly concerts.[98] Many middle class patrons also participated in this type of music sponsorship. These newly-arrived benefactors wanted music that they could enjoy both as a spectator and as a participant. Many were well-trained which stood them in good stead since hiring a professional was not always an option. As the century progressed the middle class became increasingly important as patrons of music and arbiters of musical taste.

The Viennese professional string quartet developed from these chamber music mornings. The first one, organized ca. 1795, was led by Ignaz Schuppanzigh. Along with Louis Sina (violin 2), Franz Weiss (viola) and Anton Kraft (cello), Schuppanzigh performed every Friday morning at the residence of Prince Lichnowsky and later at Prince Rasumofsky's. But these were private performances only; throughout the 1790s, string quartets, and chamber music in general, were still almost unknown in the public arena. Only during the first decade of the 1800s did Schuppanzigh's group begin performing for formal subscription concerts.[99]

This lack of public performance is confirmed by a near-complete absence of documentation of such situations. Our knowledge of private performances, although scanty, at least verifies the place of the string quartet in the salon. A simple review of these is helpful. In addition to the above-cited private concerts in the chamber of Emperor Joseph II, we know that in 1773 Charles Burney wrote about a performance of a Haydn quartet in which Carlo d'Ordonez took part.[100] The following decade, the *Pressburger Zeitung* issued a report (12 January 1782) about a concert given in Countess von Norden's rooms on 26 December 1781. The music was by "Herr Haydn" and members of the quartet included "Messrs Luig Tomasini, Apfelmayr, Weigl, and Huber". The article notes the fine reception accorded the music for which Haydn received an "enamelled golden box set with brillants" and each of the other musicians received a "golden snuff-box".[101] Michael Kelly makes mention of a "quartett party" in his *Reminiscences* during his visit to Vienna ca. 1784. Apparently due to the delayed arrival of Signor Blasi, who was travelling from Venice to take part in the production of Casti's *Il Re Teodoro*, Kelly's host, Mr. Storace decided to give a quartet party. According to Kelly, the players

---

[98] Rice, "Vienna Under Joseph II", pp. 129–30.
[99] Morrow, *Concert Life in Haydn's Vienna*, pp. 9–10; Baron, *Intimate Music*, p. 243.
[100] Cited in A. Peter Brown, "Introduction" in *Carlo d'Ordonez: String Quartets, Opus 1*, vol. 10: *Recent Researches in the Music of the Classical Era* (Madison, WI: A-R editions, 1980), p. vii.
[101] Marianne Pandi and Fritz Schmidt, compilers, "Music in Haydn's and Beethoven's Time Reported by the Pressburger Zeitung", *The Haydn Yearbook* 8 (1971): 274.

"were tolerable, not one of them excelled on the instrument he played, but there was a little science among them, which I dare say will be acknowledged when I name them: The first violin...Haydn, the second violin...Baron Dittersdorf, the violoncello...Vanhall, the tenor...Mozart...a greater treat or a remarkable one cannot be imagined".[102]   A similarly illustrious body of performers and connoisseurs can be found in the gathering at Mozart's home on 12 February 1785 where both Haydn and Mozart again took part.[103] And to the above we can add the private weekly parties sponsored by Prince Lichnowsky, Count Rasumofsky, and Nikolaus Zmeskall von Domanowecz.[104]

Outside Vienna, the string quartet enjoyed great favor, but again as a form of private music-making and not for public consumption. And as in Vienna, it was something enjoyed by both professionals and amateurs, nobility and middle class alike.[105] The quartet was valued as a serious genre for private music-making among serious players. It was the favored ensemble among courtiers, Kapelle members, princely families, and even some rulers (for example, Bavarian Elector, Prince of Fürstenberg, Frederick the Great, Friedrich Wilhelm II) across Germany at Berlin, Regensburg, Mecklenburg, Schwerin, and Oettingen-Wallerstein.[106] Performance was for the learned music lover, regardless of station, and took place in chamber concerts at court and in private homes. We have only limited documentation concerning string quartet performance, much of it anecdotal. Burney wrote about attending a concert in Hamburg on 11 October 1773, at the house of M. Westphal whom he described as "an eminent and worthy music-merchant". The performers were dilettantes.[107] A decade later, Cramer's *Magazin der Musik* noted a performance on 17 November 1782, of two quartets from Haydn's Op. 33, played in the Westphalian House.[108]

Only in the 1790s, as the genre became more complex, and as the piano assumed the function of providing domestic entertainment for amateurs, did the string quartet enter the domain of professional and concert music.[109] This

---

[102] Michael Kelly, *Reminiscences of Michael Kelly of the King's Theatre and Theatre Royal Drury Lane* (New York: J. F. J. Harper, 1826), pp. 150–1.

[103] Landon, *Haydn: Chronicle and Works*, vol. 2, pp. 508–9.

[104] Ibid., vol. 4, pp. 25–30.

[105] See the discussions by Unverricht, "Privates Quartettspiel", p. 111, and Rudolf Walter, "Die Autobiographie des Chordirektors von St. Maria auf dem Sande in Breslau Ignatz Lukas (1762-1837)", *Musik des Ostens* 8 (1982): 87.

[106] See Fiona Little, *The String Quartet at the Oettingen-Wallerstein Court: Ignaz von Beecke and his Contemporaries* (New York: Garland Publishing Inc., 1989), pp. 1–45 for a fine discussion of the role of the string quartet in Germany ca. 1770–1800.

[107] Burney, *The Present State*, p. 257.

[108] Cited in Landon, *Haydn: Chronicle and Works*, vol. 2, p. 582. Two members of the performing group are named: violinist Schick and cellist Trickler.

[109] Little, *The String Quartet*, pp. 44–5.

also coincided with the rise of music publishing in Vienna and the surrounding environs. In contrast to Paris, Vienna was slow to establish publishing houses. Most string quartet music up to the 1780s was available only in manuscript form and, according to Burney's comments, was very expensive to obtain. Thus ownership of music was effectively restricted to those who could afford it. Once the publishing firm Artaria established itself in 1778, followed by Kozeluch and Hoffmeister, the situation changed. Sheet music was much more readily available, and many of the above-named firms specialized in music that appealed to the amateur musician, for this naturally translated into higher sales. Consequently, during the decade 1780–90, music printing gradually replaced hand copies as the major way of reproducing music. For the composer, this change was revolutionary. No longer was he dependent on the good will of single person or small group of benefactors. Instead if he so desired, he could offer his music to the public at large. And, provided he wrote to the public's taste, he would be rewarded with sales.

It is not too much to suggest that the form of transmission – manuscript or published – often influenced a composer's stylistic decisions. A creative ideal might be tempered by a knowledge of place of performance, type of performer, and skill level. Just as composers did not work in a musical vacuum, any examination of the eighteenth-century string quartet should not be restricted to structural and theoretical components; rather, it should incorporate the social and cultural milieu as well.

Chapter 3

String quartet types: toward a reconsideration

Music of the late-eighteenth century still functioned in court life, but it was also a basic part of the middle class. Royalty was no longer the chief patron and commissioner of music. Increasingly, the bourgeoisie and aristocrats were important consumers both at the public concert, which became more common, and through the purchase of publications or subscriptions. At the same time, home music-making increased and there was an ever-growing number of small concerts in private domiciles; these provided entertainment for the middle class.[1] These home concerts, by necessity, could not feature large ensembles due to both the expense and the difficulties which arose in accommodating such a group. The string quartet, with its limited number of players and therefore, reduced expenses and space requirements, was the ideal medium for home entertainment. There was not, however, a single type of quartet throughout Europe. Rather, we find numerous types, each of which reflected the needs of a particular group of people or locale. Division of quartets into types – *Hausmusik, concertant*, Viennese, and less often *brilliant* – has traditionally been carried out along theoretical or formal lines. Use of these modifiers allows the researcher to begin with a predetermined set of expectations which may or may not be met. Regardless, the genre is looked at in terms of musical style, not as chamber music. While a more appropriate method of examination will be suggested below, it is important to understand the meaning of each of these divisions.

Hausmusik

The term *Hausmusik*, when linked to the string quartet, designates music intended for everyday use and for performance by musicians possessing a wide range of technical and interpretive skills. These works are typically lighter in texture (homophonic) and contain a minimal amount of interplay between the instruments. The phrasing is regular, rhythms are uncomplicated, and melodies are immediately accessible.

---

[1] See Levy, "The Quatuor Concertant", pp. 23–4, for a summation of the basic research on the social history of music for the eighteenth century. See also her fn. 1 on p. 24 for a select bibliography of this topic.

Although some works featured four parts of only modest technical requirements, it was more common to find *Hausmusik* which emphasized the first violin at the expense of the lower voices. Works such as those written by Ignace Pleyel often fit into this category; the listener is most aware of the acrobatics performed by the first violin and only minimally conscious of what the other voices are doing. From 1785 on, Pleyel's works, which circulated with great success, familiarized the bourgeois chamber music public with such a quartet style. One theory, as advanced by Finscher, was that such compositions served as a stepping stone for the middle class; the ultimate goal was to develop one's ability to understand and recognize the supremacy of Haydn's chamber works.[2]

There is another way to view the success of Pleyel's pieces: they meet a specific need on the part of musicians. Even if one does not possess great technical skills, one can still engage in music-making and enjoy high quality works. And in fact as Hickman has noted, only the first violinist need be a professional musician. Thus these *Hausmusik* pieces could and should be evaluated on their own merits, rather than as "poor" relations to the Haydn (Viennese) quartet.

The actual playing material was not restricted solely to original string quartets. Home music-making sessions often included arrangements of other popular works: charming orchestral music, larger chamber compositions, oratorios, folk songs, and above all, popular opera arias. This purely functional aspect of *Hausmusik* fed the need of a ravenous middle class for the newest opera melodies. The origin of this practice came from Paris, where from 1760 on, one could easily purchase *ariettes en symphonie* or from 1770, *Quatuors d'airs connues* or *d'airs dialogués*. In these works, the dominance of the first violin meant that players of varying abilities could come together to enjoy chamber music.[3]

The *Hausmusik* type of string quartet peaked during the years 1790-1810 and was superseded by the *quatuor brillant*, which featured an even more virtuosic first violin part. This was also the time that the *Hausmusik* quartet left the private dwelling and became part of the concert repertoire. While *Hausmusik* was frequently played before small circles up to 1800, dedicated to particular patrons, or programmed as part of a subscription concert series, the *quatuor brillant* belonged to the larger concert halls (see below) and found a home with traveling virtuosi and those that wished to hear concerto-like pieces.[4]

---

[2]   Finscher, "Zur Sozialgeschichte", p. 38.

[3]   Ibid.

[4]   Ibid. See also Paul Henry Lang, Review of *Studien zur Geschichte des Streichquartetts* by Ludwig Finscher, *The Musical Quarterly* 63 (1977): 107, who suggests that those quartets with a dominant first violin part were really performance pieces and not designed for home music-making.

The *quatuor concertant*

More popular than the *Hausmusik* type was the *quatuor concertant.*[5] The *quatuor concertant* developed in Paris during the 1770s, perhaps as a result of the *symphonie concertante*, a form in which instruments were treated in turn in a solo fashion, resulting in a homophonic, or less frequently, a dialogue texture. The actual development is clouded by the often misleading titles. Prior to 1770, quartets might be designated as symphonies or quartets, *quatuors en Symphonie*, or *quatuors et simphonies à 4 parties.*[6] For example, in 1766, la Chevardière issued six symphonies by Christian Cannabich with the title (and instructions): "Six symphonies, the first three of which may be played as octets or quartets and the three others by full orchestra obbligato". Thus the interpretation and execution of these pieces was less than definite; quality of sound varied based on the number of performers.[7]

Although centered in Paris, and less so in London, this type of quartet became common throughout the continent. The term itself was initially employed in a somewhat loose fashion, but it came to stand for a piece with specific characteristics, namely a two- or three-movement composition for two violins, viola, and cello in which some or all of the instruments have prominent passages. Those *quatuors* laid out in two movements generally opened with a sonata allegro movement and closed with either a rondo/rondeau or a theme and variations. The three-movement plan contained a slow or moderately slow middle movement in ABA, rondo, or similarly simple form. The genre was characterized by melodic material shared among all voices, a lack of fugal treatment of thematic material, short developments, and in the sonata movements, a considerably longer secondary key area in which a vast majority of the dialogue occurs.[8]

Although understood to be scored for four solo string instruments (without continuo), these were not necessarily virtuosic works. Some florid or embellished writing was common, but one did not necessarily expect brilliancy and showiness. Each player was guaranteed a share in the main melodic action – as a soloist, as

---

[5]   The two standard sources for the *quatuor concertant* are Janet Levy's excellent dissertation, "The Quatuor Concertant in Paris in the Latter Half of the Eighteenth Century", and Dieter Lutz Trimpert, *Die Quatuors Concertants von Giuseppe Cambini* (Tutzing: Hans Schneider, 1967), esp. pp. 173–206.

[6]   Trimpert, *Die Quatuors Concertants*, pp. 187–8.

[7]   Mongrédien, "Paris: the End of the Ancien Régime", p. 76.

[8]   Levy, "The Quatuor Concertant", pp. 100–101.

a participant in a momentary dialogue, or in larger alternation with the other part(s).[9]

"Concertant", in the eighteenth-century sense, referred not only to solo performance, but also to a style in which each member of the ensemble partook in the presentation of melodic material ("dialogué") or mutually created the main line of a melody.[10] The term did not necessarily imply a conversational style in which motivic material is tossed about from instrument to instrument, but rather one which allows each instrument to play a melodic passage in its entirety before receding to the background to let another take over.

The term "dialogué" was often applied to French chamber music ca. 1770. This word, frequently used interchangeably with "concertant", informed the musician and listener alike that all the instruments were important, not just the first violin, and that all took part.[11] *Dialogué* introduced the concept of conversation,[12] which in the French aesthetic, emphasized words, discourse, and the salon practice of polite exchange of ideas. Here each voice responded to another, but only after the "speaking" party had fully completed its thought. The *quatuor concertant*, with its statement and response style, was the musical equivalent of the art of conversation with which eighteenth-century France was obsessed.[13]

This art of conversation was highly valued by French theorists. L'Abbé André Morellet's *De la conversation* was fairly representative in its approach.[14] The author detailed eleven bad habits of conversation including: being inattentive, interrupting someone else or speaking simultaneously, showing off, being

---

[9]   Levy, "The Quatuor Concertant", p. 60. Employment of this criteria explains why Finscher, and those he has influenced, dismissed the *quatuor concertant* as insignificant since this means of describing the genre does not focus on those structural aspects – four-movement cycle, development of sonata form, motivic work – which are viewed as essential to the establishment of a classical prototype.

[10] Ibid., pp. 49–51.

[11] Lionel de La Laurencie, "Les Débuts de la Musique de Chambre en France", *Revue de Musicologie* 15 (1934): 222.

[12] Many published works actually included the terms "conversation" and "dialogue" on the title page. See for example, Haydn's oft-cited Op. 1, published by de la Chevardière in 1764, as *Six Symphonies ou quatuors dialogués pour deux violons, alto et basse*. See also Guillemain's 1746 publication, *Six sonates en quatuor ou conversations galantes et amusantes entre une flûte traversière, un violon, une basse de viol et la basse continue.*

[13] Barbara Hanning, "Conversation and Musical Style in the late Eighteenth-Century Parisian Salon", *Eighteenth-Century Studies* 22 (1989): 512.

[14] See also Levy's discussion of the writings of Koch (*Versuch, Lexikon*), de Momigny, and Rousseau in her "The Quatuor Concertant", pp. 203–8. The French, in particular were interested in dialogue for it allowed them to avoid a thick texture but at the same time, move beyond the simple melody plus accompaniment approach to one with exchange and enough "individualization of parts to *effect* a sense of greater activity and provide a substitute for counterpoint".

pedantic or egotistical, and dominating the conversation. (The parallels with the *quatuor concertant* are quite obvious and need little elaboration here.) Morellet cautioned against isolating a particular word at the expense of a general subject. Musically, this corresponded to a concern for too much motivic development. Thus the French practice of allowing a melody to unfold in its entirety, free of interruption, was rooted in the art of conversation.[15]

An essential part of the *quatuor concertant* was its quasi-democratic distribution of soloistic material among the four players. In theory, all four instruments played nearly equal and mutually important roles.[16] This was achieved through the rotation of melodic material within a basically homophonic texture. Composers rarely incorporated counterpoint and motivic interplay in their works; rather, they utilized texture to create contrasts and maintain interest. "The very life of the genre...depends on striking, appealing changes of texture."[17] And in fact, the term *dialogué*, used frequently on title pages to attract the attention of the French public so enamored with the art of conversation, referred mainly to texture. Its presence promised the purchaser and listener a conversation among four participants.[18]

But what kind of conversation can the listener expect? Anton Reicha, in his *Traité de mélodie*, discusses four ways to "dialogue a melody": the entire melody may be presented *in toto* by one, then another voice; phrases or ideas of a melody may be distributed among the voices; the melody may be presented with some imitation; and the melody may begin in one voice and finish in another.[19] In the *quatuor concertant*, dialogue fills out a structural outline, reinforces or extends a period, or may simply provide musical filler.[20] It may also give a sense of movement and forward motion. What the listener will not find is the cultivation of an entire movement of *conversation*, complete with interrupted statements. Conversation encompasses all four members of the group; dialogue implies restricted participation of two, possibly three members of the ensemble.

Levy estimates that no fewer than two hundred composers wrote *quatuors concertants* and that nearly thirty-six hundred such works appeared on the Parisian market during the period 1770–1800.[21] French or "transplanted" composers

---

[15]   Ibid., pp. 515–18.
[16]   Mongrédien, "Paris: the End of the Ancien Régime", p. 78. Rousseau, in his *Dictionaire*, argued that this was an impossibility since four equal parts could not be placed on an equal footing.
[17]   Levy, "The Quatuor Concertant", p. 207. For a discussion of the characteristics of the genre, see pp. 42-60.
[18]   Hanning, "Conversation and Musical Style", p. 520.
[19]   Anton Reicha, *Traité de mélodie* (Paris, 1814), p. 117. Quoted in Hanning, "Conversation and Musical Style", p. 522.
[20]   Levy, "The Quatuor Concertant", pp. 221, 226.
[21]   Ibid., p. 8.

residing in the Paris area such as Antoine Laurent Baudron, Antoine Bullant, Giuseppe Maria Cambini, Nicolas-Marie Dalayrac, Jean-Baptiste Davaux, François-Joseph Gossec, Le Chevalier Joseph-Boulogne de Saint-Georges, Pierre Vachon, Giovanni Battista Viotti, and others produced the largest number of *quatuors concertants*. Their works bore the characteristics outlined above. But a large number of German and Viennese composers also wrote for the Parisian market, tailoring their style to meet public demand. Among them were Franz Aspelmayr, Christian Cannabich, Anton Filtz, Adalbert Gyrowetz, Franz Anton Hoffmeister, Antonín Kammel, Leopold Kozeluch, Carl Stamitz, Johann Baptist Vanhall, Josef Wölfl, and Paul Wranitzky. Others, including Luigi Boccherini and Ignace Pleyel, who spent at least part of their lives in Paris composed quartets in both the Parisian and Viennese styles, orienting themselves towards different markets.

The *quatuor brillant*

The *quatuor concertant*, while still popular in Paris, did not remain static. During the 1790s some *quatuors* were written to meet the needs and demands of professional musicians. Virtuoso performers, usually violinists and no longer satisfied with the solos of the *quatuor concertant*, altered their compositional approach and conception of the French medium. These new-style *quatuors brillants* were designed as showcases for their own prowess. In contrast to the *quatuor concertant*, the *quatuor brillant* often focused on virtuosity for its own sake. Such works, initially written by Cambini, then taken up by Dalayrac, Davaux, Josephus Andreas Fodor, Gossec, Hyacinthe Jadin, and Viotti, were essentially violin concerti, some of which even contained cadenzas. There was little dialogue in these works; rather the listener expected to hear melody and accompaniment throughout, with little if no change in each instrument's roles. One positive outcome of this arrangement was that professionals and amateurs could play together, much as was previously noted with the *Hausmusik* type of quartet. The professional would assume responsibility for the first violin part, the amateurs, for the remaining voices.

Once introduced to Viennese audiences and composers, the new medium found a receptive audience alongside the *quatuor concertant* and Viennese quartet, at least through the late 1790s. The Viennese *quatuor brillant* had much in common with the *quatuor concertant* including the simple structures, the two- and three-movement sequence, and the emphasis on melody. But it differed from its French counterparts – both the *quatuor concertant* and the *quatuor brillant* – in that while the former was written for the amateur with limited skill, the latter, with its focus on virtuosity, *in all parts*, required execution by four professionals. Thus while the Viennese *quatuor brillant* was equivalent to the French form in terms of structure, it differed from it with regard to technical requirements.[22] In the hands of Viennese composers such as Paul and Anton Wranitzky, Adalbert Gyrowetz, and Franz Krommer, the medium became a showcase for the talents of several members of an ensemble.

Hickman attributed the success of the *quatuor brillant* in Vienna partly to the changing social climate. With the decline of the aristocracy and the rise of the middle class, the nobility had to reconsider its lifestyle often at the expense of maintaining private orchestras. A less costly but quite satisfactory substitute was the professional string quartet.[23] The medium showcased the technical skill of its members and revealed its ability to mimic the dramatic contrasts and effects of the orchestra. The combination of these aspects encouraged composers to take a theatrical approach when writing for the string quartet during the 1790s.

The Viennese quartet and the "classical ideal"

In Vienna, the breakdown of the older patronage system forced composers to work independently of the court. Publishing houses and public concerts became important venues for both the aspiring and established musician. Composers tailored their works to meet the taste and desires of the non-professional musician. Seeking the widest possible audience, they initially produced works based on the popular Parisian *quatuor concertant* style. The leading composers were many of the same ones associated with the *Hausmusik* type of quartet: Pleyel, Hoffmeister, Gyrowetz, Haydn, and Anton Wranitzky.

It was not long however, before the learned amateur became the more important consumer in Vienna. The typical Viennese string quartet was synonymous with music written for the well-educated noble person – the *Kenner*. It required an intellectual approach both on the part of the listener and the performer. The Viennese quartet, which culminated in the post-1780 compositions of Haydn and Mozart, was written with this connoisseur in mind and included such features as a four-movement structure, the first of which was in sonata form, intensive thematic manipulation, harmonic shocks, and counterpoint. Although *concertante* elements and a melodically prominent first violin were still evident, composers showed a greater interest in the integration of the ensemble voices.

Toward the end of the century, Viennese composers again changed their approach, based on consumer demand, and one finds a fusion of Viennese and Parisian styles as was the case with Mozart's late quartets and those of Paul

---

[22]   See Hickman, "The Flowering of the Viennese String Quartet", pp. 165–8, for an excellent discussion of the Viennese *quatuor brillant* and its relationship to the Viennese quartet, and the French *quatuor brillant* and *quatuor concertant*.

[23]   Ibid.

Wranitzky. Hickman notes that within the Viennese repertoire one can find three types of quartets existing side by side: the *quatuor concertant*, the *quatuor brillant*, and the Viennese classical quartet. Ironically, the type of quartet we have so long referred to as the "true" kind of quartet (the Viennese) was written by relatively few composers between the years 1788 and 1797: Haydn, Anton Wranitzky, Krommer, Wölfl, and Emanuel Aloys Förster.[24] The major difference between the strictly Viennese and the "fusion" quartets was that the former contained more sonata-form movements, a greater emphasis on motivic work and counterpoint (especially in the development sections) and a more varied finale structure.[25]

Perhaps due to the presence of Haydn's and Mozart's works within this category, the Viennese quartet has overshadowed all other types. Scholars have come to equate with the Viennese approach its tonal balance, idiomatic instrumental treatment, and sonorous blending of all four instruments with the entire classical chamber style.

Most see the string quartet as a further development of the divertimento; Hickman's objections have been noted in the first chapter of this study. Finscher simply states that the divertimento was the predecessor of the string quartet.[26] Similarly, Ruth Rowen opts for this evolutionary approach: "[Classical chamber] music, to be of a consistent character, required more logic and unity than was offered in the *divertimento*... In an examination of preclassical quartets, not only their deficience but also their merits must be taken into account. The basis for the Classical string quartet was there, awaiting development".[27] And later she comments:

> It was perhaps natural for the great composer [Haydn] to underrate his earlier and stylistically less mature productions. But it is fortunate that as maturer works were conceived the earlier compositions were not irrevocably destroyed. From the chamber enthusiast's point of view, these early quartets are still entertainment...while to the historian they constitute an indispensable landmark in the early history of the Classical chamber style.[28]

Rowen implies that Haydn's early works, and by extension, the divertimento genre, are not fully developed compositions. She rates them as inferior to later works which bear the designation "string quartet"; they should therefore be judged within an evolutionary context, not on their own merit.

---

24 Hickman, "The Flowering of the Viennese String Quartet", pp. 158–68.
25 Ibid., p. 168.
26 Finscher, *Studien zur Geschichte*, pp. 13, 84–105.
27 Rowen, *Early Chamber Music*, pp. 143, 153.
28 Ibid., p. 164.

If the divertimento is the precursor to the classical string quartet, when does the latter appear, and how should it be defined? Many mark the year 1781 as the start of the Classical chamber ideal. Warren Kirkendale's comments are representative:

> The word "classical" is...used primarily as a chronological and evaluative limitation, without indicating a unified stylistic period... Adler's assignment of the beginning of the Viennese classical era to the year 1781 finds a certain confirmation in chamber music. In this year, after a long pause, string quartets by Haydn again appeared: Op. 33...the year brought for Mozart the decisive move to Vienna and the friendship with Haydn; from this issued in 1782, after an equally long pause, the six quartets dedicated to the older master...The first of the new quartets introduces a fugato to the Classical sonata form.[29]

Confirmation of the importance of Haydn's Op. 33 collection and Mozart's "Haydn" quartets as the epitome of the classical chamber style is given by Finscher within the first paragraph of his study: "Mozart's six great string quartets, dedicated to Haydn, are understood to be as explicit a statement [of the Classical Style] as the standard and model which originated with the paternal friend's Op. 33, and have, in their turn, not only acted upon Haydn, but enriched the *exempla classica* canon".[30]

Recently, James Webster has argued against both the evolutionary approach and the whole idea of a unified Classical style. He views those mid-century compositions as fully developed and not as precursors to later, post-1780 works. He maintains that the divertimento is not a link between late-Baroque chamber music and the string quartet, and should be considered and evaluated on its own merit. Works such as Haydn's Opp. 9, 17, and 20 are not merely early and "less developed" examples of the string quartet, they are just as masterful as Haydn's Op. 33.[31] Webster concludes that a single uniform Classical string quartet style does not exist:

> Insofar as the Classical string quartet exists at all, it arose precisely via this new general cultivation and dissemination [of quartets in Vienna during the 1780s]; it included, but was not limited to, Haydn's quartets of the 1780s and Mozart's dedicated to him...The Classical string quartet was not a synthesis of pre-Classical genres from all over Europe, but a

---

[29] Kirkendale, *Fugue and Fugato*, pp. xxvi–xxvii. On the "long pause" in the quartet production of Haydn, see Webster's argument in his conclusion to *Haydn's "Farewell" Symphony and the Idea of the Classical Style* (Cambridge: Cambridge University Press, 1991).

[30] Finscher, *Studien zur Geschichte*, p. 9.

[31] Webster, *Haydn's "Farewell" Symphony*, pp. 335–41.

development within a single regional tradition, which became the central element in *later* explanations of the rise of the genre. "Classical" chamber music could arise only in the act of forgetting its own origins.[32]

Towards a reassessment of the string quartet

Thus the string quartet of the late-eighteenth century with its intensity, virtuosity, and orchestral-like gestures produced a far different effect than the intimate chamber style common since the 1760s. One way to account for this change is to view the quartet of the 1790s as a foreshadowing of the nineteenth-century romantic quartet.[33] This view is reinforced if one examines the medium from a structural point of view highlighting the harmonic progressions and stylistic criteria. As Hickman notes, one finds a "fundamental transformation that cuts across distinctions between Viennese and Parisian styles. Every quartet composer in Vienna, whether preferring three or four-movement structures, began to employ orchestral characteristics and a more daring harmonic idiom".[34] Such works as Paul Wranitzky's Op. 15 with its greater intensity; Krommer's Op. 19 with its chromaticism, rapid harmonic movement and use of third relations; Haydn's Op. 76 with its harmonic irregularities; and Gyrowetz's works with their formal and harmonic ambiguities reinforce Hickman's notion that a major transformation had occurred within the medium, one that notifies the listener of the upcoming romantic period.[35] But this view, as with those mentioned in Chapter 1, neglects to consider the medium as chamber music. An emphasis on harmonic and structural aspects converts the string quartet into a metaphor for the second half of the eighteenth century. As a consequence, we neglect the most unique aspect of the string quartet: the relationship of the four voices. Thus a re-evaluation of our approach is in order for a couple of reasons. One is to relieve ourselves of the baggage imposed by the categories discussed above. The second is to set aside, at least temporarily, the now commonly held assumption of the quartet as evolving into a near-perfect medium with the issuance of the works of Haydn and Mozart from the 1780s.

This is not to suggest that we throw the baby out with the bath water, but rather that we use a "different soap". Heinrich Koch's definition of the medium offers one possibility.[36] The theorist's focus on equality of voices and the conversational

---

[32]   Ibid., p. 346. See also Larsen, *Proceedings*, pp. 336–9 and 342–6, where Webster speaks to the same topic, but with less detail.

[33]   Hickman, "The Flowering of the Viennese String Quartet", p. 178.

[34]   Ibid., p. 173.

[35]   Ibid., pp. 175–7.

[36]   See Chapter 1 for a discussion of Koch's entries on the string quartet in his *Versuch* and *Musikalisches Lexikon.*

aspects of the medium has largely been ignored by modern-day scholars in lieu of harmonic and structural components. A re-evaluation of Koch's definition, taken in concert with his further emphasis on the flexibility of roles, suggests a means by which we can view the genre in general: as a form of communication, or type of discourse, between four instruments.

There is not one means of interaction; rather one can construct at least four separate and distinct "categories": lecture, conversation, debate, and polite conversation. The advantage to this is that these terms imply neither an evolutionary scheme, nor a hierarchical one. Furthermore, this method insists that we consider the relationship between the four participants as a primary feature of the string quartet instead of an ancillary one.

The lecture, as defined in the *Oxford English Dictionary*, is a "discourse given before an audience upon a given subject, usually for the purpose of instruction".[37] This suggests one voice (generally the first violin) holding forth while the other three provide a simple accompaniment. The minuet of Johann Georg Distler's Quartet No. 5 in C Major from Book 2 of 1795 is an excellent example (Ex. 3.1). Here the first violin fully commands our attention while the middle voices fill out the sonority. Similarly, many of Johann Baptist Vanhal's quartets display the lecture approach. A majority of his works are dominated by the first violin. The

Example 3.1 Johann Georg Distler, Book II, Quartet No. 5 in C Major, Menuetto

---

[37] *Oxford English Dictionary* (2nd ed., 20 vols, Oxford: Clarendon Press, 1989), vol. 8, pp. 785–6.

Example 3.1 concluded

other instruments serve as pure accompaniment, and claim no special attention. The middle movement of his Op. 1, No. 4 from ca. 1768–9 is a particularly good illustration. Here the melodic first violin dominates and is supported by a persistent pizzicato figure in the lower strings. This contrast of bowed vs. plucked only further highlights the distinction between melody and accompaniment (Ex. 3.2).

The leading melodic line may or may not be technically difficult. The above illustrations, for the most part, do not emphasize the first violinist as technical

Example 3.2 Johann Baptist Vanhal, Op. 1, No. 4, Mvt. II, mm 1-18

master, but rather as the one who commands the listener's attention. But in many lecture settings, the first violinist must be of professional calibre while the other parts can still be rendered by amateurs. Such is the case with the first movement of Luigi Boccherini's Quartet in A Major (G.213) of 1787. In this sonata form movement, the first violinist must execute a succession of scale passages, arpeggios, string crossings, and pedal points at a rapid speed. In contrast, the lower parts, which are supportive and accompanimental, are characterized by pitch repetition, monotone rhythmic patterns, and clearly non-melodic lines. Only rarely does the first violinist "calm down"; at these points, the cellist or second violinist may come forward to participate in a small exchange with the first violinist. But these moments serve more as a form of relief from the otherwise consistently florid line of the first violinist than as a textural change.

The lecture stands in stark contrast to the conversation, which can be defined as "an interchange of thoughts and words; a familiar discourse of talk".[38] In this setting, the four instruments are freed of set roles and are placed on an equal setting. Orin Moe refers to this as successive independence, and describes it as an exchange of textural roles between instruments, especially in homophonic textures. "Each instrument may take any role in any texture, from leading melodic line to accompanimental line, from secondary melodic to bass." The end result is that all instruments are released from previously stereotyped functions and may share the same material to the extent that it is technically possible.[39] The trio from Distler's previously mentioned Quartet No. 5 in C of Book II provides an excellent example of a conversation (Ex. 3.3). In contrast to the violin-dominated minuet, the trio reveals a setting in which all four instruments are fully integrated into the quartet fabric. All take part; the role-playing is fluid. A melodic line is equally at home in any of the four voices. The parts look alike and one cannot pinpoint a single instrument as the most important.

The fourth movement of Felice Giardini's Op. 14, No. 1 of the 1770s also exhibits this fluidity of function. This F-Major Prestissimo contains four equally important and independent lines. Melodic material, scales, and rapid passagework found in the first violin are just as likely to appear in the other three parts. Likewise, the sustained pitches so often associated with an accompanimental line occur in all four voices (Ex. 3.4).

The debate, which occupies a position between the conversation and the lecture, allows for more melodic equality among the voices, but at the same time, insists on a fairly fixed dispensation of roles and functions for each instrument. The thematic fragmentation and give-and-take of motivic material so characteristic of this type resemble the verbal debate which the *Oxford English Dictionary* defines as "a controversy or discussion" of "the act of engag[ing] in discussion or argument".[40] While the first violin carries the bulk of the melodic material especially when presented in its entirety, and the other instruments assume

---

[38] *Oxford English Dictionary*, vol. 3, p. 868.
[39] Orin Moe, "The Significance of Haydn's Op. 33", in *Haydn Studies: Proceedings of the International Haydn Conference, Washington D. C., 1975* (ed. by Jens Peter Larsen, Howard Serwer, and James Webster; New York: W. W. Norton and Co., 1981), p. 446.
[40] *Oxford English Dictionary*, vol. 4, p. 309.

Example 3.3 Johann Georg Distler, Book II, Quartet No. 5 in C Major, Trio

Example 3.4 Felice de Giardini, Op. 14, No. 1, Mvt. IV

Example 3.4 continued

Example 3.4 continued

Example 3.4 concluded

supportive roles, there are places where all four instruments take part in motivic exchanges, and simultaneous independence: "each voice is independent and is identifiable through melodic and/or rhythmic means".[41] What distinguishes the debate from the conversation is the fact that in the former, the ensemble members assume a particular role from which they rarely deviate. Musical lines are not interchangeable and one can easily predict who will have what kind of part and when variations will occur. The exposition of Paul Wranitzky's Op. 23, No. 5 of 1793, is an excellent example (Ex. 3.5). In this Allegro, the composer provides something for all, but dominance remains with the first violin. Following a unison opening, we are presented with a traditional lecture-like dispensation of roles: the melodic first violin is supported by an unobtrusive accompaniment (mm 11–31). The sonority is temporarily varied as the middle strings come forward in parallel motion accompanied by the first violin and cello (mm 34–37). Although the first violin resumes leadership in measure 44, this is short-lived for the three lower strings join the upper one, beginning in measure 49, for five bars of give-and-take. As the first violin again takes center stage, the second violin presents an undercurrent which, although secondary, attracts our attention. Further distracting us are the viola and cello lines which are more than mere repeated notes and sustained tones. This interplay and weaving of lines suggest independent voices, rather than a primary one with uninteresting support. But as to be expected in a musical debate, these exchanges are temporary and do not alter the hierarchy of dominance. Thus when the first violin insists on our full attention in measure 73, the other instruments return to their traditional roles of inner filler (violin 2 and viola) and harmonic support/foundation (cello). Although the lower parts have small snippets of motivic material, none truly achieves a position of leadership equal to that of the first violin. Rather the melodic and rhythmic shape of the

---

[41]   Moe, "The Significance of Haydn's Op. 33", p. 446.

lower voices provides variety to what would otherwise by a simple homophonic texture.

Example 3.5 Paul Wranitzky, Op. 23, No. 5, Mvt. I, mm 1–101

Example 3.5 continued

Example 3.5 continued

Example 3.5 continued

Example 3.5 continued

Example 3.5 concluded

The polite conversation is one in which each instrumentalist comes forward with melodic material while the others recede into the background. If we liken this to a setting where four people are talking politely amongst each other, we find that each takes a turn while the other participants listen without interruption or competition. To be polite implies that one is of a "refined manner; especially showing courteous consideration for others [i.e., not interrupting]".[42] Musically one hears a succession of solos, reinforced by unobtrusive accompaniments. The first movement of Giardini's Op. 23, No. 3 in A Major (1783) is a particularly fine example. In this Andante, Giardini presents us with a succession of lengthy solos. As each instrument comes forward, the others join together to provide a unassuming accompaniment of repeated eighth notes, sustained pitches, or simple patterns. In the exposition, Giardini places the solo first in the uppermost part, and then systematically moves lower, giving each instrument a chance to shine. While the top three voices have eleven-measure solos, the cello holds our attention for a full eighteen measures. This strong distinction between melody and accompaniment, both from an aural standpoint and a visual one, is typical of the polite conversation. A simple perusal of the parts succinctly reveals which instrument is "holding forth" and which ones are politely listening. Solos may or may not be thematically connected to surrounding ones. In the recapitulation, we are treated to the same melodic material, but this time the voicing has been rearranged. This flexibility of instrumentation underscores the conversational aspect of the work. The distinct separation of solo and accompaniment reinforces the politeness.

The visual aspect is one which provides for immediate identification. The cello part of the opening Allegro of Franz Hoffmeister's Op. 9, No. 2 of 1783 illustrates this point (Ex. 3.6). If one examines just this part, one immediately sees the blatant differences between the solo and accompanimental sections. The ten-measure melody just preceding the recapitulation (mm 141–150), with its varied rhythms and pitches, is markedly different from the rest of the movement which is characterized by repeated pitches, even eighth notes, and patterned figures. A review of the other parts reveals the same distinctions.

A polite conversation need not feature all four instruments, as may be seen with the first movement of Giuseppe Cambini's G Major Quartet, Op. 7, No. 4 (T28) of 1777–78. In this Allegro, the cello functions as a supportive and foundational instrument while the upper three strings execute their solos, one after the other and without interruptions, imitative exchanges, or give-and-take passages. Solos are lengthy; accompaniments are inconspicuous. There is no competition for the listener's attention.

---

[42]   *Oxford English Dictionary,* vol. 12, p. 31.

Example 3.6 Franz Hoffmeister, Op. 9, No. 2, Mvt. I, mm 88–162, cello part

The examples provided here are intentionally clear-cut. Not all works are as easy to categorize. Many would best be viewed as "hybrids", that is, they exhibit traits of two or more types of discourse. What remains important, however, is that even when one uses a mix, one still focuses on the chamber aspect. This is not to suggest the elimination of such terms as Viennese quartet or *quatuor concertant*. They are conveniences that convey certain structural and formal features. But these categories should be used in conjunction with ones specific to the string quartet. Such classification encourages us to go beyond the works of Haydn and Mozart. While theirs may still be seen as the zenith of the eighteenth-century genre, using a different means of examination allows us to look at the vast amount of, as yet, unexplored works without immediately subjecting them to a comparison which, for many, will surely fall short. Only then can we understand the medium as chamber music, rather than as a metaphor for the classical period. In this way, we can begin to grasp the variety and wide range of string quartets that were written during the second half of the eighteenth century.

Chapter 4

The lecture

As a group, string quartets of the second half of the eighteenth century contain more lecture movements than any other type. This is as true for the first part as the last part of the period.[1] Although the traditional view holds that, especially in light of the increasingly conversational output of Haydn and Mozart, the four voices become more independent and participatory as the century progresses, in reality, one finds that the lecture remains a viable and quite useful format well into the 1790s. Table 1 reveals the consistent incorporation of the lecture throughout the entire half century.

The ideal lecture consists of a melody plus accompaniment; the listener has no doubt about the role of each instrument. In nearly every case, the first violinist holds forth while the other ensemble members support it. The cellist provides the foundational bass and rarely deviates from this function. The second violinist may travel below the first violin either in parallel motion or some other supportive fashion, or alternatively may join with the violist to fill out the sonority. This approach is neither restricted to works from the first part of the second half of the century, nor to composers' first efforts with the genre. Rather it is a conscious choice made by those who wish to present a particular quality of sound and texture. Works by Antonín Kammel (1730 [baptized]–ca.1787), Ignace Joseph Pleyel (1757–1831), and Franz Neubauer (ca. 1760–95) are particularly good examples.

Most of Kammel's string quartets appeared during the 1770s, the first of which was his *Six quatuors concertants*, Op. 4 of ca.1770.[2] Each contains three movements and none is overly demanding. All lines are suitable for amateurs. The opening movement of the sixth quartet is representative (the exposition is given in Ex. 4.1).

---

[1] This statement is based on an examination of over 650 string quartets composed between 1750 and 1797, by sixty-two composers. This sampling, which forms a good cross-section of the genre in its eighteenth-century form, includes representative works from each decade by Austrian, Bohemian, French, German, and Italian composers, some of whom resided both in their native countries as well as others such as England and Spain. Of these works, 407 include at least one lecture movement. 134 consisted of nothing but lecture movements.

[2] Sächsische Landesbibliothek, Dresden, Mus. 3440/P/1. Numbers 3 and 4 appear in manuscript parts as Quartetto I–II and are housed at Benediktiner-Stift Kremsmünster, 120/41–2. No. 6, in manuscript form, is located at Stift Einsiedeln Musik Bibliothek, Th 71/13, ms 2327.

Table 1: A Selected List of Lectures [3]

Year	Composer	Title/Catalogue #[4] (Movement[s])
ca.1750	J. Zach	Sinfonia I (1, 2, 3)
	J. Zach	Sinfonia II (1, 2, 3)
	J. Zach	Sinfonia III (1, 2, 3)
	J. Zach	Sinfonia IV (1, 2, 3)
	J. Zach	Sinfonia V (1, 2, 3)
ca.1755–63	P. C. von Camerloher	Op. 4, No. 8 (1, 2)
1755–9	J. Haydn	Op. 1, No. 1 (1, 3, 5)
	J. Haydn	Op. 1, No. 2 (3, 4, 5)
	J. Haydn	Op. 1, No. 4 (3, 5)
	J. Haydn	Op. 1, No. 6 (1, 3, 4, 5)
	J. Haydn	Op. 2, No. 1 (2, 3, 4, 5)
	J. Haydn	Op. 2, No. 2 (1, 2, 4, 5)
	J. Haydn	Op. 2, No. 4 (1, 2, 3)
	J. Haydn	Op. 2, No. 6 (1, 2, 3, 4)
1757	F. X. Richter	Op. 5, No. 3 (3)
	F. X. Richter	Op. 5, No. 4 (3)
1759–66	A.-E.-M. Grétry	Op. 3. No. 1 (1)
	A.-E.-M. Grétry	Op. 3, No. 2 (1, 3)
	A.-E.-M. Grétry	Op. 3, No. 3 (1)
	A.-E.-M. Grétry	Op. 3, No. 4 (2, 3)
ca.1760	P. C. von Camerloher	Sinfonia in C (1, 2, 3)
	P. C. von Camerloher	Sinfonia in G (1, 2, 3)
	A. Filtz	Quadro in G (1, 2, 3)
	A. Filtz	Quatro [in A] (1, 2, 3)
	A. Filtz	Quatro [in Bb] (3)
	A. Filtz	Quattro [in F] (1, 2, 3)
1760	J. Albrechtsberger	Divertimento V[?] (1, 2, 3, 4, 5)
	J. Albrechtsberger	Divertimento VI^{to} (1, 2, 3, 4)

---

[3] See the bibliography for a full citation of each of the listed compositions.

[4] To ensure as much uniformity as possible when refering to specific compositions, standardized cataloguer identification systems have been adopted. (Cataloguers' names are given in parentheses.) Thus Beecke's works are identified with M numbers (Smart), Boccherini's works with G numbers (Gérard), Cambini with T numbers (Trimpert), Gassman with H numbers (Hill), Michael Haydn with MH numbers (Sherman–Thomas), Mozart with K numbers (Köchel), Pleyel with Ben numbers (Benton), and Vanhal by key and number (Jones). In the case of Joseph Haydn, the commonly recognized Op. numbers have been retained.

Table 1 continued

Year	Composer	Title/Catalogue # (Movement[s])
1760/64	J. Albrechtsberger	Divertimento [in A] (1, 2, 3, 4, 5)
1760s	F. Gassmann	H.431 (1, 2)
	F. Gassmann	H.435 (1, 3)
	F. Gassmann	H.461 (1)
	F. Gassmann	H.467 (1, 2, 3)
	F. Gassmann	H.471 (1, 3)
	F. Gassmann	H.475 (1, 2, 3)
	F. Gassmann	H.476 (1, 2, 3)
	F. Gassmann	H.480 (3)
	C. d'Ordonez	Op.1, No. 4 (3)
1761	L. Boccherini	G.161 (3)
	L. Boccherini	G.162 (1, 2, 3)
1768–69	J. B.Vanhal	c2 (1, 2,3)
	J. B.Vanhal	F11 (1, 2, 3)
	J. B.Vanhal	D3 (2, 3)
1769	F. Asplmayr	Op. 2, No. 1 (1, 2, 3, 4)
	F. Asplmayr	Op. 2, No. 2 (1, 2, 3, 4)
	F. Asplmayr	Op. 2, No. 3 (1, 2, 3)
	F. Asplmayr	Op. 2, No. 4 (1, 2, 3, 4)
	F. Asplmayr	Op. 2, No. 5 (1, 2, 3, 4)
	F. Asplmayr	Op. 2, No. 6 (1, 2, 3, 4)
	L. Boccherini	G.165 (1, 2, 3)
	L. Boccherini	G.166 (2)
	L. Boccherini	G.167 (1, 2, 3)
1769–70	J. Haydn	Op. 9, No. 1 (2, 3, 4)
	J. Haydn	Op. 9, No. 2 (1, 2, 3)
	J. Haydn	Op. 9, No. 3 (3)
	J. Haydn	Op. 9, No. 4 (1, 2, 3)
	J. Haydn	Op. 9, No. 5 (4)
	J. Haydn	Op. 9, No. 6 (1, 3, 4)
ca.1770	I. von Beecke	M.11 (3)
	A. Kammel	Op. 4, No. 3 (2, 3)
	A. Kammel	Op. 4, No. 6 (1, 2, 3)
1770	L. Boccherini	G.171 (1, 2, 3)
	L. Boccherini	G.174 (1, 2)
	W. A. Mozart	K.80 (3, 4)
1770s	F. de Giardini	Op. 14, No. 5 (2)
	C. E. Graf	Quartetto a F (2, 3)

Table 1 continued

Year	Composer	Title/Catalogue # (Movement[s])
	A. Zimmerman	Quartetto [in D] (1, 2, 4)
ca.1770–71	J. B.Vanhal	F6 (1, 2, 3)
	J. B. Vanhal	E1 (1, 2, 3)
1771	J. Haydn	Op. 17, No. 1 (1, 3)
	J. Haydn	Op. 17, No. 3 (2, 3)
	J. Haydn	Op. 17, No. 5 (3)
	J. Haydn	Op. 17, No. 6 (1, 2, 3)
ca.1772	F.-J. Gossec	Op. 15, No. 1 (1, 2)
	F.-J. Gossec	Op. 15, No. 2 (1, 2)
	F.-J. Gossec	Op. 15, No. 3 (1, 2)
	F.-J. Gossec	Op. 15, No. 4 (1, 2)
	F.-J. Gossec	Op. 15, No. 5 (1, 2)
	F.-J. Gossec	Op. 15, No. 6 (1, 2)
1772	I. von Beecke	M.13 (1, 2, 4)
	I. von Beecke	M.2 (2, 4)
	I. von Beecke	M.17 (2, 3, 4)
	J. Haydn	Op. 20, No. 1 (2)
	J. Haydn	Op. 20, No. 2 (3)
	J. Haydn	Op. 20, No. 5 (1, 2, 3)
	J. Haydn	Op. 20, No. 6 (1, 2, 3)
1772/73	W. A. Mozart	K.155 (1, 2, 3)
	W. A. Mozart	K.156 (1)
	W. A. Mozart	K.157 (1, 2, 3)
	W. A. Mozart	K.159 (1)
	W. A. Mozart	K.160 (2, 3)
1773	J. B. Vanhal	C1 (1, 2, 3, 4)
	J. B. Vanhal	A1 (1, 2, 3)
	J.-B. Davaux	Op. 6, No. 1 (2)
	J.-B. Davaux	Op. 6, No. 2 (2)
	J.-B. Davaux	Op. 6, No. 3 (2)
	J.-B. Davaux	Op. 6, No. 6 (1, 2)
	W. A. Mozart	K.168 (3)
	W. A. Mozart	K.169 (2, 3, 4)
	W. A. Mozart	K.170 (1, 2, 3)
	W. A. Mozart	K.171 (4)
	W. A. Mozart	K.172 (1, 2)
	W. A. Mozart	K.173 (3)
	J. Schmitt	Op. 5, No. 1 (1)

Table 1 continued

Year	Composer	Title/Catalogue # (Movement[s])
	J. Schmitt	Op. 5, No. 2 (3)
	J. Schmitt	Op. 5, No. 3 (1, 2, 4)
	J. Schmitt	Op. 5, No. 4 (1, 2, 4)
	J. Schmitt	Op. 5, No. 5 (1, 4)
	J. Schmitt	Op. 5, No. 6 (1, 2, 3)
	P. Vachon	Op. 7, No. 1 (1, 2, 3, 4)
	P. Vachon	Op. 7, No. 2 (3)
	P. Vachon	Op. 7, No. 3 (2, 3)
	P. Vachon	Op. 7, No. 5 (2)
1773–4	G. M. Cambini	T.1 (3)
1774	I. von Beecke	M.6 (2, 3, 4)
	G. Brunetti	Op. 2, No. 1 (1, 2, 3, 4)
	G. Brunetti	Op. 2, No. 2 (1, 2)
	G. Brunetti	Op. 2, No. 3 (1, 2, 3, 4)
	G. Brunetti	Op. 2, No. 4 (1, 3, 4)
	G. Brunetti	Op. 2, No. 5 (1, 3, 4)
	G. Brunetti	Op. 2, No. 6 (2, 3, 4)
	G. Brunetti	Op. 3, No. 2 (1, 2)
	G. Brunetti	Op. 3, No. 3 (1)
	G. Brunetti	Op. 3, No. 5 (1, 2)
	G. Brunetti	Op. 3, No. 6 (2)
ca.1775	P. Vachon	Op. 5, No. 1 (2)
	P. Vachon	Op. 5, No. 2 (2)
	P. Vachon	Op. 5, No. 3 (3)
	P. Vachon	Op. 5, No. 4 (3)
	T. Giordani	Op. 8, No. 5 (2)
	T. Giordani	Op. 8, No. 6 (2)
1775	J.-B.-S. Bréval	Op. 1, No. 1 (2)
	J.-B.-S. Bréval	Op. 1, No. 2 (2)
	J.-B.-S. Bréval	Op. 1, No. 5, (2, 3)
	J.-B.-S. Bréval	Op. 1, No. 6 (3)
1776–8	L. Boccherini	G.190 (1, 3)
	L. Boccherini	G.192 (2, 3)
ca.1777	N.-J. Chartrain	Op. 8, No. 4 (2)
	N.-J. Chartrain	Op. 8, No. 6 (1, 2, 3)
	M. Haydn	MH. 308 (2, 3)
ca. 1778	N.-J. Chartrain	Op. 4, No. 1 (2, 3)
	N.-J. Chartrain	Op. 4, No. 5 (2)

Table 1 continued

Year	Composer	Title/Catalogue # (Movement[s])
b.1780	N.-M. Dalayrac	Op. 7, No. 5 (2)
1779	J. B. Vanhal	G7 (1, 3, 4)
ca.1780	J. B. Vanhal	G8 (1, 2, 3, 4)
	J. B. Vanhal	c1 (1, 2)
1780	C. Cannabich	Op. 5, No. 2 (2)
	G. M. Cambini	T.43 (3)
	G. M. Cambini	T.45 (3)
	G. M. Cambini	T.46 (3)
	G. M. Cambini	T.47(2)
	I. von Beecke	M.14 (1, 2, 3, 4)
	L. Boccherini	G.206 (1, 3)
1780/81	J. Albrechtsberger	Op. 2, No. 2 (1)
	J. Albrechtsberger	Op. 2, No. 3 (1)
	J. Albrechtsberger	Op. 2, No.5 (1)
	J. Albrechtsberger	Op. 2, No. 6 (1)
ca.1781	M. Haydn	MH. 309 (1, 2, 3)
	M. Haydn	MH. 313 (2, 3)
1781	L. Boccherini	G.207 (1, 2)
	L. Boccherini	G.208 (1)
	L. Boccherini	G.209 (1)
	J. Haydn	Op. 33, No. 2 (2, 4)
	J. Haydn	Op. 33, No. 3 (3)
	J. Haydn	Op. 33, No. 4 (3, 4)
	J. Haydn	Op. 33, No. 5 (1, 2, 3, 4)
1781-1783	J. Albrechtsberger	Op. 7, No. 1 (1)
	J. Albrechtsberger	Op. 7, No. 2 (1, 2, 3)
	J. Albrechtsberger	Op. 7, No. 3 (1, 2, 3)
1782	J. A. Fodor	Book 4, No. 1 (2)
	J. A. Fodor	Book 4, No. 5 (1, 2)
	J. A. Fodor	Book 4, No. 6 (2)
1782-3	I. J. Pleyel	Ben. 301 (1, 2, 3)
	I. J. Pleyel	Ben. 302 (1, 2, 3)
	I. J. Pleyel	Ben. 303 (1, 2)
	I. J. Pleyel	Ben. 304 (1, 2, 3)
	I. J. Pleyel	Ben. 305 (1, 2, 3)
	I. J. Pleyel	Ben. 306 (1, 2, 3)
1782-6	P. Vachon	Op. 11, No. 2 (2, 3)
	P. Vachon	Op. 11, No. 3 (1)

Table 1 continued

Year	Composer	Title/Catalogue # (Movement[s])
	P. Vachon	Op. 11, No. 4 (2)
	P. Vachon	Op. 11, No. 6 (2)
ca.1783	M. Haydn	MH. 311 (1, 2)
	M. Haydn	MH. 312 (2, 4)
1784	J. Fiala	Op. 1, No. 1 (2, 4)
	J. Fiala	Op. 1, No. 3 (3)
	J. Fiala	Op. 1, No. 5 (2, 3)
	J. Fiala	Op. 1, No. 6 (3)
1785	J. B. Vanhal	C7 (1, 2, 3)
	J. B. Vanhal	A4 (1, 2, 3, 4)
	J. B. Vanhal	Bb10 (1, 2, 3, 4)
	I. J. Pleyel	Ben. 313 (1, 2, 3, 4)
	I. J. Pleyel	Ben. 314 (2, 3, 4)
	I. J. Pleyel	Ben. 315 (1, 2, 3, 4)
	I. J. Pleyel	Ben. 316 (3, 4)
	I. J. Pleyel	Ben. 317 (1, 3, 4)
	I. J. Pleyel	Ben. 318 (1, 2, 3, 4)
1785–7	J. B. Vanhal	Eb11 (2, 3)
1786	J. B. Vanhal	g2 (2)
	J. Haydn	Op. 42 (3)
	I. J. Pleyel	Ben. 322 (1, 3)
	I. J. Pleyel	Ben. 324 (2)
1787	J. Haydn	Op. 50, No. 3 (3)
	J. Haydn	Op. 50, No. 5 (2, 3)
	J. Haydn	Op. 50. No. 6 (3, 4)
	L. Boccherini	G.213 (1, 2, 3)
1788	J. Haydn	Op. 54, No.1 (1, 2, 4)
	J. Haydn	Op. 54, No. 2 (1, 2, 4)
	J. Haydn	Op. 54, No. 3 (1, 2, 3)
	J. Haydn	Op. 55, No. 3 (3)
	L. Boccherini	G.215 (1, 3)
	C. D. von Dittersdorf	*Sei Quartetti*, No. 2 (2)
	C. D. von Dittersdorf	*Sei Quartetti*, No. 3 (1, 2, 3)
	C. D. von Dittersdorf	*Sei Quartetti*, No. 4 (2)
	C. D. von Dittersdorf	*Sei Quartetti*, No. 5 (1, 2, 3)
	C. D. von Dittersdorf	*Sei Quartetti*, No. 6 (2, 3)
	V. Pichl	Op. 13, No. 1 (3)
	V. Pichl	Op. 13, No. 2 (3)

Table 1 continued

Year	Composer	Title/Catalogue # (Movement[s])
	V. Pichl	Op. 13, No. 3 (2)
	I. J. Pleyel	Ben. 343 (2)
	I. J. Pleyel	Ben. 346 (2, 3)
	I. J. Pleyel	Ben. 347 (2, 3)
1788/90	F. Fiorillo	Op. 6, No. 1 (1, 2, 3)
	F. Fiorillo	Op. 6, No. 2 (1)
1789	L. Boccherini	G.216 (2)
	L. Boccherini	G.217 (1, 2)
	G. Brunetti	Quartetto I [in A] (1, 2, 3, 4)
	A. Teyber	Op. 2, No. 1 (2, 3)
	A. Teyber	Op. 2, No. 2 (2)
ca.1790	I. von Beecke	M.15 (1, 2, 3, 4)
	I. von Beecke	M.3 (2)
	I. von Beecke	M.16 (2, 3)
	J. A. Fodor	Op. 11, No. 6 (2)
	A. Gyrowetz	Op. 3, No. 1 (1, 2, 3)
	A. Gyrowetz	Op. 3, No. 3 (1, 2, 3)
	F. Danzi	Op. 5, No. 1 (1, 2)
	F. Danzi	Op. 5, No. 2 (1, 2)
	F. Danzi	Op. 5, No. 3 (1, 2)
	F. Danzi	Op. 6, No. 1 (1, 2)
	F. Danzi	Op. 6, No. 2 (1, 2)
	F. Danzi	Op. 6, No. 3 (1, 2)
1790	J. Haydn	Op. 64, No. 2 (2)
	J. Haydn	Op. 64, No. 3 (2, 3)
	J. Haydn	Op. 64, No. 4 (1, 2, 3)
	J. Haydn	Op. 64. No. 5 (2, 4)
	L. Boccherini	G.218 (1, 2)
	L. Boccherini	G.219 (1, 2)
	P. Wranitzky	Op. 10, No. 6 (2, 3)
1790–1	L. Kozeluch	Op. 32, No. 2 (1, 2)
	L. Kozeluch	Op. 32, No. 3 (2)
	L. Kozeluch	Op. 33, No. 1 (2)
	L. Kozeluch	Op. 33, No. 2 (1, 2)
	L. Kozeluch	Op. 33, No. 3 (2, 3)
1791	G. Brunetti	Quartet [in g] (2, 3)
	F. Fränzl	Op. 1, No. 1 (3)
	F. Fränzl	Op. 1, No. 2 (1, 2, 3)

Table 1 continued

Year	Composer	Title/Catalogue # (Movement[s])
	F. Fränzl	Op. 1, No. 3 (2)
	F. Fränzl	Op. 1, No. 5 (1, 2, 3)
	F. Fränzl	Op. 1, No. 6 (3)
	F. Hoffmeister	Op. 14, No. 1 (2)
	F. Hoffmeister	Op. 14, No. 2 (1, 2, 3)
	F. Hoffmeister	Op. 14, No. 3 (3, 4)
1792	L. Boccherini	G.220 (1, 2)
	L. Boccherini	G.221 (1, 2, 3)
	L. Boccherini	G.222 (1)
	L. Boccherini	G.223 (2)
	L. Boccherini	G.224 (1)
	L. Boccherini	G.225 (1, 2)
1793	F. Neubauer	Op. 7, No. 1 (3)
	F. Neubauer	Op. 7, No. 3 (2)
	P. Wranitzky	Op. 23, No. 4 (2)
	P. Wranitzky	Op. 23, No. 5 (2)
	F. Krommer	Op. 1, No. 1 (2)
	A. Gyrowetz	Op. 3, No. 2 (1, 2, 3)
	A. Gyrowetz	Op. 3, No. 4 (2, 3)
	A. Gyrowetz	Op. 3, No. 6 (1, 2, 3)
	J. Haydn	Op. 74, No. 3 (2)
1794	F. Benda	Quartetto in Eb (1, 2, 3, 4)
	F. Benda	Quartetto in F (1, 2, 3, 4)
	L. Boccherini	G.226 (1)
	L. Boccherini	G.227 (2)
	L. Boccherini	G.228 (1, 2)
	L. Boccherini	G.230 (1, 2)
	L. Boccherini	G.231 (1, 2)
	J. L. Eybler	Op.1, No. 1 (2)
	J. L. Eybler	Op. 1, No. 2 (3)
	J. L. Eybler	Op. 1, No. 3 (3)
1795	H. Jadin	Op. 1, No. 1 (4)
	H. Jadin	Op. 1, No. 2 (1, 2, 3, 4)
	H. Jadin	Op. 1, No. 3 (2, 4)
	L. Boccherini	G.234 (2, 3)
	J. G. Distler	Opp. 1–2, No. 6 (3)
ca.1796	M. Haydn	MH. 310 (1, 2, 3)
1796	F. Krommer	Op. 5, No. 3 (2)

Table 1 concluded

Year	Composer	Title/Catalogue # (Movement[s])
1797	F. Krommer	Op. 7, No. 1 (4)
	F. Krommer	Op. 7, No. 3 (1, 4)
	J. Haydn	Op. 76, No. 1 (2, 3)
	J. Haydn	Op. 76, No. 2 (2, 4)
	J. Haydn	Op. 76, No. 5 (3)

Example 4.1 Antonín Kammel, Op. 4, No. 6, Mvt. I, mm 1–56

Example 4.1 continued

Example 4.1 continued

Example 4.1 concluded

This Allegro con spirito features a melodically dominant first violin, a foundational cello, and texture-enriching second violin and viola. Thematic material, nearly always presented by the first violin, is rhythmically and musically varied. Triadic lines are balanced with scale passages; a sixteenth-note run is surrounded by slower surface rhythms. In contrast, the second violin part reveals less variety for it either parallels the first violin line or fills out the harmony in conjunction with the viola. The latter is achieved through broken intervals, repeated pitches, and measured tremelos. Neither middle voice is melodically independent. Both are essential for enriching the sonority and offering support.

There is no interplay between the voices except at the opening of the development. Here a four-measure second violin-cello duet is answered by a first violin-viola one. From the beginning to end of the movement, the lecture continues nearly unabated. Only with the strategically placed unisons and parallel octaves does the melody plus accompaniment texture momentarily cease. Even in such places where the number of lines is effectively reduced to one, it is the lower parts which are incorporated into the top line. In this way, Kammel maintains the primacy of the first violin part.

Many of Ignace Pleyel's quartets bear similar qualities. Most of the composer's more than eighty quartets were written between the years 1787 and 1795. Although twentieth-century scholars have not assessed his works in an overly positive manner,[5] during his day, especially the 1780s and early 1790s, Pleyel was among the most popular of composers. His quartets, many of which were offered for sale to the public rather than a specific patron, reflected the interests and desires of a large portion of the musical community, both performing and listening.

Pleyel's Quartet in Eb Major (Ben 302) from his Opus 1 collection of 1782–3, consists of three movements, all of which are lectures. The work is characterized by a continuous emphasis on the first violin as melodic leader with the lower voices providing harmonic and textural support. This relationship is particularly evident in the first movement, an Allegro in sonata form. While the uppermost voice is charged with the unfolding of thematic material, the lower ones provide accompaniment in the form of harmonic foundation, repeated figures, and supportive lines which contain little rhythmic and melodic variety. Whereas the lower voices are suitable for amateurs, the first violin part requires a performer who can easily execute string crossings, passages in the upper register, decorated arpeggios, and multiple stops. Neither the second violin nor the viola parts demand these skills. Melodic material in the lower voices is only present when the instruments travel in unison or parallel octaves as in, for example, the opening three bars. After this, the instruments assume their respective roles. The first violin is occasionally paralled by the second violin but more often is supported by unobtrusive filler lines and a functional bass (Ex. 4.2).

The second movement, a Minuet and Trio in Eb and Ab Major respectively, offers but minimal relief from the consistently homophonic texture. While the minuet maintains the purely dominating role of the first violin, the trio presents some interplay between the upper three voices; the cello retains its position as

---

[5]   Kirkendale, in *Fugue and Fugato*, p. 182, describes the later quartets as "superficial" while H.C. Robbins Landon assesses the works as "debased pseudo-Haydn". See *Haydn: Chronicle and Works*, vol. II: *Haydn at Eszterháza 1766-1790* (Bloomington, IN: Indiana University Press, 1978), pp. 360–1.

Example 4.2 Ignace Pleyel, Ben 302, Mvt. I, mm 1–89

Example 4.2 continued

Example 4.2 continued

Example 4.2 continued

Example 4.2 concluded

foundation (Ex. 4.3). The last movement, a four-part adagio-presto alternation, returns us to the lecture format.

Example 4.3 Ignace Pleyel, Ben 302, Trio

The 1790s saw composers still writing lectures with great frequency. More than ten years after the appearance of the seminal works of Haydn and Mozart which featured a more integrated and conversational approach, many such as Franz Neubauer continued to use the lecture format as a viable means of organizing the four members of the ensemble.

Of Neubauer's twenty-five quartets, all but three are extant. Most of these works are in three movements and a vast majority appear to have been written with the musical amateur in mind. Although Richard Sjoerdsma notes that Neubauer was interested in moving away from the first violin-dominanted style,[6] the composer still found it useful as a means of concluding his Op. 7 collection of 1793.[7] The last movement in the final quartet (Op. 7, No. 3), a Rondo in C major, is a full-blown lecture. The listener's focus remains firmly fixed on the first violin. It is this part that has all the thematic material and technical display. The lower strings are pure support: repeated notes and figures, sustained pitches, and minimal rhythmic and melodic variety (Ex. 4.4). Even the *minore* section, where one would traditionally expect a timbral change, features the first violin. Both from a visual and aural perspective, one has no doubt as to the role of each instrument (Ex. 4.5).

To the above-named works, we might add any number of the more familiar quartets by Wolfgang Amadeus Mozart and Joseph Haydn, both from their early years up through their later ones. By way of illustration, we turn to Mozart's K.155; all three movements are excellent examples of the lecture. K.155 is the first of a set of six quartets (K.155–160), all of which were written in Italy at the end of 1772 and the beginning of 1773. These three-movement works with their clear, transparent textures have received a mixed reception among scholars. Karl Geiringer labels them as "orchestral in conception".[8] In contrast, Daniel Heartz and Roger Hickman argue that they are true quartets since all require a solo cello; they reject the possibility that the lowest line might be rendered either as a continuo

6   See Richard Dale Sjoerdsma's criticial edition of Neubauer's works in *Recent Researches in the Music of the Classical Era*, vol. 21: *Franz Christoph Neubauer: Chamber Music* (Madison, WI: A-R Editions, 1985), pp. viii–ix; and his "The Instrumental Works of Franz Christoph Neubauer (1760-1795)" (PhD diss., Ohio State University, 1970), p. 153.

7   Parts of Op. 7 are revisions of Op. 6. The first movement of Op. 7, No. 3 corresponds to the first movement of Op. 6, No. 1, and the opening movement of Op. 6, No. 4 forms the basis for Op. 7, No. 1. Although the main difference is the tempo indications, there are also some structural changes. See Sjoerdsma, "The Instrumental Music", pp. 109–10, for a discussion of this.

8   Karl Geiringer, "The Rise of Chamber Music", in *New Oxford History of Music*, vol. 7: *The Age of Enlightenment: 1745–1790* (London: Oxford University Press, 1973), p. 559.

Example 4.4 Franz Neubauer, Op. 7, No. 3, Mvt. II, mm 1–18

Example 4.5 Franz Neubauer, Op. 7, No. 3, Mvt. II, minore section

Example 4.5 continued

Example 4.5 continued

Example 4.5 concluded

part or by a string bass. Heartz points to the abundance of lyric melodies and the contrapuntal texture as indicative of the quartet genre.[9] Still others, less decisive, see these works as a combination of orchestral, divertimento-like techniques, especially the Mannheim crescendo-*walze* and the *coup d'archet*, and genuine chamber writing.[10]

K.155 is representative of the set as a whole in its emphasis on the outer parts to carry the burden of melodic and harmonic interest while the middle parts fill out the texture and sonority. The final movement, a D Major molto allegro in rondo form, exhibits these characteristics. All the melodic material is assumed by the first violin while the others provide support. Whereas the rondo theme presented by the first violin is buttressed with octave doubling and parallel movement in the second violin, the episodes feature a soloistic first violin with only the barest of accompaniments. Continuous domination by the first violin is offset by punctuating remarks in the lower instruments (Ex. 4.6).

One might attribute this emphasis on a light, homophonic texture to the fact that K.155 is one of Mozart's earliest quartets. The basic assumption would be that as he continued to write in this genre, he works would become more conversational. But even in his "Haydn" quartets, long considered exemplary

9   Daniel Heartz, *Haydn, Mozart and the Viennese School: 1740–1780* (New York: W. W. Norton and Co., 1995), pp. 46–8.
10   Konold, *The String Quartet*, pp. 74–5.

examples of perfect quartet writing, Mozart continued to include lecture movements. In the case of K.421 and K.458, the lecture becomes the basis for the trio and as such, provides a strong contrast to the debate minuets. Marianne

Example 4.6 Wolfgang Amadeus Mozart, K.155, Mvt. III, mm 1–32

Danckwardt, for example, states that with K.458, composed in 1784, Mozart finally learned how to write a quartet. In particular she points to both the motivic and thematic work and their simplicity, and the goal-oriented writing.[11] In light of this one might conclude that the lecture trio simply provides a relief from the more complex texture of the surrounding movements. Alternatively, one can view it as yet another form of discourse between four conversants. The former reduces the importance of the trio, the latter points out the difference minus the pejorative aspects.

One advantage of the eighteenth-century string quartet was that it needed so few players, especially when compared with an orchestra. This was of particular benefit to those with limited resources and limited space. A second advantage was that of the few players required, not all, if any needed to be highly skilled. Many quartets, such as those by Johann Baptist Vanhal (1739–1813) could be rendered by amateurs on all four parts.

The vast majority of Vanhal's string quartets feature the first violin with simple support. Rather than viewing this as a static and undeveloped approach to the genre,[12] one should evaluate this regularity merely as a consistent method of writing for the first violin in a manner of a solo instrument plus accompaniment. Many movements are near-perfect examples of the lecture, and several, such as those found in Op. 6, highlight the accessibility of Vanhal's works to musicians of limited ability.

The six quartets which make up Op. 6 probably date from the last two years of Vanhal's visit to Italy. All are in a three-movement, fast – slow – fast sequence. Compared to Vanhal's earlier quartets, these works are simpler, scaled-down, and require no soloistic technique. The E-major quartet (E1) fits this description. Laid out as a binary slow movement surrounded by two quick sonata form ones, the entire work can be executed by amateurs. Even though the lecture format is heard throughout the quartet, each movement has a unique sound. In the opening Allegro, large portions of homophony are separated by the strategic use of unisons. The lyrical Adagio comprises a melody supported by a patterned accompaniment, while in the concluding Presto, the rapid surface rhythm of the supporting voices provides a stable underpinning to the dominant first violin. In all movements, none of the parts is technically demanding. Even the first violin part can be played by someone with limited skill.

By his late 40s, Vanhal apparently had made a conscious decision not to compose any more quartets. Jones attributes this to the fact that the musician

---

[11]   Marianne Danckwardt, "Mozarts 'ganz neue besondere Art' zu schreiben: der Kopfsatz aus dem Streichquartett KV 458 (1784)", *Mozart Jahrbuch* (1984–85): 24–31.

[12]   Jones, "The String Quartets", pp. 227–8, notes that this consistency is only regarded negatively if one uses the works of Haydn and Mozart as benchmarks, for only then does one receive a "blinkered and misleading view of the string quartet in the eighteenth century".

realized he could not compete with Haydn and Mozart; their works were simply on a different intellectual and artistic level. Moreover, since Vanhal neither had a specific patron nor was a businessman (like Pleyel and Hoffmeister), he had to find some way to support himself, and thus made a commercial decision to turn to other genres.[13]

The Opp. 3 and 4 collections of Placidus Cajetan von Camerloher (1718–82) are comparable with many of Vanhal's works. These two sets of quartets, both titled "sinfonien", were published during his lifetime. Each contains twelve works. The C-Major quartet from Op. 3,[14] dating from ca. 1760, is representative and points up some of the difficulties in assessing the genre during the third quarter of the century. In keeping with the ambiguousness of terminology so common during that time period, the labeling of this three-movement work as "Sinfonia a 4tro" simply tells us that it contains four parts: two violins, viola, and basso. None of the lines is rhythmically complex, nor does any require a player of great skill. Subtle manipulations of the bow, gradual gradations of sound, and individuality of lines are all absent. Frequent alternations of forte and piano as well as triadic themes suggest a possible orchestral performance. But at the same time, the emancipation of the viola from the bass line as well as the handling of the voices is, in principle, similar to that found in a string quartet.[15] Not unlike the Vanhal work discussed above, this C-major quartet highlights a melodically dominant first violin and three accompanying voices. Just as the lower lines are technically accessible to the amateur, so too is the top voice. All the parts can be played in first position thus providing the interested string player with a rewarding, but at the same time, not too challenging piece to play (Ex. 4.7).

In contrast to the all-amateur type, other lectures require at least one player, nearly always the first violinist, to possess greater facility than the other members of the ensemble. Sometimes this means only a moderately better player; other times, the first violin part requires a performer of professional calibre. Within the output of the Italian-born cellist, Luigi Boccherini (1743–1805), one finds examples of both.

Scholars have not always been kind in their assessment of Boccherini's nearly one hundred quartets. Inevitably this is due to the expectation that the eighteenth-century quartet, in its "classical" form must contain of motivic development and follow the path taken by Joseph Haydn.[16] In Boccherini's case, however, and as

---

[13] Ibid.

[14] "Sinfonia a 4tro [Op. 3]", manuscript parts, Fürstlich Oettingen-Wallerstein'sche Biblio thek Schloß Harburg, HR III 4½ 4°727.

[15] Sandberger, "Zur Geschichte des Haydnschen Streichquartetts", p. 54.

[16] Konold, *The String Quartet*, p. 64, refers to Boccherini's "negligible stylistic evolution". Michael Tilmouth, in a harsher assessment comments that "During the . . . same period in which Haydn had dyamically revolutionized the form Boccherini was content with a virtually static art, albeit one of abundant charm and grace". See *The New Grove*, s. v. "String

**Example 4.7 Placidus Cajetan von Camerloher, *Sinfonia a 4tro* [in C Major],
Mvt. I, mm 1–70**

Example 4.7 continued

Example 4.7 concluded

shall be seen as we return to his works many times, the Italian composer's output does not follow the same progression as Haydn's. Rather, throughout his life, he employed a variety of discourses based on the situation. His music does not reveal a "neat" chronological progression from texturally simple *Hausmusik* to the motivic style associated with the Viennese quartet. Instead, he varied his textural choices from work to work. Just as a conversation is as likely to appear early in Boccherini's output as later, so too does the composer employ the lecture, with its varying degress of difficulty for the first violin, throughout his entire career.

Some of his quartets, such as the Quartettino in Bb, G.220,[17] are ideal examples of *Hausmusik*/lecture: melodic first violin, harmonic foundation cello, and filler inner voices. The first violin part, while dominant, is not so hard as to preclude performance by only the most advanced string player. This two-movement work of 1792, bears all the characteristics one would expect to find in the lecture. The opening a Maestoso assai, in sonata form, is particularly illustrative. Throughout the entire movement, the first violin never relinquishes its role as the carrier of the melody. Variety in this part comes from the degree of embellishment and changes in surface rhythm. While the first seven measures present the melody in an unadorned fashion, the following ones become increasingly florid. Only with the recapitulation in measure 28 does the first violin return to its original state. This calmer mode does not remain for long, however, as Boccherini again increases the activity. The listener's continued focus on the upper part is ensured by the uniformity of the lower three voices. Throughout the movement the second violin and viola play repeated notes, rhythms, and patterns. The cello part serves as the harmonic underpinning. While all four voices are necessary, a sense of hierarchy and position is obvious. The first violinist must be far more facile than those executing the lower lines, thus making this a perfect piece for a group consisting of one skilled player and three amateurs (Ex. 4.8).

This is not the only instance in which Boccherini requires a skilled first violinist. His Op. 8 (G.165–170) of 1769, demands such a performer; the remaining parts can, for the most part, be executed by players of only minimal facility. G.165, for example, consists of three lecture movements, all dominated by the first violin. The cello, together with the viola, plays the simplest of lines, while the second violin part varies between moving in parallel motion with the upper voice, working with the viola to provide sonoric filler, or simply rendering a slightly more active accompaniment. All these features are immediately found in the exposition of the opening Allegro vivace. The near continuous sixteenth notes of the top voice are offset both by the slower moving accompaniment of the inner voices as well as the regularity of the bass line. Measure 16 finds a change

---

[17]   Together with G. 221–25, this quartet was published as Op. 44.   Manuscript copies are located at both the Staatsbibliothek zu Berlin Preußischer Kulturbesitz, M596, and the Bibliothèque de l'Opéra (Paris), Réserve 507/7.

Example 4.8 Luigi Boccherini, G220, Mvt. I

Example 4.8 continued

Example 4.8 continued

Example 4.8 continued

Example 4.8 concluded

in the second violin's accompanimental part but no refocusing of the listener's attention (Ex. 4.9).

There are a host of eighteenth-century composers whose quartets seem designed for this combination of skilled and less-skilled players. Lack of space precludes a review of all of them, but a brief mention of some works by Gaetano Brunetti (?1744–98), Pierre Vachon (1731–1803), Adalbert Gyrowetz (1763–1850), and Franz Danzi (1763–1826) will suffice.

Example 4.9 Luigi Boccherini, G165, Mvt. I, mm 1–23

Example 4.9 concluded

Nearly all of Brunetti's 451 compositions are chamber pieces; of these, the string quartets number more than forty.[18] Not all these works are dominated by the

---

[18]   Forty-four quartets are readily available at the Library of Congress in Washington D. C.: Opp. 2–5 plus twenty other unpublished works (M452.B9 case). In addition, twenty-seven quartets, in manuscript form, are held at the Bibliothèque Nationale, Paris. F Pn Ms. 1634–35, bundled together, duplicate Opp. 2–3. The remaining fifteen are in loose parts and have numbers attached to them: 37, 42, 43, 45, 46, 44 (F Pn Ms. 1636, 1–6); 48–50, 52, 53, 55 (F Pn Ms. 1637, 1–6); 56, 57 (F Pn Ms. 1638, 1–2); and 58 (F Pn Ms. 1639). For a discussion of these Paris manuscripts, see Klaus Fischer, "Die Streichquartette Gaetano Brunettis (1744–1798) in der Bibliothèque Nationale in Paris im Zusammenhang mit dem Streichquartett des 18. Jahrhunderts", in *Bericht über den Internationalen Musikwissenschaftlichen Kongress, Bayreuth 1981*(ed. by Christoph-Hellmut Mahling and

first violin. Some require the participation of the lower voices; we shall have occasion to return to these in later chapters.

Brunetti does not restrict himself to melody plus meager accompaniment in his lecture movements. In many, the lower voices have some periods of increased surface rhythm which give at least the illusion of participation. But regardless of the degree of perceived involvement, the first violin outshines the other voices. The final movement of an A Major quartet[19] is typical. In this sonata form Allegretto non molto, the first violin part is both active and demanding. There is no confusion regarding the role of each instrument. From the opening melody presented by the first violin with the barest of support, to the arpeggios and exacting passagework, this movement requires a violinist of professional calibre. The sustained pitches, repeated eighth notes, and lower register of the bottom three voices ensure that nothing covers up the activity of the top line (Ex. 4.10). This separation of parts is maintained throughout the movement and becomes even more pronounced during the development. Measures 90–127 in particular highlight a concerto-like approach to the top line while the lower voices recede even further into the background (Ex. 4.11).

Example 4.10 Gaetano Brunetti, Quartet in A Major, Mvt. III, mm 1–34

Sigrid Wiesmann; Kassel: Bärenreiter, 1984), pp. 350–59.
19   Manuscript parts, Bibliothèque Nationale, Paris, Ms 1637, 6.

Example 4.10 concluded

Example 4.11 Gaetano Brunetti, Quartet in A Major, Mvt. III, mm 90–127

Example 4.11 concluded

A similar distinction between melody and accompaniment can be found in some quartets by Pierre Vachon, a French violinist and composer who lived and worked in Paris, London, and Berlin. Vachon's quartets have fallen into obscurity; this is unfortunate as they are highly idiomatic for the instruments and reveal a variety of structure, melody, and texture.[20] Throughout his multiple sets, Vachon requires his violinists to execute pedals, double stops, barriolage, and intricate bowing techniques; performers must also have the facility to move easily into the upper positions. But he did not use his quartets merely as a study of technique. Vachon explored texture and sonority as well. Most often, this investigation is achieved by attending to the relationship between the four voices. His Op. 11 quartets,[21] for example, demonstrate an awareness of string texture, sonority, and idiomatic possibilities, especially for the violin. This last feature is particularly evident in the middle movement of the sixth quartet. Surrounded by two debates, this three-part Andante with its lecture format displays a strong separation between melody and accompaniment. While the uppermost part must be a executed by a skilled performer, the other ones can easily be relegated to amateurs. The melodic first violin, filled with lyricism, varied rhythms, and rapid figuration stands in contrast to the sustained pitches, supportive, and slow moving lower lines (Ex. 4.12).

Example 4.12 Pierre Vachon, Op. 11, No. 6, Mvt. II, mm 47–64

---

[20] For a discussion of Vachon's quartets, see Lionel de la Laurencie, *L'École Française de Violon de Lully a Viotti: Études d'Histoire et d'Esthétique* (3 vols, Paris: 1922–24; Geneva: Minkoff Reprints, 1971), and Philippe Oboussier, "The French String Quartet, 1770–1800", in *Music and the French Revolution* (Cambridge: Cambridge University Press, 1992), pp. 74–92.

[21] *Six Quatuors concertants. . .* Op. XI (Paris: Sieber, [1782–6]). Printed parts are available at the Library of Congress, Washington D. C., M452.A2V2 Op. 11.

Example 4.12 concluded

While Vachon's compositions require facility primarily in the lower positions, Franz Danzi's quartets Opp. 5–6 require the same in all positions. Although Danzi's fame derives primarily from his music for the theater, he is also known as a prolific writer of instrumental music. Among these are two sets of quartets, Opp. 5–6.[22] Both consist of three works each, and every movement is a set of figural variations. All contain a demanding top part and "amateur-friendly" lower ones. Even when the original melody is given to one of the bottom parts, the figuration in the first violin obscures it. Thus this melodic material becomes part of the sonority, rather than a distinct entity. The listener remains focused solely on the first violin.

The first movement of Op. 6, No. 2 is typical. After a leisurely unfolding of the theme (mm 1–28), the first violin launches into rapid scales, arpeggios, and passagework; successful execution requires quick and easy movement about the instrument. At times, the first violin is freed of the responsibility of producing the melody; this may be delegated to either the second violin (mm 29–56) or the cello (mm 57–84). In these places, the florid nature of the first violin part continues to demand the listener's attention; the original tune becomes secondary. Moreover, the contrast of surface rhythms and pitch variety between the upper and lower voices further reinforces the lecture aspect of the movement. Example 4.13 clearly illustrates this point. To ensure audibility, Danzi has placed the full melody in the cello's middle to upper register. The repeated pitches, sustained notes, and other supportive movement of both the second violin and viola suggest that the listener's attention will remain with the cellist. This, however, is not the case; the top line is so ornate that the balance of power is completely shifted to that voice.

---

22   "Trois Quatuors pour deux violons, alto et violoncelle [Op. 5]," manuscript parts, Badische Landesbibliothek, Donaueschingen, Musik Ms 302. "Trois Quatuors pour deux violons alto e violoncello [Op. 6]," manuscript parts, Badische Landesbibliothek, Donaueschingen, Musik Ms 303. Both works were published in Munich, probably during the early part of the 1790s.

Throughout this variation we are treated to arpeggios, figuration, string crossings, octave leaps, and passagework. Thus the melody becomes just another

Example 4.13 Franz Danzi, Op. 6, No. 2, Mvt. I, mm 57–84

Example 4.13 concluded

part of the octave leaps, and passagework. Thus the melody becomes just another support. Unless one makes a concerted effort to find it and listen specifically for it, the theme is absorbed into the accompaniment and overshadowed by the virtuosic nature of the first violin line.

Many of Adalbert Gyrowetz's quartets require a similarly skilled first violinist in order to ensure a satisfactory reading. Gyrowetz wrote at least forty-two string quartets, and possibly as many as forty-five.[23] The early works, those pertinent to this study, are two- or three movement compositions, most of which are dominated by lyricism. Although Hickman finds these to be in the *quatuor concertant* style,

---

[23]   While the works list in the *New Grove* makes reference to forty-five works, Hickman, in his "The Flowering of the Viennese String Quartet", pp. 162–3, reduces this number to forty-two noting that those dedicated to the Prince of Wales are duplicates of works in another set.

not all are so easily categorized.[24]   Use of such a label papers over the fact that some are pure lectures; *Trois Quatuors Concertants*, Op. 3[25] has two such exceptions. Both the first and third quartets, with the emphasis firmly placed on the first violin, are fine examples of the lecture. Throughout these three-movement works, the cello provides a harmonic foundation while the two middle voices often work as a unit to fill in the sonority. The Allegro of the B-flat quartet (No. 3) shall serve as an illustration.

This sonata form movement exhibits all the expected characteristics of a lecture: focus on the first violin, supportive inner voices, and foundational cello. While the first violin part must be executed by a skilled player, the lower parts require performers with only minimal skills. Interplay between the instruments is limited; any give-and-take is restricted to the less stable sections. Following a four-measure unison opening, the first violin presents the melody over a supportive and unobtrusive accompaniment. The slower surface rhythm and repetitive nature of the lower voices stand in stark contrast to the variety of the upper line. Measures 23–30 bring a small interchange between the first violin and the two middle voices; the unison passage which follows leads us into another section of first violin domination complete with string crossings, rapid scales, and arpeggios. Even when the second violin and viola come forward in measure 39 with melodic material, the first violin refuses to cede its prominent position. The slow-moving melodic snippets produced in the middle voices are constantly interrupted with sixteenth-note runs. After two unsuccessful attempts to attract our attention, the middle voices return to their supportive roles while the first violin takes center stage, remaining there until the end of the exposition. While at times the second violin line may parallel that of the first, there is no redistribution of roles and functions for any of the instruments.

The beginning of the development recalls the opening of the movement, but this time there are two such unison passages. Most of the twenty-six measure development features the first violin, but there is also a suggestion of independence amongst the voices. Snippets of the primary group's material can be heard in the various parts and there is less melody plus accompaniment texture. The recapitulation returns us to both familiar material and dispensation of roles.

---

[24]   Hickman, in his "Vojtěch Jírovec and the Viennese String Quartet", in *Janáček and Czech Music: Proceedings of the International Conference, Saint Louis, 1988* (ed. by Michael Beckerman and Glen Bauer; Stuyvesant, New York: Pendragon Press, 1995), p. 186, is fairly explicit about the connection between Gyrowetz and the *quatuor concertant*. Characterizing these works as tuneful, simple, and light, Hickman asserts that they feature the essence of the genre as conceived by Boccherini and Pleyel. He does, however, note that these works differ from the French quartet in the frequent harmonic diversions in the exposition and the formal ambiguity at the start of the recapitulation. See "Six Bohemian Masters", p. 167. Note that this differentiation is based on formal aspects, rather than modes of interaction.

[25]   Berlin: Hummel, [1790?].

The above examples reveal a consistent emphasis on the first violin by incorporating technical requirements which naturally draw the listener's attention. But composers also had the option of manipulating the accompaniment. For example, the lower voices can be reduced to the barest possible presence as found in the second movement of Pleyel's C Major quartet (Ben 346) of 1788. Even the most cursory visual inspection reveals the dominant-subservient relationship of the four lines. The repetitiveness of the lower voices is strikingly different from variety of the top line. Movement in the second violin part stands out as unusual; its appearance is nearly always due to a paralleling of the first violin part. Thus even when another part seems remotely melodic, it is subsumed under the more noticeable first violin part (Ex. 4.14).

Example 4.14 Ignace Pleyel, Ben 346, Mvt. II, mm 17–32

Example 4.14 concluded

Less overt are those accompaniments which one might refer to as "minimal". The first movement of Vachon's Op. 11, No. 3 aptly illustrates this. In this Moderato, the first violin is firmly established in the leadership position. The repetitive accompanimental figures and limited interplay ensure that the lower voices do not intrude. Still other composers choose to provide a more active accompaniment while still maintaining the balance of power; this is achieved when the first violin's part consistently demands our attention with its technical requirements and position as bearer of melody. The opening movement of Joseph Haydn's first "Tost" quartet (Op. 54, No. 1) meets this description.

Although Haydn's early quartets are exemplary examples of lectures, the composer never completely forsook this approach. Even the landmark Op. 33, often viewed as the epitome of the classical Viennese chamber style, contained fine illustrations of the lecture.[26] With each successive set, Haydn continued to incorporate a variety of discourse styles. The six quartets of Opp. 54–55 (1788) were no exception.

Johann Tost, the dedicatee of these works, served as violinist at Esterháza during the years 1783–88. According to John Baron, it was Tost's "custom" to acquire the exclusive rights to new chamber works for a period of three years during which time any performance would require his presence.[27] It is possible that Haydn, aware of this, knew that whatever he wrote would need an accessible and public-friendly approach. The quartets were sent to London ready for presentation during the 1789 season and were highly successful. The Longman and Broderip

[26]   See Blume, "Josef Haydns künstlerische Persönlichkeit", pp. 29–30, 32; Bruce Alan Brown, "Maria Theresa's Vienna", in *The Classical Era: From the 1740s to the end of the 18th Century* (Englewood Cliffs, New Jersey: Prentice Hall, 1989), pp. 120–1; Landon, *Haydn: Chronicle and Works*, vol. 1, pp. 228–30; and James Webster, "Did Haydn 'Synthesize' the Classical String Quartet", in *Haydn Studies*, pp. 338–9.

[27]   John Herschel Baron, *Intimate Music: A History of the Idea of Chamber Music* (Stuyvesant, New York: Pendragon Press, 1998), pp. 218–9.

edition makes mention of their performance with the inscription "performed at the Professional Concert Hanover Square 1789".[28]

With one exception (Op. 55, No. 2), at least one lecture movement appears in each quartet. The first three in particular, feature the first violin in three out of the four movements. This is not achieved simply by reducing the activity of the lower instruments but rather by stressing the concerto-like difficulty of the upper part. The opening movement of the set illustrates this point. A visual examination of this G Major Allegro con brio reveals activity in all voices. While the first violin part is constantly varied; in contrast, the lower voices vacillate between typical accompaniment and melodic snippets. At times, one or more of the lower voices will respond to the first violin line, moving with a similar surface rhythm or contour. But rather than suggesting a dialogue or interchange, the lower voices offer punctuation to the continuously active and melodically dominant first violin (mm 24–32). At times, the discourse resembles a lecture/debate hybrid, especially in the development. Measures 80–86 with their imitative activity involving all voices might make one rethink a lecture categorization, but the technical requirements of the first violin – use of upper register, rapid scales, arpeggios, passagework, and octaves – are not typical of the lower voices. This easily allows the listener to distinguish the first violin from the other three parts, and encourages one to focus primarily on that instrument, thus reinforcing the roles of lecturer and listener/supporter.

While the lecture's traditionally featured instrument is the first violin, a composer will occasionally choose to highlight another one. Thus the two violins might exchange roles. Aurally there may be no difference in sonority, but from the players' and observers' perspectives, the balance of power has shifted. In the case of Joseph Schmitt's (baptized 1734–91), Op. 5, No. 2, it is the viola that takes center stage in the Trio.

Schmitt's *Six quatuors*, Op. 5[29] date from 1773. All the quartets contain at least one lecture movement, and only two do not contain more. All but the final quartet are four-movement works; the sixth is laid out in three. Of particular interest is the second quartet. As three of the four movements are debates, the lecture Minuet and Trio stand in sharp contrast. Even more interesting is the fact that while the Minuet features the first violin, the Trio highlights the viola. The latter, with its darker sonority, provides a timbral contrast but at the same time maintains the lecture approach of the former. The minimal technical requirements suggest that Schmitt

---

[28]   For a good discussion of the background of the Tost quartets, see Landon, *Haydn: Chronicle and Works*, vol. 2, pp. 635–41.

[29]   Joseph Schmitt, "Six quatuors a deux violons, taille et basse. . . oeuvre Cinquieme", manuscript parts, Akademiska Kapell, Lunds, Saml. Kraus 399. In published form, the imprint reads Amsterdam: Hummel, [1773]. This unpublished set also contains a duplet basso part, suggesting perhaps a two-instrument reading of the basso line.

was more interested in quality of sound than a display of showmanship (Ex. 4.15). Furthermore, as composers often allowed secondary instruments to come forward in a Trio or rondo episode, Schmitt's use of the viola is in keeping with traditional practices.

Example 4.15 Joseph Schmitt, Op. 5, No. 2, Trio

The lecture provided the composer with the means to explore a particular texture, timbre, and a melodic hierarchy. It also offered a unique opportunity for amateur and professional musicians to play together. Inevitably it was the first violin part which required the most facility, both from a technical as well as musical standpoint. This disparity of skill levels in no way diminished the ability of the four members of the ensemble to feel the intimacy inherent in the medium. Because it established a sense of hierarchy and position within the ensemble, performers and listeners alike were presented with something comfortable and familiar. Each instrumentalist had a set function within the ensemble. Thus when a composer did choose to make alterations – i.e., place the melodic line in another part –, he could exploit certain elements such as timbre for the express purpose of providing an aural contrast. This did not upset the balance of power; it merely offered respite and momentary change. Rather than treating the lecture as a poor cousin of the Viennese debates and conversations of Haydn and Mozart, it should be regarded as but one type of discourse available to the four members of a string quartet.

Chapter 5

The polite conversation

The polite conversation, most closely associated with the *quatuor concertant*, shares certain characteristics with the lecture. Both feature a homophonic texture thereby allowing the listener to focus on one melody at a time with little, if any, distraction. Secondly, both types meet the needs of a wide variety of performers; amateurs as well as professionals can be satisfied, and often these musicians are able to play together in the same ensemble.

Although not as plentiful as the lecture, the polite conversation emerged as one of the most commonly found types of quartet of the second half of the eighteenth century.[1] While the majority of the earliest ones appeared in works by French composers, by the fourth quarter of the century, one was just as likely to find such an approach in works by non-French composers. Like the lecture, the polite conversation remained a viable means of organizing the four voices well into the 1790s as illustrated in Table 2.

Table 2: A Selected List of Polite Conversations [2]

Year	Composer	Title (Movement[s])
1759–66	A.-E.-M. Grétry	Op. 3, No. 1 (2)
	A.-E.-M. Grétry	Op. 3, No. 5 (1)
1760s	C. d'Ordonez	Op. 1, No. 3 (2)
	F. Gassmann	H.480 (2)
1761	L. Boccherini	G.159 (1, 2)
	L. Boccherini	G.160 (1)
	L. Boccherini	G.161 (2)
1768	A. L. Baudron	*Sei Quartetti*, No. 1 (1, 2)
	A. L. Baudron	*Sei Quartetti*, No. 2 (1, 2, 3)
	A. L. Baudron	*Sei Quartetti*, No. 3 (1, 3)
	A. L. Baudron	*Sei Quartetti*, No. 4 (1, 2, 3)
	A. L. Baudron	*Sei Quartetti*, No. 5 (1, 2)
	A. L. Baudron	*Sei Quartetti*, No. 6 (1, 2, 3)

---

[1] A popular approach, the polite conversation appeared in at leastone movement in 37% of the quartets examined. Of these, a full 100 contained nothing but polite conversations. For a partial listing, see Table 2.

[2] See the bibliography for a full citation of each of the listed compositions.

Table 2 continued

Year	Composer	Title (Movement[s])
1769	L. Boccherini	G.168 (2)
ca.1770s	C. E. Graf	*Quartetto a F* (1)
1770s	F. de Giardini	Op. 14, No.1 (2)
	F. de Giardini	Op. 14, No. 3 (3)
	F. de Giardini	Op. 14, No. 4 (2, 3)
	F. de Giardini	Op. 14, No. 5 (1, 3)
	F. de Giardini	Op. 14, No. 6 (1, 3)
1773	J.-B. Davaux	Op. 6, No. 1 (1)
	J.-B. Davaux	Op. 6, No. 2 (1)
	J.-B. Davaux	Op. 6, No. 3 (1)
	J.-B. Davaux	Op. 6, No. 4 (1, 2)
	P. Vachon	Op. 7, No. 6 (3)
1773–4	G. M. Cambini	T.1 (Op. 1, No. 1) (1)
1774	G. Brunetti	Op. 2, No. 2 (3)
	G. Brunetti	Op. 2, No. 6 (1)
	G. Brunetti	Op. 3, No. 1 (1, 2)
	G. Brunetti	Op. 3, No. 6 (1)
ca.1775	T. Giordani	Op. 8, No. 1 (1, 2, 3)
	T. Giordani	Op. 8, No. 2 (1, 3)
	T. Giordani	Op. 8, No. 3 (2, 3)
	T. Giordani	Op. 8, No. 4 (1, 2)
	T. Giordani	Op. 8, No. 5 (1, 3)
	P. Vachon	Op. 5, No. 5 (1)
1775	J.-B.-S. Bréval	Op. 1, No. 1 (1, 3)
	J.-B.-S. Bréval	Op. 1, No. 2 (1, 3)
	J.-B.-S. Bréval	Op. 1, No. 3 (1, 2, 3)
	J.-B.-S. Bréval	Op. 1, No. 4 (1, 2, 3)
	J.-B.-S. Bréval	Op. 1, No. 5 (1)
	J.-B.-S. Bréval	Op. 1, No. 6 (1, 2)
1776	E.-B.-J. Barrière	Op. 1, No. 1 (1, 2)
	E.-B.-J. Barrière	Op. 1, No. 2 (1, 2, 3)
	E.-B.-J. Barrière	Op. 1, No. 3 (1, 2)
	E.-B.-J. Barrière	Op. 1, No. 4 (1)
	E.-B.-J. Barrière	Op. 1, No. 5 (2)
	E.-B.-J. Barrière	Op. 1, No. 6 (1)
	G. M. Cambini	T.13 (1, 2)
	G. M. Cambini	T.14 (1, 2, 3)

Table 2 continued

Year	Composer	Title (Movement[s])
	G. M. Cambini	T.15 (1, 2)
	G. M. Cambini	T.16 (1, 2)
	G. M. Cambini	T.17 (1, 2, 3)
	G. M. Cambini	T.18 (1, 2)
1776–8	L. Boccherini	G.190 (2)
	L. Boccherini	G.192 (1)
ca.1777	N.-J. Chartrain	Op. 8, No. 1 (2)
	N.-J. Chartrain	Op. 8, No. 2 (1, 2, 3)
	N.-J. Chartrain	Op. 8, No. 3 (1, 2)
	N.-J. Chartrain	Op. 8, No. 4 (1, 3)
	N.-J. Chartrain	Op. 8, No. 5 (1, 2)
1777–8	G. M. Cambini	T.25 (1, 2)
	G. M. Cambini	T.26 (1, 2)
	G. M. Cambini	T.27 (1, 2)
	G. M. Cambini	T.28 (1, 2)
	G. M. Cambini	T.29 (1, 2)
	G. M. Cambini	T.30 (1, 2)
b.1778	G. A. Kreusser	Op. 9, No. 5 (2)
ca.1778	N.-J. Chartrain	Op. 4, No. 2 (1, 2)
	N.-J. Chartrain	Op. 4, No. 3 (3)
	N.-J. Chartrain	Op. 4, No. 4 (1, 2)
	N.-J. Chartrain	Op. 4, No. 5 (3)
	N.-J. Chartrain	Op. 4, No. 6 (2, 3)
1778	G. M. Cambini	T.37 (1, 2)
	G. M. Cambini	T.38 (1, 2)
	G. M. Cambini	T.39 (1, 2)
	G. M. Cambini	T.40 (1, 2)
	G. M. Cambini	T.41 (1, 2)
	G. M. Cambini	T.42 (1, 2)
1779	J.-B. Davaux	Op. 9, No. 1 (1)
	J.-B. Davaux	Op. 9, No. 2 (1, 2)
	J.-B. Davaux	Op. 9, No. 3 (1)
	J.-B. Davaux	Op. 9, No. 5 (1, 2)
	J.-B. Davaux	Op. 9, No. 6 (1)
1779–82	G. M. Cambini	T.55 (1, 2)
	G. M. Cambini	T.56 (1, 2)
	G. M. Cambini	T.57 (1, 2)
	G. M. Cambini	T.58 (1, 2)

Table 2 continued

Year	Composer	Title (Movement[s])
	G. M. Cambini	T.59 (1, 2)
	G. M. Cambini	T.60 (1, 2)
b.1780	N.-M. Dalayrac	Op. 5, No. 1 (1, 2)
	N.-M. Dalayrac	Op. 5, No. 2 (1, 2)
	N.-M. Dalayrac	Op. 5, No. 3 (1, 2)
	N.-M. Dalayrac	Op. 5, No. 4 (1, 2)
	N.-M. Dalayrac	Op. 7, No. 3 (2)
	N.-M. Dalayrac	Op. 8, No. 1 (1)
	N.-M. Dalayrac	Op. 8, No. 2 (2)
	N.-M. Dalayrac	Op. 8, No. 3 (2)
	N.-M. Dalayrac	Op. 8, No. 4 (1)
	N.-M. Dalayrac	Op. 8, No. 6 (1)
	N.-M. Dalayrac	Op. 11, No. 1 (1, 2)
	N.-M. Dalayrac	Op. 11, No. 2 (1, 2)
	N.-M. Dalayrac	Op. 11, No. 3 (1, 2)
	N.-M. Dalayrac	Op. 11, No. 4 (1,2)
	N.-M. Dalayrac	Op. 11, No. 5 (1, 2)
	N.-M. Dalayrac	Op. 11, No. 6 (1, 2)
1780	G. M. Cambini	T.43 (1)
	G. M. Cambini	T.44 (1, 2, 3)
	G. M. Cambini	T.45 (1)
	G. M. Cambini	T.46 (1)
	G. M. Cambini	T.47 (1)
	G. M. Cambini	T.48 (1)
1781	L. Boccherini	G.209 (2)
	L. Boccherini	G.210 (1)
	L. Boccherini	G.211 (1)
	L. Boccherini	G.212 (2)
	G. M. Cambini	T.78 (1, 2)
	G. M. Cambini	T.79 (1, 2)
	G. M. Cambini	T.80 (1, 2)
1782	G. M. Cambini	T.97 (1, 2)
	G. M. Cambini	T.98 (1)
	G. M. Cambini	T.99 (1, 2)
	G. M. Cambini	T.100 (1, 2)
	G. M. Cambini	T.101 (1)
	G. M. Cambini	T.102 (1)
	J. A. Fodor	Book 4, No. 1 (1)

Table 2 continued

Year	Composer	Title (Movement[s])
	J. A. Fodor	Book 4, No. 2 (1, 2)
	J. A. Fodor	Book 4, No. 3 (1, 2)
	J. A. Fodor	Book 4, No. 4 (1)
	J. A. Fodor	Book 4, No. 6 (1)
	F. de Giardini	Op. 23, No. 3 (1, 2, 3)
	F. de Giardini	Op. 23, No. 4 (1, 2, 3)
1782/3	F. Hoffmeister	Op. 9, No. 1 (1, 2, 3)
	F. Hoffmeister	Op. 9, No. 2 (1, 2, 3)
	F. Hoffmeister	Op. 9, No. 3 (1, 2, 3)
	F. Hoffmeister	Op. 9, No. 4 (1, 2, 3)
	F. Hoffmeister	Op. 9, No. 5 (1, 2)
	F. Hoffmeister	Op. 9, No. 6 (1, 2)
1782/5	J.-B.-S. Bréval	Op. 18, No. 4 (1, 2, 3)
1782–6	P. Vachon	Op. 11, No. 4 (1)
ca.1783	M Haydn	MH. 311 (3)
1784	J. Fiala	Op. 1, No. 1 (1, 3)
	J. Fiala	Op. 1, No. 2 (1, 2, 3)
	J. Fiala	Op. 1, No. 3 (1, 2)
	J. Fiala	Op. 1, No. 4 (1, 3)
	J. Fiala	Op. 1, No. 5 (1)
	J. Fiala	Op. 1, No. 6 (1, 2)
1785	I. J. Pleyel	Ben 314 (1)
	I. J. Pleyel	Ben 317 (2)
1786	I. J. Pleyel	Ben 320 (1)
	I. J. Pleyel	Ben 321 (2)
	I. J. Pleyel	Ben 323 (1)
	I. J. Pleyel	Ben 324 (1)
1788	L. Boccherini	G.215 (4)
	V. Pichl	Op. 13, No. 1 (2)
	V. Pichl	Op. 13, No. 2 (2)
	V. Pichl	Op. 13, No. 3 (1, 3)
	I. J. Pleyel	Ben 343 (3)
	I. J. Pleyel	Ben 349 (1, 2)
	I. J. Pleyel	Ben 347 (1)
1788/90	F. Fiorillo	Op. 6, No. 3 (2, 3)
	F. Fiorillo	Op. 6, No. 4 (1, 2)
	F. Fiorillo	Op. 6, No. 6 (1, 2)
1789	L. Boccherini	G.216 (1)

Table 2 continued

Year	Composer	Title (Movement[s])
	A. Teyber	Op. 2, No. 2 (2)
	A. Teyber	Op. 2, No. 3 (2)
ca.1790	J. A. Fodor	Op. 11, No. 1 (1, 2)
	J. A. Fodor	Op. 11, No. 2 (1, 2)
	J. A. Fodor	Op. 11, No. 3 (1, 2)
	J. A. Fodor	Op. 11, No. 4 (1)
	J. A. Fodor	Op. 11, No. 5 (1)
	J. A. Fodor	Op. 11, No. 6 (1, 3)
	A. Gyrowetz	Op. 3, No. 2 (1, 2, 3)
1790	F. de Giardini	Op. 29, No. 1 (1, 2, 3)
	F. de Giardini	Op. 29, No. 2 (1, 2, 3)
	F. de Giardini	Op. 29, No. 3 (1, 2, 3)
	F. de Giardini	Op. 29, No. 4 (3)
	F. de Giardini	Op. 29, No. 5 (1, 2, 3)
	F. de Giardini	Op. 29, No. 6 (1, 2, 3)
1791	G. Brunetti	Quartet in g (1)
	F. Fränzl	Op. 1, No. 1 (1, 2)
	F. Fränzl	Op. 1, No. 3 (1, 3)
	F. Fränzl	Op. 1, No. 4 (1, 2, 3)
	F. Fränzl	Op. 1, No. 6 (1, 2)
	F. Hoffmeister	Op. 14, No. 3 (1)
1792	L. Boccherini	G.223 (1)
	F. Neubauer	Op. 3, No. 1 (1, 2)
	F. Neubauer	Op. 3, No. 3 (1)
1793	P. Wranitzky	Op. 23, No. 1 (4)
	P. Wranitzky	Op. 23, No.4 (1)
	P. Wranitzky	Op. 23, No. 5 (2)
	F. Krommer	Op. 1, No. 1 (1, 3)
	F. Krommer	Op. 1, No. 2 (2)
	F. Krommer	Op. 1, No. 3 (1, 2, 3)
	F. Krommer	Op. 3, No. 1 (1, 3)
	F. Krommer	Op. 3, No. 2 (1, 2, 3)
	F. Krommer	Op. 3, No. 3 (3)
	A. Gyrowetz	Op. 3, No. 1 (1, 2, 3)
	A. Gyrowetz	Op. 3, No. 3 (1, 2, 3)
	A. Gyrowetz	Op. 3, No. 4 (1)
	A. Gyrowetz	Op. 3, No. 5 (1, 2)

Table 2 concluded

Year	Composer	Title (Movement[s])
1794	L. Boccherini	G.227 (1)
	F. Krommer	Op. 4, No. 1 (1)
1795	J. G. Distler	Opp. 1–2, No. 5 (1)
1796	F. Krommer	Op. 5, No. 1 (3)

Polite conversations can be identified by the presence of long, uninterrupted melodies, part or voice exchange, and a strong contrast – both visually and aurally – between melody and accompaniment. Some of these characteristics are more apparent than others, and not all appear consistently in the four voices of the ensemble. For example, some quartet movements may reveal but two members engaged in a polite conversation. Such is the case with Antoine Laurent Baudron's (1742–1834) *Sei Quartetti*.[3]

Although most of Baudron's works are for the theater, he did write at least one set of quartets – *Sei quartetti* – during the 1760s.[4] While Philippe Oboussier finds these works to be a shared experience of equality among all four instruments,[5] in reality, the democracy extends only to the two violins. The upper voices are virtually indistinguishable in range, function, technical requirements, and the amount of melodic material assigned to each. Throughout the set, the role of melodic leader is constantly rotated between the two upper voices. There is no give-and-take between the two violins, just a polite waiting for one to finish so the other can begin. Material is not developed; instead, Baudron introduces a wealth of ideas, each presented one after the other.

This is not to say that the viola and cello never have the opportunity to come forward. Often they are assigned one solo per movement. But in contrast to the treatment of the upper voices, the lower voices are usually paired in parallel thirds and the solo, consistently found in the development and less stable sections, is a short, three- to four-measure snippet. Neither instrument presents either primary or secondary group material in sonata form movements. Thus the overall impression is not a polite conversation among equals, but rather a violin conversation with lower voice accompaniment. This distinction is readily seen in the final movement of the second quartet.

---

[3] *Sei quartetti per due violini, alto, e violoncello obligati* (Paris: Berault, [1768]). Printed parts are available at the Library of Congress, Washington D. C., M452.B333 (case) 1768.

[4] His Op. 3, listed as lost in *The New Grove*, is probably the same as the *Sei quartetti*.

[5] Philippe Oboussier, "The French String Quartet, 1770–1800", in *Music and the French Revolution* (Cambridge: Cambridge University Press, 1992), p. 76.

The last of three movements, this Allegro in sonata form opens with the two violins moving in parallel motion over a simple viola-cello accompaniment. Once the first violin assumes full possession of the melody, the second violin joins the lower voices in support with broken chords, simple quarters, and occasional measures of parallel motion. Only in measure 21 does the second violin come forward, replacing the first violin as the dominant one. The roles of the two upper voices are fully exchanged; the accompanimental figures, previously in the second violin, are now at home with the first violin. The equality of the two parts is seen easily by a simple comparison of measures 5–12 and 21–26 (Ex. 5.1). Both melodies are technically comparable and while the accompanimental lines are not identical, they are similar in requirements and certainly subservient to the uppermost line. Meanwhile, the cello and viola continue unabated in their supportive roles with sustained and repeated pitches, and simple rhythms. This rotation of melodic prominence continues to the end of the exposition, broken only by a final burst of parallel motion.

Example 5.1a   Antoine Laurent Baudron, *Sei Quartetti*, No. 2, Mvt. III, mm 5–12

Example 5.1b   Antoine Laurent Baudron, *Sei Quartetti*, No. 2, Mvt. III, mm 21–26

Like the exposition, the twenty-seven measure development features rotating leadership by the violins. Only at the conclusion of this section does the cello come forward with a small solo which leads directly to the recapitulation and a return to the polite conversation between the two upper voices.

Although most composers of polite conversations feature the violins when there are only two participants, some choose to highlight a less expected pairing. In the first movement of his A-major quartet (Ben 314) from Op. 3 (1786),[6] Pleyel

---

[6]   I[gnace] Pleyel, *Six Quatuors Concertants pour deux violons, alto et basse. . .* Oeuvre III (Paris: Sieber, [1786]). Printed parts are available at the Library of Congress, Washington D. C., M452P723. The title page identifies Pleyel as Joseph Haydn's student ("Composés

directs the listener to the first violin and cello. Although the solos are not marked as is common in many *quatuors concertants*, the distinction between melody and accompaniment is immediately apparent and there are no distractions to draw our attention away from thematic material. Underneath the melody, the second violin moves in either parallel motion or repeated figures, while the viola maintains its unobtrusive line throughout.

The movement opens with an elaborate first violin solo of fourteen measures. After two measures rest, the soloist returns, this time paralleled briefly by the second violin. The solo, which continues in an increasingly ornate fashion for another ten measures, is marked by figuration, use of the upper register, and large leaps. When the sixteen-measure cello solo begins in measure 29, the first violinist recedes into the background with repeated pitches, regular rhythms, and pure subservience (Ex. 5.2). The latter returns to prominence in bar 46 but with more reserve than previously; up to the double bar, which marks the conclusion of the first half, the two violins are more closely connected, moving much of the time in parallel motion.

Example 5.2 Ignace Pleyel, Ben 314, Mvt. I, mm 19–45

Example 5.2 concluded

The same separation of primary and secondary material is evident in the second half of the movement. The contrasting B section which immediately follows the double bar is distinguished by slightly shorter solos and a seemingly quicker pace. Twelve measures of first violin dominance give way to fourteen measures of cello, which in turn yield to sixteen measures of the first violin. After a short cello melody, the two polite conversationalists travel in parallel motion to the fermata (m 112) which heralds a return to the opening "A" material.

Underneath all this has been the violist whose steady repetition of pitches and rhythms has provided a stable background. This accompanimental line stands in strong contrast to the ones discussed; there is no confusion regarding the role which this particular part plays. The second violin parts bears similar qualities although the occasional paralleling of a melodic line has been noted.

A polite conversation may also occur between three members of the quartet. The characteristics of a two-voice conversation easily allow for an additional participant. Many of Italian-born Giuseppe Maria Cambini's (?1746–1825) more than 170 quartets are fine illustrations.

Cambini is often portrayed as one of the primary figures in the development of the French string quartet. He is, in actuality, one of many who made contributions; his output, however, is far larger than that of his contemporaries. The majority of Cambini's quartets (126) are two-movement works.[7] Trimpert notes that this emphasis on the "shorter structure" was in keeping with composers of similar type quartets. It is interesting to note that only at the beginning and end of his quartet-writing career did Cambini include a fourth movement.[8] Regardless of the number of movements, execution of Cambini's quartets requires four knowledgeable performers; the violin parts can be particularly demanding.[9] In any given work, one might be called upon to render sixteenth-note and triplet passages, wide leaps, octaves, chromatic movement, bariolage, harmonics, and/or double stops.

Not all quartets are equally difficult. Some, such as the E Major quartet (T18) from Op. 3 (1776),[10] provide us with an excellent illustration of a less-demanding three-voice polite conversation. The first movement, an Allegro in sonata form, allows the viola to join the violins in dialogue leaving the cello to provide the harmonic foundation. Throughout the movement, we hear solos from primarily the two violins; the viola's contribution, restricted to the development, is not atypical with regard to how that instrument is integrated. Entering just prior to the recapitulation, the viola brings a change of sonority. This darker timbre, coupled with its appearance in the least stable section of the movement, increases the tension of the development. In many respects, the introduction of an "unfamiliar" sound is comparable to the restlessness which one traditionally expects to find in

---

[7]   Far fewer include an additional movement; thirty-eight contain three movements.

[8]   Trimpert, *Die Quatuors concertants*, pp. 59–63, suggests that a composer's decision regarding number of movements may be connected to his/her nationality or then-current location. Two-movement works were in fact quite common during the eighteenth-century; Trimpert points to such composers as Abel, J.C. Bach, Bréval, Cannabich, Dalayrac, St. George, Kreusser, Gossec, Neubauer, and A. Stamitz as representative composers. Only the Viennese classicists showed a preponderance for four-movement works. The fact that we see this as the norm reflects our modern-day restricted view of the period.

[9]   Trimpert's assessment of equality among the four voices is not quite accurate (Ibid., pp. 110–11). Although he notes that the first violinist simply "has more notes", he neglects to point out that many of the works can best be described as a virtuosic first violin part accompanied by amateur-level lower parts.

[10] A facsimile transcription appears in Kenneth Cooper, *Three Centuries of Music in Score: Facsimiles of Scores Made Under the Works Projects Administration*, vol. 10: *Chamber Music IV: Classical String Duos and Quartets (1769–c.1859)* (foreword by Susan T. Sommer; New York: Garland Publishing, Inc., 1990), pp. 131–202.

the development. The return to familiar thematic material and an emphasis on the violins reinforces the stabilizing function of the recapitulation.

Thus the movement can be viewed as a three-voice polite conversation, not necessarily among equals, but one in which whomever is "speaking", regardless of how often or for how long, demands the listener's undivided attention. Supporting lines, in all accompanying voices, are characterized by simple rhythms, pitch repetition, and regularity.

While the above discussion has highlighted polite conversations between either two or three voices, there are a number of examples which incorporate all four. The concluding movement of Jean-Baptiste Sébastien Bréval's (1753–1823) Op. 1, No. 3 is a particularly fine illustration.

By 1775, Bréval had already established his credentials as a performing cellist and instructor. With his *Six Quatuors concertantes pour deux violons, alto et basse*,[11] he made his entrance into the publishing world. Despite the absence of the phrase "et dialogué" which consistently appears on all of Bréval's other quartet publications, this particular collection still contains the characteristic rotation of material common to the French *dialogué*.[12] An examination of the last movement of the third quartet reveals the composer's approach as he incorporates all four voices into a polite mode of discourse. This sonata form Presto opens with the two violins moving in octaves accompanied by the viola. Following a lyrical unfolding of the melody in the first violin with simple accompaniment in the lower three parts, the rotation of material begins. This "traveling" line is always distinguished by its steady eighth notes which stand in contrast to the slower surface rhythm of the surrounding parts. The first instrument to come forward is the viola: for twelve measures, it moves in continual eighth notes while the remaining instruments produce sustained pitches. After "handing" the material over to the first violin, the viola returns to simple repeated quarter notes. When the second violin comes to prominence, its former line is assumed by the now subservient first violin. Thus this part rotation applies not only to the solo but to the accompaniment as well (Ex. 5.3). A two-measure cadence concludes the exposition.

The development is neither technically difficult for any instrument nor is it texturally different from the exposition. The first violin melody is supported by either sustained pitches or patterned accompanimental figures. Only in measure 88 does another instrument replace it as the focus of our attention: the viola. The eighth-note passage of this alto voice is reminiscent of the contour found in the exposition's corresponding line. A repetition of this part by the lowest voice of the

---

[11]   Op. 1 (Paris: de la Chevardiere, [1775]).   Printed parts are held by the Bibliothèque du Conservatoire, Brussels, 6443.

[12]   Viano, "Jean-Baptiste Bréval", pp. 140–1. Not all the movements conform to expectation. While the majority are polite conversations and contain those features typical of *dialogué* works, five are lectures. These inevitably appear in middle and third movements.

Example 5.3   Jean-Baptiste Sébastien Bréval, Op. 1, No. 3. Mvt. III, mm 37–61

Example 5.3 concluded

ensemble shifts our concentration yet again. But it is not just the primary line that receives new voicing.   The viola now renders the previously heard basso part. Thus, just as with the violins in the exposition, the lower voice treatment ensures a democratic distribution of material. The recapitulation, which begins in measure 119, reviews the first twenty-one bars before moving to the secondary group, which is presented in a manner similar to that found in the exposition. While none of the voices are particularly "soloistic", all partake in the presentation of interesting thematic material. No single part interrupts another; the listener has no doubt about which instrument should receive full attention.   Accompaniments serve to enrich and support the melody; they neither compete with nor distract from it.

This last mentioned aspect – the presence of long, intact melodies – is a particularly distinctive feature of the polite conversation. These uninterrupted themes may appear in any voice, thereby reinforcing the idea of four equal, but polite conversants. This absence of interplay among the voices and interjection of competing ideas provides the researcher with a concrete means of identifying this type of quartet even when it is not composed by a French composer. Representative movements by Tommaso Giordani (ca. 1733–1806) and Pleyel will illustrate this point.

Between 1771 and 1790, Giordani published more than thirty sets of instrumental works, two of which were of string quartets: Opp. 2 and 8 from the

1770s. Op. 8[13] contains numerous polite conversations. A succession of lengthy solos, all unhampered by competing lines, is the rule rather than the exception in such movements as the second one of the fourth quartet. Democracy is reinforced by the similar technical requirements in the lines; this pertains not only to the solo parts, but to the accompanimental ones as well. The politeness is revealed with the presence of long, intact solos which are allowed to begin and end without interruption and disturbance.

The Allegretto Grazioso opens with a sixteen-measure rondo theme in the first violin. Broken chords in the viola and second violin, and punctuating eighth notes in the cello provide a stable background for the melody. Measure 17 introduces the second violin as soloist. For the next twenty bars, this instrument fully occupies our attention. The line is, at times, enriched by parallel motion in both the first violin and viola; other times those same instruments play repeated pitches and rhythmic figures. The cello maintains its foundational status. The ensuing rondo theme returns us the the original dispensation of roles. The minore section which follows features a cello–viola–cello succession of solos. In all instances, each melody is allowed to unfold unhindered and without intrusive "remarks" by other voices. Support is rendered by broken chords or intervals, and sustained pitches. The final presentation of the rondo theme and concluding coda return us to a melodic first violin.

Throughout the movement, Giordani consistently places one instrument in the forefront. This succession of prominence, rather than a concentration of melodic material in one voice only, is one means of distinguishing the polite conversation from the lecture. The lack of interaction between the voices is what separates the former from the four-voice conversation.

This absence of interplay is also found in the first movement of Pleyel's F Major quartet (Ben 347).[14] In this Allegro vivace, one finds a succession of solos. Politeness is maintained by the almost rigid distinction of "talking" and "listening" roles. After two eight-measure phrases, each of which begins with a four-measure unison passage, the first violin requests our complete attention. The steady eighth-note fluttering in the middle voices coupled with the cello quarter-note punctuation on the first and third beats only heightens the difference between melody and support. The eleven-bar cello solo which follows presents a stark shift of emphasis. The lowest voice, now a melodic one, is filled with variety of rhythm, contour, and figuration, and stands in sharp contrast to the first violin whose line

---

[13] *Sei quartetti* . . . Op. 8 (London: Napier [c. 1775]).

[14] This quartet, like many others by Pleyel, appeared in multiple publications with vary- ing opus numbers. The source for this particular study was the *Seventh Sett of Six Quartettos for Two Violins, Tenor, and a Violoncello*. . . Op. 20 (London: Forster, [1788]). To avoid confusion, one should consult Rita Benton, *Ignace Pleyel: A Thematic Catalogue of his Compositions* (New York: Pendragon Press, 1977).

has been reduced to a repeated rhythmic pattern. The following second violin solo, complete with rapid figuration and large leaps, again presents something new for the listener. Occasionally Pleyel enriches that part by allowing the first violin to parallel the melodic line or even engage in a moment of imitation. The viola's increased surface rhythm, beginning in measure 58, is exceptionally noticeable as this instrument has been virtually hidden up to this point. Moreover, the sixteenth notes, string crossings, and octave leaps are so different from what that instrument has been previously assigned that the listener cannot help but notice the viola's transformation. Example 5.4 provides a visual illustration of this.

The re-emergence of the first violin as dominant in measure 63 brings with it a reference to previously heard material. The uppermost voice repeats the second violin solo, while the lower part now plays the supportive line formerly rendered by the first violin. This part exchange thus provides the listener with material that is familiar, but also ensures a slightly different sound due to the unique physical makeup of the instruments themselves. The first violin is featured continuously up to the close of the exposition; at times it is joined by the second violin and viola in parallel motion. The cello, with one brief exception, has returned strictly to a harmonic and foundational position.

The development and recapitulation maintain this rotation of melodic prominence. The former presents us with a second violin–viola–cello sequence. Solos are shorter than in the exposition, but they remain distinct and self-contained. Only after a small amount of give-and-take between the cello and first violin does the latter demand the listener's sole attention. A grand pause heralds the recapitulation. Although the layout and sequence of events mirror those in the exposition, Pleyel changes the instrumentation of each solo. Thus musical democracy is achieved by redistributing the melodic and accompanimental material. Although the structure and texture of the exposition and recapitulation are similar, the sonority changes due to the revoicing.

This musical democracy is a hallmark of the polite conversation. There are many examples where one finds the same material traveling from voice to voice. It is this variety of timbre that relieves the monotony of continuous repetition. In the last movement of his Op. 18, No. 4 of 1785,[15] Bréval treats the listener to such changes. Incorporating all four voices into the fabric, the composer allows each to take his or her turn as the bearer of melody. This rotation is applied to the accompanimental lines as well for even the supportive lines are repeated by various voices. This three-part Presto opens with a twelve-bar first violin melody accompanied by sustained pitches and simple repeated eighth notes. Measure 13 brings a second violin melody joined midway with octave doubling by the upper

---

[15] The entire work has been newly edited and printed in Viano, "Jean-Baptiste Bréval", vol. 2, pp. 83–102.

Example 5.4 Ignace Pleyel, Ben 347, Mvt. I, mm 36–73

Example 5.4 concluded

voice. Having thus presented the listener with the concept of hearing one melody
at a time, Bréval then goes about the business of moving not only the thematic
material from voice to voice, but the subsidiary ones as well. The cello requests
our attention in measure 29. The accompaniment seems simple enough: a
sixteenth-note fluttering figure in the viola with constant reference to the note "d"
allows us to feel a sense of stability while the two violins alternate in the execution
of a short figure. Because it is the upper voices that share this snippet, the listener
only hears one voice playing a repeated figure. When the surface rhythm of the
cello melody increases, that of the supporting voices decreases so that the listener
can maintain his or her focus on the bass voice. Measure 46 brings a repeat of this
entire section, but with a redistribution of parts. The cello part is now heard in the
first violin; the second violin takes over the viola line; and the figure shared by the
violins is now executed by the two lowest voices. The fact that this figure can now
be heard as two lines, due to the octave disparity, provides a slight thickening of
the texture. Only with measure 58, as the first violin now extends the
passagework, does the voice exchange cease to function (Ex. 5.5). The second
violin solo, which begins in measure 68, continues the sixteenth-note activity
begun by the upper part.

**Example 5.5   Jean-Baptiste Sébastien Bréval, Op. 18, No. 4, Mvt. III,
mm 29–66**

Example 5.5 continued

Example 5.5 concluded

The minore middle section features mainly the first violin. The texture may thicken momentarily, but in general the listener is more aware of the sixteenth-note passagework in the first violin than the occasional eighth-note movement in the lower voices. With the return of G Major, one is given the chance to review previously heard material with one small exception: bars 12–28 have been deleted.

Similar instances of voice exchange can be found in the works of Nicolas-Joseph Chartrain (ca. 1740–93). His thirty-six quartets, issued in six sets during the first half of the 1780s, reveal the pitfalls of blanketly labeling a musician as a composer of *quatuors concertants* simply due to the wording on a title page. Although *Six Quatuors Dialoguées. . .* Op. 4.[16] with its inclusion of the term "dialoguées", and Op. 8, entitled *Six Quatuors Concertant*, suggest that one might expect a stereotypical *quatuor concertant*, a more thorough investigation reveals otherwise. We shall have occasion to return to these works in the next chapter. At this point it is sufficient to note that although we turn our attention to the final movement of Op. 4, No. 5, it is the only movement of this particular quartet which is a polite conversation.

Preceded by a sonata form debate and lecture in ABA form, this Presto in F Major features a democratic distribution of both melodic and accompanimental lines; this sharing occurs primarily in the violins with one exception. Following a six-measure unison opening, the two upper voices proceed in parallel motion. Small interjections by the two lower voices provide textural interest to the otherwise first-violin dominated section. The second violin emerges from its supportive role in measure 47 and holds our attention for the next eighteen bars with not only a quicker surface rhythm, but use of the upper register, arpeggios, and triplet figuration. In contrast, the first violin part, varied up to this point, is reduced to a limited amount of parallel motion, sustained pitches, and nonobtrusive figures. Measure 65 once again finds the first violin as the carrier of

---

[16]   Paris: Berault, 1778 (?). Printed parts are available at the Library of Congress, Washington D. C., M452A2C44.

thematic material, while the second violin recedes into the background with lower pitches and repeated rhythmic patterns.

The contrasting B section begins as the opening did – with a unison passage incorporating all four voices. An eight-measure first violin solo followed by a slightly longer second violin one again reinforces the concept of politely waiting for one instrument to finish before the other begins. The entrance of an active viola in measure103 pushes both violins into the background. The supensions which make up this supportive material form the same foundation for the cello triplets, which echo those just recently heard in the viola line. What makes this repetition so interesting is that the violins have now switched lines. The silent viola merely duplicates the lack of activity previously found in the cello part (Ex. 5.6). The cadence returns us to the opening A section although Chartrain bypasses

Example 5.6 Nicolas-Joseph Chartrain, Op. 4, No. 5, Mvt. III, mm 103–122

the initial unison material. Rather than a verbatim repetition, he chooses to invert the violin parts; thus the first violin line now appears in the second violin and vice versa. This wholesale switching of parts does not extend to the lower voices. Here, as in the opening A section, both the viola and cello provide the barest of support with repeated eighth notes, sustained pitches, and punctuating quarter notes. Neither part is thematically integrated; instead the two offer a backdrop upon which a melody can be played and listened to without interruption.

Polite conversations feature a strong contrast between melody and accompaniment. This is discernable not only from an aural perspective, but from a visual one as well. One need only peruse the variation movement of Cambini's Quartet in Bb (T57) to find a concrete example. (The entire movement is reproduced in Ex. 5.7.) Many of Cambini's quartets offer this same means of identification. The substantial solos for the violins and viola as found in the opening movement of his G major quartet (T28), allow the composer to highlight the distinction between rhythmically and melodically varied soloist (talker) and the repetitive and regular supporter (listener). Solos are long and unencumbered; any interplay between the voices would destroy the listener's ability to attend to the speaker (Ex. 5.8). Thus the importance lies not with which instrument is placed in the solo position, but rather with the fact that only one occupies center stage at a time.

Not all polite conversations contain each of the ingredients discussed above: long, intact solos which may appear in any voice, rotation of prominence, part exchange, and strong differentiation between melody and accompaniment. A composer may choose to feature one or more depending on the desired quality of sound and texture. Some works, however, have several of these ingredients within a single movement; an examination of a movement from Franz Anton Hoffmeister's (1754–1812) Op. 9, No. 1 and from Ferdinand Fränzl's (1767–1833) Op. 1, No. 4 reveals how this recipe can be used to create an ideal polite conversation.

Hoffmeister's Op. 9 is but one of fourteen sets issued by the composer during his lifetime. Totalling fifty-seven quartets, not all are for the traditional two violin, viola, and cello arrangement.[17] Op. 9[18] consists of six two- or three-movement works, all of which are polite conversations and reflective of the *liebhaber* taste.[19] The opening movement of the C Major quartet, an Allegro in sonata form, is a

---

[17] Dianne James, in the introduction to her edition of Hoffmeister's Op. 14 quartets (Wellington, New Zealand: Artaria Editions, c1998), suggests that this number may be erroneous. She notes that the composer wrote thirty-four quartets between 1781 and 1806.

[18] *Six Quatuors Concertantes pour 2 Violons, Alto viole et Basse*...Oeuvre IX (Vienna: Christoph Torricella, [1783]).   Printed parts are available at Benediktiner-Stift, Kremsmünster, Fasc. 70, nr. 316–321.

[19] Fiona Little, *The String Quartet at the Oettingen-Wallerstein Court: Ignaz von Beecke and his Contemporaries* (New York: Garland Publishing, Inc., 1989), pp. 122–5.

Example 5.7 Giuseppe Maria Cambini, T57, Mvt. II

Example 5.7 continued

Example 5.7 continued

Example 5.7 continued

Example 5.7 continued

Example 5.7 concluded

D.C. al Fin

Example 5.8 Giuseppe Maria Cambini, T28, Mvt. I, mm 1–75

Example 5.8 continued

Example 5.8 continued

Example 5.8 continued

Example 5.8 concluded

fine illustration of how the various aspects of a polite conversation can be successfully combined. Example 5.9 reproduces the exposition.

The movement opens in a traditional lecture fashion: emphasis on the first violin with support provided by a harmonically and texturally enriching pair of middle voices and a foundational bass line. Only when the second violin enters in measure 22 with the melody do we become aware that perhaps this is not just a simple lecture. The repetition of this line by the first violin in measure 30 suggests a democratic treatment of thematic material. The appearance of the viola in a position of melodic importance in measure 42 followed by the cello in a similar fashion eight bars later confirms this democracy; the fact that each phrase is allowed to be heard without competition and in its entirety points to a polite conversation. Measure 60 returns leadership to the first violin; note the second violin line. Bar 71 brings an exchange of parts between the two violins. Only after this rotation is the first violin allowed to come forward to finish the exposition in the role of melodic leader. With the exceptions noted above, both the viola and cello have maintained their purely subsidiary roles. Their parts, neither technically demanding nor distinctive, have formed the foundation upon which the thematic material may stand. Thus, throughout the exposition, Hoffmeister combines the various ingredients – long, intact solos, unobtrusive accompaniments, democratic dispensation of melodic material, and part exchange – to create a successful polite conversation.

The development features a continuous rotation of distinction between the two violins. While some repetition of material is heard at the start of this section, the listener is more aware of a succession of solos than anything else. Motivic development is not a factor nor does the composer make any attempt to integrate the lower two instruments into the melodic fabric. Rather Hoffmeister maintains the homophonic texture throughout, concentrating on the presentation of ideas by

Example 5.9 Franz Anton Hoffmeister, Op. 9, No. 1, Mvt. I, mm 1–94

Example 5.9 continued

Example 5.9 continued

Example 5.9 continued

Example 5.9 continued

Example 5.9 concluded

the upper two voices, one after the other with no interruption. Following a grand pause, the recapitulation begins. After a nearly verbatim repetition of the opening, Hoffmeister introduces a lengthy cello solo, different from before. The remainder of the movement follows the exposition rather closely with changes in voicing for the solos. As with the exposition, the conscious separation of melody and accompaniment, inclusion of undisturbed lines, and democratic distribution of leadership work together to maintain a polite mode of communication between the four voices.

Many of these same characteristics are present in the opening movement of Ferdinand Fränzl's Op. 1, No. 4.[20] During his lifetime, Fränzl composed nine quartets – the six which make up Op. 1, from the early 1790s, and three of Op. 6 (c1800). The latter, owing to the later date, fall outside the scope of this study. All the quartets of Op. 1 are three-movement works; each begins with a sonata form and with one exception, concludes with a rondo. While many of the movements are polite conversations, Fränzl also makes use of the lecture (both the second and fifth quartets contain nothing but lectures). Franzl's approach to the former is different than that of Hoffmeister, but no less effective. For example, the Allegro from the F Major quartet (No. 4) contains lengthy solos, a strong distinction between melody and accompaniment, little interplay between the voices, and a rotation of prominence between the voices. This is particularly noticeable in the exposition and recapitulation. The former spotlights solos by the two violins and cello; the latter highlights the upper strings.

The development features primarily the first violin, but a viola solo towards the end reminds us that Fränzl is not interested in domination by a sole part, but instead chooses to allow another voice to share the spotlight. The increased surface rhythm, and unisons and parallel octaves which follow suggest a more integrated ensemble, but this is short-lived (Ex. 5.10). That this activity should occur toward the end of the development only heightens the feeling of arrival and stability a few measures later as we once again hear the familiar material and texture in the recapitulation.

Lastly, mention should be made of those movements that might best be described as "not so polite". Such settings bear the typical characteristics of the polite conversation, but also reveal a greater integration of parts. The presence, for example, of a more active accompanimental line forces the listener to attend not only to the solo but to the other voices as well, for the latter now have interesting ideas. The first movement of Václav Pichl's (1741–1805) Op. 13, No. 3 provides an excellent illustration of this.

---

[20]   *Six quatuors pour deux violons, alto & basse. . .* Op. 1 (Paris: Offenbach, 1791; 2nd ed., Paris: Andre, 1799). Printed parts are available at University of Pennsylvania Rare Book Room, RBC Folio M452.F7op. 1.

Example 5.10 Ferdinand Fränzl, Op. 1, No. 4, Mvt. I, mm 150–174

Example 5.10 concluded

The three quartets which comprise Pichl's Op. 13 appeared in 1788,[21] some nine years after his first efforts in the genre (Op. 2). Dedicated to Dittersdorf with whom he had served at Nagyvárad, these three-movement works offer a good cross-section of discourse types. Of the nine movements, nearly half are polite conversations; the remaining ones are lectures and debates. The third quartet's opening Allegro non troppo is of particular interest because although it contains the expected featues of a polite conversation – lengthy, uninterrupted solos, democratic distribution of melodic prominence, and part exchange – it also reveals an active accompanimental line that not only supports the solo, but is interesting in itself.

The homorhythmic opening allows Pichl to firmly establish the key of E-flat major while immediately focusing our attention on the first violin. Over a backdrop of parallel motion and quick surface rhythm, the upper voice presents the opening melodic material. Measure 11 brings a near identical repetition of the majestic beginning followed by increased technical display by the first violin in the form of arpeggios, sixteenth notes, and large leaps. Textural variety is provided by the middle instruments: the second violin vacillates between paralleling some of the less "active" measures and simple repeated eighth notes while the viola, obviously supportive, varies the surface rhythm and contour of its line. A twelve-measure cello solo, beginning in bar 27, marks an abrupt change for that instrument. In contrast to the earlier heard simple repeated eighth notes, this line now is characterized by rhythmic and melodic variety, triplets, string crossings, and double stops. Measure 40 brings another change: even though the melodic leadership has shifted back to the first violin, the lower three parts refuse to recede

---

21   The title page of the 1788 print appears as follows: Wenceslao Pichl, *Tre Quartetti a due Violini, Viola, & Violoncello*...Opera XIII (Berlin: Hummel, [1788]). Printed parts are available at the Library of Congress, Washington D. C., M452P58Op. 13 (case).

into the background. Instead, the four voices offer a more tightly knit fabric than what has preceded. When the viola and cello parts are reduced to sustained pitches, punctuating quarters, and repeated eighth notes, the two violins engage in eight measures of part exchange; every other measure finds the instruments switching parts. Thus while we hear the same material, the act of moving the line from one voice to another provides novelty and a fresh sound (Ex. 5.11). A momentary interjection by the lower instruments informs us that the part exchange is over. The resumption of leadership by the first violin is reinforced by the less prominent parallel motion below. Again, while the texture has been enriched and interest can be found in the lower parts, it is the top voice which earns the label of melodically dominant.

Example 5.11 Václav Pichl, Op. 13, No. 1, Mvt. I, mm 50–57

The short eighteen-bar development which begins in measure 76, features solos by both the first violin and cello. Each is distinct, long, and clearly separated from the other lines. As to be expected, the cello politely waits to begin its solo, entering only when the first violin has cadenced. Technical displays by the soloists stand in stark contrast to the rather mundane nature of the accompaniment. The recapitulation presents our familiar material with few alterations. A viola solo prior to the closing is new and replaces the part exchange of the violins from the exposition.

What is noteworthy about this movement is that although Pichl adheres to the principle of polite conversation by incorporating those characteristics we have come to expect, he adds a twist. The increased activity in the supporting lines, the almost snippet-like rotation of material in the violins, and the homorhythmic passages all suggest a greater integration of parts. A similar "lack of politeness" can be found in works by Nicolas-Marie Dalayrac (1753–1809) and Franz Krommer (1759–1831).

All thirty-six of Dalayrac's string quartets were written and issued in sets of six (Opp. 4, 5, 7, 8, 10, and 11) prior to 1780. In general, his works feature a a great deal of part rotation. The two violin parts are quite similar in character and technical requirements. The cello is almost uniformly excluded from taking part in the melodic democracy; the viola, however, is included routinely. While the title page of many of the works, with the inclusion of the term *quatuor concertant*, suggests that these are simply polite conversations, a more detailed examination reveals otherwise. Dalayrac's Op. 8[22] is a fine illustration. The violin parts appear interchangeable; the composer neither assigns specific roles nor does he require a greater facility on the instrument from one performer or the other. Thus the second violin's solo material is likely to be as difficult as that of the first. Moreover, the fluidity of the second violin – as a soloist, paired with the first violin in parallel motion, or working in tandem with the viola – makes it difficult to assign to this instrument a particular function. Interplay between the instruments often occurs in both the exposition and development. Dalayrac may either pair the middle voices against the first violin, or set the upper instruments against the lower ones. These characteristics are found in the opening movement of the fifth quartet.

This Allegro ma non tanto is a fine example of a polite conversation with "a little something extra". The opening first violin melody, with its periodic rests, is punctuated by second violin echoes. The simple quarter note, quarter-note rest accompaniment of the viola and cello ensure that we are not distracted from the treble voices. Measure 9 begins with a repetition of this material but this time the violins have switched places; the viola and cello merely reiterate their previous

---

[22]   *Six Quartetto Concertants*, Op. 8 (Paris: Durieu, [b. 1780]). Printed parts are available at the Library of Congress, Washington D. C., M452 D212 Op. (Case).

lines. Although the second violin, now in the leadership position, begins familiarly, it concludes the phrase with a different and more taxing line. Following the unison cadence, Dalayrac returns the top voice to the forefront; the second violin and viola are paired and provide snippet-like interjections for a couple of measures before joining the cello as pure accompaniment. Continued rotation of prominence, as well as short sections of give-and-take between the first violin and middle voices, contrast with the longer solos supported by simple accompaniment. Just when we think that Dalayrac has forsaken the polite conversation, measure 57 places us on familiar ground. Four measures of passagework by the first violin is supported by the barest of accompaniment. The two violins then switch positions, repeat the material, and continue in parallel octaves to close the exposition (Ex. 5.12).

Example 5.12 Nicolas-Marie Dalayrac, Op. 8, No. 5, Mvt. I, mm 1–66

Example 5.12 continued

Example 5.12 continued

Example 5.12 concluded

The development recalls the beginning of the movement but soon gives way to a lengthy viola solo. The modest accompaniment of both violins and the cello guarantee that full attention will be paid to the triplet arpeggios, sixteenth-note scales, and other passagework of the tenor voice (Ex. 5.13). The recapitulation bypasses Group I material and concentrates on Group II, with a near identical sequence of events.

Example 5.13 Nicolas-Marie Dalayrac, Op. 8, No. 5, Mvt. I, mm 84–97

This overview reveals two aspects to the movement. The part exchange, rotation of prominence, melody-accompaniment dichotomy, and lengthy viola solo are in keeping with a polite conversation. At the same time, however, the degree of integration and activity of at least the top three voices suggest a "less courteous" approach. Since the modes of discourse devised for this study are artificial and necessarily rigid, it is inevitable that not all works will be easily categorized. What is interesting then is to see how hybrids are constructed, which ones work well together, and which particular form of communication is chosen as the dominant one.

A similar mixing can be found in several of Franz Krommer's works. His quartets, which were written during the two decades surrounding 1800, were issued in more than twenty sets. During his lifetime, Krommer was regarded, along with Haydn, as one of the leading quartet composers and was considered a serious rival of Beethoven.[23]

Krommer's first five publications (Opp. 1, 3, 4, 5, and 7) are of interest as their dates of issuance fall within the time frame of this study. Although the majority of the movements are polite conversations, one also finds debates, hybrids, conversations, and lectures. The opening movement of Op. 4, No. 1 (1794) for example is what one might call a "classic" polite conversation. Labeled solos in the individual parts, distinct separation of melody and accompaniment, and part exchange readily provide us with a way to identify the mode of discourse.

Categorizing the corresponding movement of the second quartet, however, is not so easy. In this sonata form Vivace, Krommer moves back and forth between the polite conversation and the conversation. Long, uninterrupted solos by each instrument are accompanied by simple sustained pitches, repeated quarters, and broken intervals in eighths. Part exchange further enhances the democratic distribution of material. (Compare Examples 5.14a and 5.14b.) This rotation occurs not just with the two violins but between the first violin and cello, and elsewhere, between the viola and cello. Extending the principle of part exchange to all four instruments lends a greater sense of equality among the voices; it is not just that each has a chance to come forward, but that the same material can be found in these voices. Further connection to the conversation derives from the interplay among the voices. A small section of give-and-take between the two lower instruments in measures 11–16 pulls the listener's attention away from the first violin. Measures 56–67 allow us to eavesdrop on an animated conversation between the lowest and two upper voices while the viola provides the barest of support. Thus, by the time we reach the end of the exposition, Krommer has engaged the members of the ensemble in two types of conversation: one polite, and one less so.

---

[23]   *The New Grove*, s. v. "Krommer, Franz", by Othmar Wessely, p. 278.

Example 5.14a Franz Krommer, Op. 4, No. 2, Mvt. I, mm 68–82

Although the development focuses on the first violin, the lower voices are not idle. Melodic activity based on the opening five pitches of the movement provides an undercurrent upon which the top voice rests. As the first violin becomes increasingly technical, our attention is drawn solely to that part. The recapitulation follows the course laid out in the exposition with few changes. A small amount of revoicing of the solos ensures that we hear something different from what was previously presented.

Example 5.14b Franz Krommer, Op. 4, No. 2, Mvt. I, mm 118–132

The polite conversation remained an attractive means of organizing the four voices of the string quartet up through the end of the eighteenth century. Its most readily identifiable feature – the presentation of long, uninterrupted melodies – allowed for participation by all, but at the same time, ensured that each instrument would receive a listener's full attention. This democratic treatment offered countless options, especially with regard to timbre. As each instrument could be given either a leading or supportive role, composers had the unique opportunity to explore sonority and texture in ways unavailable to composers of other genres. Thus the democratic nature of the discourse plus the sonic possibilities offered a viable and attractive approach to the medium that appealed to performer, listener, and composer alike.

The sheer number of these conversations suggests that rather than dismissing them as a mere episode in the history of the string quartet, they need to be acknowledged and incorporated into any discussion of the genre. The emphasis on fluidity of function as well as the timbral possibilities of the ensemble has remained basic to the string quartet up to the present day.

Chapter 6

The debate

The debate, so often found in the works of the Viennese masters, is commonly regarded as the epitome of the classical era string quartet; ironically, only a very small number of such eighteenth-century works consist solely of this type of movement. Moreover, when compared with either the lecture or the polite conversation, considerably fewer compositions contain even one debate.[1] In spite of this numerical discrepancy, scholars have focused on this corpus as representing the essence of the genre. This may be explained by the presence of such works as Joseph Haydn's Opp. 20, 33, 50, and 64, and Mozart's "Haydn" quartets, but it also points out our lack of familiarity with the vast quartet output of the time period. Table 3 provides a partial listing of the many debates written during the second half of the eighteenth century. Although Mozart's and Haydn's works are well represented, it is also interesting to view the names of the many other composers whose works are often overlooked. While it is not the intent here to perpetuate the myth that the Viennese approach (the "debate") is the archtype of the genre, it is helpful to examine and understand what makes a work such as Haydn's Op. 33 such a fine illustration of the debate.

In late 1781, Haydn wrote to various music lovers and patrons offering them handwritten copies of his newest quartets at six ducats a work. In his letter, Haydn stated that the works were "written in a new and special way (for I haven't composed any for ten years)". Soon after, the publishing firm Artaria announced in the Vienna *Zeitung* that these works would be available in four weeks. Haydn was irate and in a letter to the publisher dated 5 January 1782, complained of the potential loss of income as subscribers would naturally opt to obtain the entire set through Artaria at a lower cost. To appease the composer, Artaria delayed publication until 17 April.[2] The first performance of these quartets took place on Christmas Day 1781, at the home of Countess von Nordon. Attending the concert were the Russian Grand Duke Paul (later Tsar Paul II), his consort Maria Feodorovna (Haydn's piano pupil), Duke Friedrich Eugen von Württemberg and his consort, Prince Ferdinand, and Princess Elisabeth of Württemberg. All four

---

[1]   As with previous chapters, these comments are based on the sampling of 650 quartets from the second half of the eighteenth century. While a mere 1% consist of all debate movements, nearly 30% of the works contain at least one debate movement. Such a disparity suggests that composers thought of this means of organizing the voices as just one option and not the ultimate goal.

[2]   For a basic recounting of these events see Landon, *Haydn: Chronicle and Works*, vol. 2, pp. 453–6, 461–2; and Finscher, *Studien zur Geschichte des Streichquartetts*, pp. 238–40.

Table 3: A Selected List of Debates [3]

Year	Composer	Title (Movement[s])
1755–59	J. Haydn	Op. 1, No. 3 (5)
	J. Haydn	Op. 2, No. 6 (5)
1757	F. X. Richter	Op. 5, No. 6 (3)
ca.1760s	F. Gassmann	H.461 (2)
	F. Gassmann	H.480 (2)
1760s	C. d'Ordonez	Op.1, No. 1 (2, 3)
1761	L. Boccherini	G.163 (2)
	L. Boccherini	G.164 (2)
1769–70	J. Haydn	Op. 9, No. 1 (1)
	J. Haydn	Op. 9, No. 4 (4)
	J. Haydn	Op. 9, No. 5 (3)
ca.1770	A. Kammel	Op. 4, No. 3 (1)
	A. Kammel	Op. 4, No. 4 (1, 2, 3)
1771	J. Haydn	Op. 17, No. 2 (1)
	J. Haydn	Op. 17, No. 4 (3)
	J. Haydn	Op. 17, No. 6 (4)
1772	J. Haydn	Op. 20, No. 1 (1, 3, 4)
	J. Haydn	Op. 20, No. 2 (2)
	J. Haydn	Op. 20, No. 3 (1, 2, 4)
	J. Haydn	Op. 20, No. 4 (3, 4)
1772/73	W. A. Mozart	K.156 (2)
	W. A. Mozart	K.158 (1)
	W. A. Mozart	K.159 (2, 3)
	W. A. Mozart	K.160 (1)
1773	W. A. Mozart	K.168 (1)
	W. A. Mozart	K.169 (1)
	W. A. Mozart	K.171 (1)
	W. A. Mozart	K.172 (4)
	W. A. Mozart	K.173 (1, 2)
	J. Schmitt	Op. 5, No. 1 (4)
	J. Schmitt	Op. 5, No. 2 (1, 2, 4)
	J. Schmitt	Op. 5, No. 5 (2)
	P. Vachon	Op. 7, No. 2 (1, 2)
	P. Vachon	Op. 7, No. 3 (1)

---

[3]   See the bibliography for a full citation of each of the listed compositions.

Table 3 continued

Year	Composer	Title (Movement[s])
	P. Vachon	Op. 7, No. 4 (1, 2)
	P. Vachon	Op. 7, No. 5 (1, 3)
	P. Vachon	Op. 7, No. 6 (1)
	J. B. Vanhal	A1 (4)
1774	I. von Beecke	M6 (1)
	G. Brunetti	Op. 2, No. 2 (4)
ca.1775	P. Vachon	Op. 5, No. 2 (3)
	P. Vachon	Op. 5, No. 3 (1, 2)
	P. Vachon	Op. 5, No. 5 (2)
	P. Vachon	Op. 5, No. 6 (1, 2)
	T. Giordani	Op. 8, No. 2 (2)
	T. Giordani	Op. 8, No. 6 (1)
ca.1777	M. Haydn	MH. 308 (1)
ca.1778	N.-J. Chartrain	Op. 4, No. 5 (1)
ca.1780	I. von Beecke	M9 (1)
	J. B. Vanhal	c1 (4)
ca.1781	M. Haydn	MH. 313 (1)
1781	J. Haydn	Op. 33, No. 1 (3, 4)
	J. Haydn	Op. 33, No. 2 (1)
	J. Haydn	Op. 33, No. 3 (1, 4)
	J. Haydn	Op. 33, No. 4 (1)
	J. Haydn	Op. 33, No. 6 (1, 2)
1781–3	J. G. Albrechtsberger	Op. 7, No. 1 (2)
1782	J. A. Fodor	Book 4, No. 5 (3)
	W. A. Mozart	K.387 (1, 2)
1782–6	P. Vachon	Op. 11, No. 2 (1)
	P. Vachon	Op. 11, No. 5 (1, 2, 3)
	P. Vachon	Op. 11, No. 6 (1, 3)
ca.1783	M Haydn	MH.312 (1, 3)
1783	W. A. Mozart	K.421 (1, 2, 4)
	W. A. Mozart	K.428 (4)
1784	W. A. Mozart	K.458 (1, 3, 4)
1785	W. A. Mozart	K.464 (1, 3)
	W. A. Mozart	K.485 (1, 2, 3, 4)
	I. J. Pleyel	Ben 316 (1, 2)
1785–7	J. B. Vanhal	Eb11 (1)
1786	J. B. Vanhal	g2 (1, 3)
	W. A. Mozart	K.499 (1, 3, 4)

Table 3 continued

Year	Composer	Title (Movement[s])
	J. Haydn	Op. 42 (1)
	I. J. Pleyel	Ben 320 (3)
	I. J. Pleyel	Ben 323 (2, 3)
	I. J. Pleyel	Ben 324 (3)
1787	J. Haydn	Op. 50, No. 1 (2)
	J. Haydn	Op. 50, No. 2 (1, 3)
	J. Haydn	Op. 50. No. 3 (1,)
	J. Haydn	Op. 50, No. 4 (1, 2)
	J. Haydn	Op. 50, No. 5 (1, 4)
	J. Haydn	Op. 50, No. 6 (1, 2)
1788	J. Haydn	Op. 54, No. 3 (4)
	J. Haydn	Op. 55, No. 1 (1, 2, 4)
	J. Haydn	Op. 55, No. 2 (2, 4)
	J. Haydn	Op. 55, No. 3 (1, 2, 4)
1788	C. D. von Dittersdorf	*Sei Quartetti*, No. 1 (3)
	C. D. von Dittersdorf	*Sei Quartetti*, No. 2 (1)
	C. D. von Dittersdorf	*Sei Quartetti*, No. 4 (1)
	V. Pichl	Op. 13, No. 1 (1)
	V. Pichl	Op. 13, No. 2 (1)
	I. J. Pleyel	Ben 343 (1)
	I. J. Pleyel	Ben 344 (1, 2, 4)
	I. J. Pleyel	Ben. 346 (1)
1789	A. Teyber	Op. 2, No. 1 (1)
	A. Teyber	Op. 2, No. 2 (1)
	A. Teyber	Op. 2, No. 3 (1, 4)
b.1790	P. Wranitzky	Quartet in A (3)
ca.1790	I. von Beecke	M3 (1, 3)
	I. von Beecke	M5 (1, 2)
1790	W. A. Mozart	K.589 (3, 4)
	W. A. Mozart	K.590 (3)
	J. Haydn	Op. 64, No. 1 (1, 3, 4)
	J. Haydn	Op. 64, No. 2 (4)
	J. Haydn	Op. 64, No. 3 (1, 4)
	J. Haydn	Op. 64, No. 4 (4)
	J. Haydn	Op. 64, No. 5 (1)
	J. Haydn	Op. 64, No. 6 (1, 2)
	F. de Giardini	Op. 29, No. 4 (2)
	P. Wranitzky	Op. 10, No. 6 (1)

Table 3 concluded

Year	Composer	Title (Movement[s])
1790–1	L. Kozeluch	Op. 32. No. 1 (1, 2, 3)
	L. Kozeluch	Op. 32, No. 3 (3)
	L. Kozeluch	Op. 33, No. 1 (1)
	L. Kozeluch	Op. 33, No. 3 (1)
1791	F. Hoffmeister	Op. 14, No. 1 (1, 3)
	F. Hoffmeister	Op. 14, No. 3 (2)
1793	F. Neubauer	Op. 7, No. 2 (2)
	F. Neubauer	Op. 7, No. 3 (1)
	P. Wranitzky	Op. 23, No. 4 (3)
	P. Wranitzky	Op. 23, No. 5 (1)
	J. Haydn	Op. 71, No. 1 (1, 2, 4)
	J. Haydn	Op. 71, No. 2 (1, 2,)
	J. Haydn	Op. 71, No. 3 (1, 2, 3)
	J. Haydn	Op. 74, No. 1 (1, 2,)
	J. Haydn	Op. 74, No. 2 (1, 4)
	J. Haydn	Op. 74, No. 3 (4)
1794	J. L. Eybler	Op. 1, No. 1 (2)
	J. L. Eybler	Op. 1, No. 2 (4)
	F. Krommer	Op. 4, No. 2 (2)
	F. Krommer	Op. 4, No. 3 (2)
1795	L. Boccherini	G.234 (1)
	L. Boccherini	G.235 (1)
	J. G. Distler	Opp. 1–2, No. 4 (1)
	J. G. Distler	Opp. 1–2, No. 5 (3)
	H. Jadin	Op. 1, No.1 (1)
	H. Jadin	Op. 1, No.3 (1, 3)
1796	L. Boccherini	G.237 (1, 2)
	F. Krommer	Op. 5, No. 3 (4)
1797	J. Haydn	Op. 76, No. 1 (1)
	J. Haydn	Op. 76, No. 2 (1)
	J. Haydn	Op. 76, No. 4 (2, 3, 4)
	J. Haydn	Op. 76, No. 5 (2, 4)
	F. Krommer	Op. 7, No. 1 (1, 2)
	F. Krommer	Op. 7, No. 2 (1, 3, 4)
	F. Krommer	Op. 7, No. 3 (3)

members of the ensemble were professional musicians: Luigi Tomasini, Franz Aspelmayr, Joseph Weigl, and Thaddäus Huber.

Many scholars have attached an immense significance to Haydn's words, "a new and special way".[4] Adolf Sandberger understood this phase to indicate that Haydn had worked out the creative crisis of Op. 20. With Op. 33, Haydn's new way was evident with the motivic work and the interplay of the instruments. Following this line, Friedrich Blume stated that Haydn needed the long pause in order to "repair" the damage of Op. 20.[5] A contrasting view was presented by Jens Peter Larsen who noted that the "motivische Arbeit" was actually present in the symphonies of the 1770s. Haydn's words, "new and special way", were not so much an indication of a turning point in his style but a selling slogan.[6] This more commercial interpretation was adopted by Mark Bonds and Georg Feder, among others. The former noted that Beethoven had done the same thing to increase sales of his Opp. 34 and 35.[7] A semi-compromise, proposed by Finscher, attempted to incorporate the sales pitch idea into the notion that after a ten-year pause in quartet writing, Haydn's artistic personality had matured. In essence, the creative crisis posed by Op. 20 was resolved with the classical style of Op. 33.[8]

Finscher's entrance into the debate subtly shifted the focus from the "new and special way" to the notion of the long pause and the model of crisis resolution. Hubert Unverricht, Charles Rosen, Daniel Heartz, and Reginald Barrett-Ayres noted the "newness" of Op. 33 and explained it as a goal which was finally attained after a protracted struggle.[9] Not all scholars agreed with this view

---

[4] See Landon, *Haydn: Chronicle and Works*, vol. 2, pp. 578–9, for a complete summary and set of citations for the basic debate. The present summary draws heavily on Landon.

[5] Blume, "Josef Haydns künstlerishce Persönlichkeit", p. 40.

[6] A similar view was expressed by Leonard Ratner who saw the impetus for lively partwriting and extended phrases as derived from the symphonies of the 1700s. See Leonard G. Ratner, "Eighteenth-Century Theories of Musical Period Structure", *The Musical Quarterly* 42 (1956): 452.

[7] Mark Evan Bonds, "Haydn's 'cours complet de la composition' and the *Sturm und Drang*", in *Haydn Studies* (ed. by W. Dean Sutcliffe; United Kingdom: Cambridge University Press, 1998), pp. 159–60.

[8] Finscher, *Studien zur Geschichte des Streichquartetts*, pp. 240–4. For Finscher, this resolution meant the establishment of a new popular tone, use of rondos for finale movements, a return to simplicity and folk tone, inclusion of a stylized dance minuet, use of slow movements with lyrical melodies, and regularity of themes and period construction.

[9] Hubert Unverricht, "Das Divertimento für Streicher", in *Zur Entwicklung der Kammermusik in der zweiten Hälfte des 18. Jahrhunderts* (Blankenburg: Michaelstein, 1986), p. 70 highlighted the role of Op. 33 as a means of solving the problems of earlier sets. Charles Rosen, *The Classical Style: Haydn, Mozart, Beethoven* (New York: W. W. Norton and Co., Inc., 1972), pp. 116–7, focused on the "revolution" in Haydn's style. Daniel Heartz, *Haydn, Mozart, and the Viennese School: 1740–1780* (New York: W. W. Norton and Co., Inc. 1995), p. 324, promoted the idea that only with Op. 33 was Haydn able to put the string quartet on a par with the symphony. Reginald Barrett-Ayres, *Joseph Haydn and the String Quartet*

however. Among the most notable critics was James Webster, who, in a series of publications, argued against the notion of a single long pause, the "new way" of composition, and the primacy of Op. 33.[10] Noting two pauses rather than a single one (1757/59–1770/72 and 1772–1781), Webster found that Haydn's quartet writing did not achieve regularity until Op. 50 of 1787. Furthermore, each set, prior to and including Op. 33, seemed to solve different compositional problems.[11] For Webster, the most significant aspect about Op. 33 was that for the first time, Haydn chose to publish on his own initiative; these were the first works intended for public consumption rather than for a specific patron. Thus the importance of Op. 33 lay not with its establishment of a mature "classical" style, but with the realization that a composer could sell his works to the public at large.

The six quartets of Op. 33 are an interesting mix of discourse types. While the second quartet, to which we shall shortly return, provides us with all but a conversation, the first quartet contains conversations and debates; the fifth quartet contains nothing but lectures. Once one realizes that Op. 33 does not present a uniform approach to the four voices, it loses its position as the prototype of the classical quartet and becomes instead, a fine set of works, some movements of which are excellent examples of the debate.

The opening movement of the second quartet, an Eb major Allegro moderato cantabile in sonata form, is a particularly good illustration of a debate. Despite the first violin's consistently dominant position, one hears small amounts of interplay in both the stable exposition and recapitulation, and more give-and-take in the development. The uppermost part, while clearly more difficult and technically demanding, does not completely overshadow the other instruments. Each of the lower three voices has a distinct identity; the tossing back and forth of short snippets allows these participants a presence in the texture without detracting from the prominence of the top instrument.

The placement of melodic material in the first violin at the movement's opening ensures that our attention is immediately focused on that instrument. The simple accompaniment in the lower voices further guarantees the primacy of the upper voice. Measures 12–14 however suggest that not all is melody plus

---

(London: Barrie and Jenkins, 1974), pp. 156–6, 166, 170, notes Haydn's new and lighter touch. Only with Op. 33 could the composer create music for listener and player both.

[10] The following writings by Webster provide a good cross section and summary of his arguments: "The Bass Part" (PhD diss.); "The Chronology of Haydn's String Quartets", *The Musical Quarterly* 61 (1975): 17–46; Review of *Studien zur Geschichte des Streichquartets* by Ludwig Finscher, *Journal of the American Musicological Society* 28 (1975): 543–49; and "Towards a History of Viennese Chamber Music in the Early Classical Period", *Journal of the American Musicological Society* 27 (1974): 212–47.

[11] This idea has been embraced by Orin Moe in his "Texture in the String Quartets of Haydn", pp. vii, 275.

accompaniment: a decorated broken triad, derived from measure two, appears successively in all four parts (Ex. 6.1). This small interruption is enough to make

Example 6.1 Joseph Haydn, Op. 33, No. 2, Mvt. I, mm 1–14

the listener take notice and reconsider the relationship of the voices, for although Haydn returns to a homophonic texture, the increased activity in all parts is suggestive of greater interaction (mm 19–20, 29–32).

It is in the development that we truly realize how far the composer has moved beyond what might otherwise be a standard lecture approach. Small ideas are shared among all four voices; a fragment may as easily appear in the cello as the first violin (mm 33–4). Question and answer sections involve not just the two violins, but the lower voices as well (compare mm 42–43 with mm 45–48 in Ex. 6.2). And lastly, one passage relegates the first violin to sustained pitches while the lower three voices converse (mm 51–53). To balance the temporary near equality of voices, Haydn returns the first violin to unrivaled prominence with a burst of figuration which also signals the recapitulation in measure 63. As with the exposition, the upper voice is securely ensconced in the leadership position; the lower voices support and periodically come forward to remind us of their presence.

Example 6.2 Joseph Haydn, Op. 33, No. 2, Mvt. I, mm 42–48

Thus while this debate preserves the dominance of the first violin, the traditional roles are suspended in selected areas. At these moments, all four voices become active participants. What is interesting is that this interaction comes in the form of small snippets passed back and forth rather than a democratic distribution of melodic material or a rotation of prominence. It is this lively exchange that allows us to distinguish the debate from other forms of discourse.

Examples of quintessential debates can be found not just in Haydn's output, but in that of his Viennese contemporaries as well. Hoffmeister's Op. 14, No. 3 of 1791, contains just such an illustration. Dianne James describes the three quartets of Op. 14 as "modest in scope and emotional depth, [but ones which] reveal Hoffmeister as a craftsman of refined musical sensibilities".[12] Although James points to the length of the first movements as indicative of the Viennese quartet, not all display the interaction one expects of a debate. For example, the first movement of Op. 14, No. 3 is really a polite conversation between first violin and cello. It is the second movement of this quartet which meets our criteria for a debate.

This multi-sectioned Adagio cantabile in A Major bears many of the characteristics found in the opening movement of Haydn's Op. 33, No. 2. The initial eight measures clearly introduce the first violin as the bearer of thematic material. The melodic and rhythmic variety of that instrument stand in strong contrast to the regularity and repetitiveness of the lower voices (Ex. 6.3).

Example 6.3 Franz Hoffmeister, Op. 14, No. 3, Mvt. II, mm 1–8

---

[12]   Franz Anton Hoffmeister, *String Quartet in d, Op. 14, No. 3* (ed. by Dianne James; Wellington, [New Zealand]: Artaria Editions, c1998), p. iii.

Increased activity in the viola and then the cello during the next eleven measures however, reveals a different approach to the voices and suggests that the composer does not intend to use a lecture approach in this slow movement.

Bar 28 brings a confirmation of this suspicion. Alternating duets between the lower and upper voices force us to constantly shift our focus of attention. One homorhythmic measure (m 40) allows us to catch our breath before the composer returns to four-part interaction. In contrast to the opening of this movement, measures 28–54 present us with four voices whose parts "look" alike both rhythmically as well as melodically (Ex. 6.4). As with the Haydn example discussed above, the small snippets which are tossed back and forth create the

Example 6.4 Franz Hoffmeister, Op. 14, No. 3, Mvt. II, mm 28–54

Example 6.4 concluded

impression of equality. A change of mode from major to minor brings with it a less interactive approach. Although all four voices have similar surface rhythms, the first violin is clearly "in charge" and it is here that we find the majority of melodic interest. This emphasis on the first violin is reinforced even further when the composer returns us to A Major in bar 82. Whereas the top voice is filled with rapid scales, arpeggios, and figuration, the lower voices move in placid repeated eighth notes. Temporary "lapses" grant the lower parts some independence and toward the end of the movement the earlier duet and more interactive textures return to remind us of what we have already heard. The movement is an interesting mix of first violin prominence and near-equal treatment of all four voices. The difference lays in the presentation of material. Integration of all four voices seems to require that the composer only work with fragments whereas the dominance of one voice over the others allows for both complete melodies and passagework.

Historically, Haydn and his Viennese contemporaries have overshadowed others who wrote debate-style movements. As a result, musicologists have given only minimal attention to the numerous other composers who used this same manner of discourse. For example, Pierre Vachon, most often discussed in conjunction with the Parisian *quatuor concertant,* included a number of debates in his quartets, yet the composer's name is curiously excluded from most examinations of the genre outside France.

Vachon's Op. 11[13] provides us with the opportunity with which to view the composer's approach to the medium. With the exception of the fourth quartet, all others contain at least one debate movement; the last includes two fine examples. In both the first and last movements of this sixth quartet, Vachon reveals a pair of violins with similar activity levels. Although the first violin retains dominance, the second violin participates in the unfolding of thematic material and the presentation of melodic fragments. The viola, while not as melodically independent, takes a lively role in the textural fabric. At times it engages in either parallel motion or imitation; elsewhere its line is independent and prominent. Rarely is it relegated to the role of uninterested bystander. The cello, labeled "basso" in the print, provides a solid accompaniment for the upper three voices. Although the least distinctive of the four parts, it lends directional clarity to the movements through its role as provider of harmonic foundation. The first movement, a Moderato in sonata form, will serve as illustration.

The opening twelve bars immediately establish the first violin as the leader of the group, but active commentary by the second violin, including a foreshadowing of melodic material, preclude our focusing solely on the former. The lower voices, while considerably slower in surface rhythm and obviously supportive, contain movement and variety (mm 1–12). After a four-measure lull in all parts, the violist requests our attention with its sixteenth-note arpeggios. Not to be outdone by the violist's prominence, the first violinist resumes its leadership role and with a burst of activity demands complete subservience from all others; this is given in the form of measured tremelos. A return to the opening material follows, but this time the viola is incorporated into the motivic fabric; the result is a series of imitative entrances which yield to first violin dominance with periodic interjections by the second violin. The upper voices then join in parallel octaves, thereby effectively reducing the texture to three voices. Just when we think Vachon has completely ignored the potential of four-voice interaction, he introduces thirteen bars of such activity. Although the first violin is noticeably more demanding, and the lower voices often travel in octaves, the listener will find something of interest in all parts to listen to. With a return to the opening material and roles, the exposition is brought to a close (Ex. 6.5).

The sixteen-measure development features the first violin. Although initially reminiscent of the opening bars, the section soon becomes a vehicle for the top voice to move in increasingly quicker surface rhythms. While facility in the upper positions of the instrument is not required, the performer must be able to execute scale figures at a rapid speed and render varied rhythms flawlessly. The

---

[13]   Pierre Vachon, *Six Quatuors Concertants. . .* Op. XI (Paris: Sieber, [1782–6]). Printed parts are available at the Library of Congress, Washington D. C., M452. A2V2 Op. 11.

Example 6.5 Pierre Vachon, Op. 11, No. 6, Mvt. I, mm 1–64

Example 6.5 continued

Example 6.5 concluded

recapitulation, while not a verbatim repetition of the exposition, reviews previously heard materials and textures. The interplay between the violins and the integration of the cello and viola in the secondary material reveal a distinct set of identities. Consequently, while the first violin retains melodic prominence, the other voices do not recede into the background. The combination of individuality and retention of roles so characteristic of the debate is carefully maintained throughout this movement.

Many composers wrote debates of a less learned sort, i.e., light debates. These were more accessible to larger groups of people, both listeners and performers. As the century wore on and the options available for the less skilled player decreased, the light debate had the advantage of allowing for continued participation by those with less facility.

Joseph Schmitt's "Quartetto" in G Major,[14] like his previously discussed Op. 5, provides an excellent starting point for this discussion. The entire quartet is an interesting mix of debate (second movement), light debate (first movement, trio), and lecture (menuetto, fourth movement). By varying the relationship of the voices from movement to movement, the composer can manipulate the degree of integration. Just as the lecture allows the first violinist to dominate the ensemble,

---

[14]   [Joseph] Schmid [Schmitt], "Quartetto a Violino Primo, Violino Secundo, Viola, e Basso", manuscript parts, The Hague, Haags Gemeente Museum, VII-4151.

the debate provides greater opportunity for all four voices to mingle. In contrast, the light debate offers a little bit of both. The first violin remains firmly in the leadership position, but the lower voices, with their light surface rhythms and varied lines, demand that we notice them. Although interaction and four-voice participation is minimal, the overall impression is one of greater activity and engagement.

The exposition of the opening Allegro moderato neatly illustrates these points. The imitative opening immediately suggests four independent voices but by measure 5, the first violin has emerged as dominant. Parallel motion in the second violin and a unison close to the phrase only heighten the notion that the first violin is primary. A short give-and-take passage between the two violins (mm12–15), set over repeated eighth notes in the lower voices, leads to a more extended one which incorporates all parts (mm16–22) (Ex. 6.6). Following this, the first violin

Example 6.6 Joseph Schmitt, "Quartetto" in G, Mvt. I, mm 1–22

Example 6.6 concluded

once again emerges as the most technically demanding: use of the higher register, continuous sixteenth notes, and string crossings stand in contrast to the punctuating eighths of the second violin and stepwise movement of the viola and cello. Measure 27 returns us to parallel motion between the violins, and then between first violin and viola; this is followed by an unadulterated highlighting of the first violin. Although the lower voices move, their repeated patterns simply provide a thicker backdrop upon which the upper voice can rest. With the change in surface rhythm at measure 42, Schmitt alters the relationship of the parts. While the first violin continues with the thematic material, paralleled by the second violin, the cello emerges with a countermelody that weaves in and out of the upper voices. The viola, moving steadily, offers yet another line for the listener to consider.   Only with the final five bars of the exposition do the lower voices relinquish their independence and return to simple punctuating quarter notes.

Even the most demanding phrases of the first violin part are not beyond the capability of a moderately skilled amateur. The lower voices, easily rendered by less facile performers, ensure that the work will be attractive to a number of musicians. Texturally, the interaction never requires extreme concentration from the listener. Schmitt manages the four voices in such a way that one is rarely required to focus on more than one important part at a time; consequently, give-and-take is minimized and the greater variety in the supporting lines provides an illusion of independence suggestive of interaction without sacrificing a homophonic texture.

Hyacinthe Jadin's (1769–1802) Op. 1, No. 1 exhibits similar characteristics. The composer's first four publications consist of twelve quartets in four sets (Opp. 1–4). With one exception, all are four-movement works laid out in the traditional Viennese fashion.[15] Jadin's first effort in the genre bears a dedication to Joseph Haydn;[16] this has sparked some debate. Philippe Oboussier notes that the works of Op. 1 recall the unpredicatability and humor of Haydn.[17] This is refuted by Horst Walter who finds that although these are four- movement works, they are markedly different from Haydn's own and decidedly French in taste.[18] Whatever the case, these are neither difficult nor concert works; rather they seem to be designed for performance by amateurs and within the confines of the private room. Textures are clear, and there is minimal interplay between the voices. Even when the lower voices come forward, Jadin carefully maintains the traditional functions of each instrument. The Minuet of the first quartet aptly illustrates these points. Although there is some independence among the voices, the first violin retains dominance throughout. The entire minuet is reproduced in Example 6.7.

With its continual melodic presence and highest pitches, the first violin establishes itself as the key melodic instrument. The texture is enhanced by the

---

[15] Op. 4, No. 1 is a two-movement work.

[16] Hyacinthe Jadin, *Trois Quatuors pour deux Violons[,] Alto[,] et Basse*...Oeuvre 1 (Paris: Hedler, [1795]). Printed parts are available at Státní Oblastní Archiv v Třeboni, CS-K 106 K23. First written notice of Op. 1 appeared with the announcement in the *Journal de Paris* on 5 September 1795. The set was first published in the *Magasin de musique*.

[17] Philippe Oboussier, "The French String Quartet, 1770–1800", in *Music and the French Revolution* (Cambridge: Cambridge University Press, 1992), pp. 87–8. For a general survey of Jadin's quartets, see Oboussier, "Une Révélation Musicale: Les Quatuors de Hyacinthe Jadin", in *Le Tambour et la Harpe: Oeuvres, pratiques et manifestations musicales Jous la Révolution* (ed. by Jean-Rémy Julien and Jean Mongrédien; Paris: Éditions du May, 1991), pp. 221–40.

[18] Horst Walter, "Haydn gewidmete Streichquartette", in *Joseph Haydn: Tradition und Rezeption* (ed. by Georg Feder, Heinrich Hüschen, and Ulrich Tank; Regensburg: Gustav Bosse Verlag, 1985), p. 20.

Example 6.7 Hyacinthe Jadin, Op. 1, No. 1, Minuet

rhythmic variety and lack of merely simple repeating pitches in the second violin, viola, and cello. Although one might make a case for greater integration of the four parts, the fabric remains light and easily accessible to the listener. First violin emphasis is not achieved by assigning that instrument difficult passages, and in fact, none of the parts are technically challenging; all can be executed in the first position. Instead, Jadin ensures, through careful spacing of the lines, that the melody always remains in the highest-pitched voice. This guarantees the best possible projection. The cello, which bears the responsibility of harmonic foundation, is always the lowest part. While that line does move, one finds that the motion takes the form of arpeggios and scales, both of which aid in the establishment of tonalities. The middle voices, carefully placed so as not to obscure the top one, fill out the sonority with parallel motion and supportive, but not competing, lines.

Just as the light debate provides accessible works for the less sophisticated listener, so too does it offer the less skilled performer the opportunity to engage in intimate music making. Whereas some debates, like their lecture counterparts, require only a skilled first violinist, others allow for execution by four amateurs. Pierre Vachon's Op. 5 is typical.[19] This set, as with many of Vachon's quartet publications, exhibits a great variety of structure, melody, tempo, key, and discourse types. The upper voices are given melodic roles of varying proportions. The lowest line, however, is consistently presented as a figured bass part. Cooper suggests that this is due to the English practices where it was usual to have a harpsichord reinforce the bass up to about 1770; one may also consider that the inclusion of numbers could have been a publisher ploy to reach the widest possible audience.[20] Within this collection of two- and three-movement works, one finds polite conversations, debates, lectures, and various hybrids. Of the fifteen movements, nearly half are debates.

This intent to offer a work of widespread appeal with limited technical requirements is seen with the final movement of the second quartet. This Allegro in sonata form contains give-and-take of small snippets, independent voices, and varied sonorities achieved through the combination of different voices. The first violin retains its dominant position, not through technical display, but with melodic prominence.

From the very start of this movement, Vachon presents not a melody plus accompaniment texture, but a more integrated ensemble. The lowest voice provides a harmonic foundation upon which the upper three can display their melodically interesting lines. Initially the first violin moves by itself, answered by the middle voices which travel in parallel motion. Shortly after, however, the violins are established as partners, advancing first in imitation and then in parallel motion. Measure 9 finds the opening material now placed in the viola, while the response, originally in the middle voices, has moved to the first violin. Repetition of this phrase finds the second violin joining the viola. (This opening section is reproduced in Ex. 6.8.) Only in measure 17 does the first violin resume its position as the focus of attention; increased activity in the lower voices beginning in measure 21 ensures that the listener does not forget their presence. With the

---

[19]   Pierre Vachon, *Six Quartettos for two violins, a tenor and bass* [Op. 5] (London: Napier, [ca.1775]). Printed parts available at the Library of Congress, Washington D. C., M452.V2. Op. 5 case. This set is also reproduced in Cooper, *Three Centuries*.

[20]   Ibid., p. 68. Figured bass parts appear in other quartets as well including Carl Friedrich Abel's Opp. 12 and 15 of 1775 and c.1780 respectively. Much has been written about publishers who, unilaterally opted to add numbers to quartets for the sole purpose of boosting sales.

Example 6.8 Pierre Vachon, Op. 5, No. 2, Mvt. III, mm 1–16

cadence five bars later, Vachon reduces the texture to two voices moving in parallel motion: a violin duet is answered by a second violin/viola duet. A first violin melody supported by repeated eighth notes in the lower voices concludes the exposition.

The development, reminiscent of the movement's opening, features a consistently active first violin with commentary provided by the middle voices. Following two parallel octave snippets which incorporate all four instruments, Vachon increases the give-and-take between the two violins. Interspersed between the subphrases is a short cello eighth-note figure which calls attention to that previously ignored voice. Upon the cello's return to a purely harmonic role, the viola enters to increase the numbering of interacting instruments to three. This thicker texture heralds the recapitulation, which begins in measure 68, and follows a near verbatim repetition of the transition and secondary material of the exposition.

Throughout the movement, one finds a great deal of independence among the upper three voices. These parts are often intertwined, usually in the form of short snippets tossed back and forth. The leadership position of the first violin is reinforced not only by its being the one instrument to bear a melody by itself, but also in its everpresent role as a participant in the give-and-take sections. This domination is achieved through melodic variety and activity, but not through technical display. The entire part could easily be rendered by the average amateur; one is never required to move past third position and there are no difficult or taxing passages. Intricate bowings, passagework, and large leaps are absent. The second violin and viola parts, also easily played by amateurs, are nearly identical in their requirements. The same types of figures and bowings appear in all three parts. Only the lowest line is simpler: twice the cellist is asked to go beyond first position, and in these situations, one must merely move the left hand a whole step in order to play the "e".

Despite the lack of bravura, these works can be satisfying for both the performer and the listener. Much of this interest derives from the activity and uniqueness of the various parts. One of the identifying features of a debate is that even though the first violin retains melodic dominance, the other voices, often subservient, are still independent and interesting. There are any number of works by Haydn and Mozart that can be used to illustrate this feature, but to do this would be to state the obvious.[21] Less well-known and yet worthy of our attention

---

[21] Debate movements appear in Haydn's Op. 20, Nos 1–4; Op. 33, Nos 1–4; Op. 42; Op. 50, Nos 1–6, Op. 54, No. 3; Op. 55, Nos 1–3; Op. 64, Nos 1–6; Op. 71, Nos 1–3; Op. 74, Nos 1–3; and Op. 76, Nos 1–5. Mozart includes debates in K.80, K.156, K.158–60, K.168–173, K.387, K.421, K.428, K.458, K.464, K.485, K.499, K.575, and K.589–590. It is important to note that in only one situation – Mozart's K.485 – is the entire quartet comprised of debate movements. More often than not, the debate is just one part of the work and its placement is far from uniform.

are a host of other works; two by Carlo d'Ordonez (1734–86) and Anton Teyber (baptized 1756–1822) will illustrate.

Ordonez's twenty-seven string quartets[22] hold an important place in the history of the new instrumental style of the third quarter of the eighteenth According to A. Peter Brown, the least advanced show a connection to the trio sonata and *sinfonia a quattro* traditions;[23] others reveal the influence of the sonata da chiesa and divertimento.[24] Nearly all the quartets contain fugues or show fugal influences. Ordonez is not unique in this respect. He is part of a group of composers including Albrechtsberger, Florian Gassmann, Matthias Georg Monn, and Christoph Sonnleithner whose works routinely incorporate fugues and fugal techniques; their compositions were often programmed as part of Joseph II's own chamber concerts.[25] It is this emphasis on contrapuntal devices that links Ordonez with the more conservative Viennese composers of the day and separates him from his more popular contemporaries such as Karl Ditters von Dittersdorf, Vanhal, and Pichl.[26] While Ordonez's fugal writing has received much attention, one should not overlook the fact that the composer used a variety of discourse types, even within a single set. His Op. 1 reveals this diversity.

Ordonez probably composed this set of quartets during the mid-1760s. They were not published, however, until 1777, by Guere in Lyon.[27] Despite the fact that the majority of these four-movement works are conversations and debates, the composer does not neglect the lecture and the polite conversation; these last-named types are found in the inner movements. In a manner similar to other debates examined in this chapter, Ordonez successfully reconciles a dominant first violin with active and independent lower voices. The third movement of the first quartet is a fine illustration. In this A Major minuet and trio, the first violin consistently bears the melodic material. The other voices, rather than serving as mere support, move independently with interesting and varied lines. Some sustained and/or repeated pitches are evident, but those instances are minimal. The second half of the minuet, as shown in Example 6.9, reveals how the composer uses such "accompanimental" devices to actually move the line forward. The first violin, with its melody, remains steadily in the forefront. The

---

[22] To this number, A. Peter Brown, in the *New Grove,* mentions nine other quartets attributed to Ordonez: one doubtful and eight spurious.

[23] Brown, *Carlo d'Ordonez: String Quartets, Opus 1*, p. vii.

[24] A. Peter Brown, "An Introduction to the Works of Carlo d'Ordonez", in *Music East and West: Essays in Honor of Walter Kaufmann* (ed by Thomas Noblitt; New York: Pendragon Press, 1981), pp. 253–4.

[25] See Kirkendale, *Fugue and Fugato* for an exhaustive discussion. See also Heartz, *Haydn, Mozart, and the Viennese School*, p. 474.

[26] A. Peter Brown, "The Chamber Music with Strings of Carlos d'Ordonez: a Bibliographic and Stylistic Study", *Acta Musicologica* 46 (1974): 259.

[27] An announcement in the Parisian *Almanach Musical* appeared in 1778.

sustained notes of the first violin allow the middle voices to come forward; note that this movement occurs only when the topmost voice has reached a temporary lull. While the second violin moves in stepwise descent, the viola retains the same pitch in two-measure groupings. Rather than regarding this repetition as monotonous, one can interpret the two quarter notes as "pick-ups" to the next measure thus leading the listener forward. The cello part further reinforces this movement with its two-measure groupings of half-step ascents. The increased surface rhythm of the first violin beginning in measure 13, along with the quicker alternation of dynamics, creates tension. The homorhythmic and near homorhythmic movement of all four voices beginning in measure 15 only heighten the effect.

Example 6.9 Carlo d'Ordonez, Op. 1, No. 1, Mvt. III, mm 9-18

The trio further points up the independence of the voices. The opening melody, set in parallel motion in the violins, is answered by the lower voices. Rather than providing a simple harmonic underpinning or unobtrusive accompaniment, the viola and cello offer a rhythmic, and at times melodic, counterpoint. In the second half, a section of give-and-take between the outer voices is offset by a slower surface rhythm in the middle parts. As the cello continues in eighth and quarter notes, the violins progress in alternating quarter and half notes set in a startling contrast of piano and sforzando respectively; the viola, with its monotone line, provides a rhythmic counterpoint with its over-the-bar line ties. Only in the final two measures do the four voices come together as a unit (Ex. 6.10).

Example 6.10 Carlo d'Ordonez, Op. 1, No. 1, Mvt. III, mm 26–34

In both the minuet and trio, Ordonez carefully maintains the hierarchy of voices. Even though the first violin never relinquishes its position as melodically dominant, the lower voices are given interesting and independent lines. Rarely does any one voice recede into simple accompaniment. Rhythmic movement and variety of contour enhance the texture of the ensemble. Furthermore, from a performer's perspective, these lower lines offer the participant a chance to take part in the shaping of the line without the responsibility of bearing the melody.

This same sense of independent, yet hierarchical parts is evident in some of the movements which make up the six quartets of Anton Teyber's Opp. 1–2 of 1788.[28] Notwithstanding his position as first court organist at Dresden (1787–91), Teyber (baptized 1756–1822) spent most of his productive life in Vienna working as a composer, pianist, organist, and cellist. His Opp. 1–2 fit the stereotypical image of the Viennese quartet: excluding the final quartet, the classic four-movement structure is maintained throughout with only minor alterations.[29] This image is perpetuated if one examines only the opening movements, for these are often debates. Beyond this however, one finds that Teyber incorporates a wealth of discourse types; middle and final movements are as likely to be lectures and polite conversations as debates or conversations. For example, Op. 2, No. 1 opens with a debate, is followed by a lecture/debate hybrid, and concludes with two lecture movements. The opening debate of Op. 2, No. 3 stands in sharp contrast to the following polite conversation. Teyber then finishes the quartet with a lecture sandwiched between two debate sections. Notwithstanding this diversity of movement types, Teyber's debates are fine illustrations of his ability to provide all the instruments with interesting parts while still preserving the melodic dominance of the first violin. The opening Allegro of Op. 2, No. 3 serves to illustrate this.

In this sonata form movement, the first violin consistently demands our attention as the primary bearer of thematic material. To support it, Teyber is not content to merely assign simple repeated notes and punctuating quarters. Instead, the lower voices are active and independent; at times they are even given some melodic material.

The movement opens with the expected dispensation of parts: melodic first violin, texture enriching middle voices, and foundational cello. Measure 5 requires that we refocus our attention: the near continuous sixteenth-note fluttering in the second violin stands in contrast to the sustained pitches of the first violin and repeated eighth notes of the lower voices. Four measures later, the first violin joins the second, and the two upper voices move in parallel motion while the lower ones continue placidly. Measure 19 brings three bars of unison movement in all parts, followed by the same number of homorhythmic ones to close the phrase (Ex. 6.11). Bar 25 returns us to a slower surface rhythm and first

---

[28] Op. 1 was published in Vienna, 1788. Op. 2 appeared in Dresden. Manuscript parts of the entire set can be found at the Staatsbibliothek zu Berlin Preussischer Kulturbesitz, M5441. Manuscript parts of Op. 2 are part of the collection at the Gesellschaft der Musikfreunde, 6278.

[29] The sixth quartet is different in that although it maintains the order and expected forms for the first two movements, the conclusion is a single extended setting in three distinct sections: Allegro–Tempo di Minuetto–Presto. Binding this sequence together is the close thematic and rhythmic relationship of the Allegro and Presto.

Example 6.11 Anton Teyber, Op. 2, No. 3, Mvt. I, mm 1–24

violin domination, but once again this is shortlived; the sixteenth-note fluttering of the second violin provides a continuous rippling of sound upon which the upper line can rest. The texture is enriched by the coupling of the viola with the first violin, and punctuated every other measure by the cello. The parts are then rearranged in bar 37: while the first violin assumes the fluttering line, the lower instruments join together to produce the slower, more melodious part. Seven measures later, the second violin, viola and cello assume the quicker moving line, but this time the sixteenths move in scale patterns rather than the broken intervals found earlier in the violins. Meanwhile, the first violin has been reduced to producing widely spaced sustained pitches. Just when the listener thinks that the first violin has relinquished its dominant position for good, that instrument bursts forth with ten measures of rapid passagework; its placement in the upper register ensures our attention. Offset by the most mundane of accompaniments – even repeated eighth notes – the first violin moves increasingly higher and higher. Even the second violin countermelody in measure 51 does not detract from this line.

Having completed this bravura passage with a solo c'''', the first violin cedes domination to the second violin for ten bars. The outer instruments provide the barest of support; the viola, only slightly more active, occasionally travels in parallel motion. The quicker surface rhythm of the second violin is maintained even when it returns to its secondary role; its pedal point serves as a background to the first violin–cello duet. The pairing of voices shifts yet again in measure 73 as the violins offer the listener sustained pitches followed by a moderately-paced melody in parallel octaves; the lower voices take over the quicker surface rhythm. Teyber then introduces a series of short duets: the first one, between the outer voices, is succeeded by one featuring the two violins; following this the second violin and cello join together, and then finally, Teyber returns us to the upper instruments. Throughout these passages, the accompanying voices have remained supportive and undemanding of the listener's attention. One simply notices the changing timbres and registers. From measure 101 to the end of the exposition, Teyber focuses on the first violin as the bearer of the thematic material. Small melodic interruptions by the second violin and viola offer respite, but not a true shift of function. Similarly, the increased activity in all the voices, while noticeable, does not reorder the function and role of each instrument. The independence and uniqueness of each line achieved through melodic and rhythmic variety reinforces the integration of the instruments, and at the same time, solidifies the relationship of the various voices.

The development, which opens with a ten-bar unison passage, reviews the opening material. A duet between the outer voices, followed by one between the inner ones, provides the listener with a variety of sonorities and contours. Although a perusal of the parts reveals the greatest variety and activity in the first violin and the least in the cello, all four voices contribute to the quartet fabric and together form an integrated whole. Rarely is one part, even the cello or viola, relegated to a mere sustained pitch for any longer than a couple of measures. More frequently, little snippets appear in the lower voices which, when interspersed with the upper ones, provide an interesting and everchanging counterpoint. By the time we reach the recapitulation, Teyber has presented us with four independent voices, each of which maintains a particular relationship to the other voices. The recapitulation follows the path laid out in the exposition with modifications to allow for deletion of some material and the harmonic changes.   The first violin part, while certainly the most melodically and technically interesting, does not completely overshadow the other voices. The second violin and viola fulfill their function as textural and harmonic filler, but in such a way as to provide both the performer and listener with unique and satisfying parts.   The cello, admittedly fulfilling the function of harmonic provider, also has moments of thematic display and is allowed to interact with the other voices.

This independence, so frequently mentioned above, is most easily seen in the development sections of sonata form movements. It is here that many composers choose to engage the instruments in interaction. Rather than examine an entire movement, several selected development sections will provide us with concrete illustrations of how composers approach the task of moving short snippets about from one instrument to another without a deterioration into chaos. We begin with the concluding movement of Brunetti's Op. 4, No. 4. In this B flat Major Presto, the composer retains the traditional roles of each instrument (melodic first violin, texture enriching middle voices, foundational cello); within these confines, he creates independence.   The interaction of the four parts coupled with varied pairings creates a kaleidoscopic effect that holds our interest throughout the entire development. The introduction of the first violin on its own at the beginning of this section immediately focuses our attention on that instrument. The material, drawn from the movement's opening, is already familiar and therefore merely reminds us of Brunetti's original theme before contrapuntal layers are added. The syncopation of the entering middle voices and the steady quarters of the lowest voice effectively alter the texture and sonority without obstructing the upper voice. A repetition of the phrase with its sequence of events follows. From this point to the end of the development, the surface rhythm of all the voices increases. The lower ones may move together in parallel quarters, alternating measures of eighth notes, or even punctuating offbeats. Brunetti varies the pairings so that at times the middle voices move together; in other instances the lower voices respond to each other. In all cases, the upper voice weaves in and out of this activity. So as not to overburden the listener, Brunetti sets the measures in which the lower voices move the quickest against a sustained pitch in the first violin. The net result is alternating registers of activity which produce a give-and- take effect between the first violin and one of the other instruments. Example 6.12, which reproduces the entire development, provides a visual image of the four integrated voices. The absence of continuously repeated pitches, reiterated rhythmic or melodic figures, and patterned accompaniments suggests that the lower lines are more than just support. While the first violin certainly retains dominance due in no small part to its register, movement, and studied separation from the lower voices, the second violin, viola, and cello offer the listener and performer independent lines that are integral to the texture and sonority.

Example 6.12 Gaetano Brunetti, Op. 4, No. 4, Mvt. III, mm 38–70

Example 6.12 concluded

Intertwined yet independent voices are also found in the first movement of Chartrain's Op. 4, No. 5.[30] In this Allegro, one finds that the first violin dominates, but only slightly. It often shares melodic responsibility with the second violin; the two instrumental parts are frequently interwoven. In the development, this relationship is turned on its head for the two violins appear to switch roles. While the viola and cello parts can still be described as supportive, the upper lines are varied and interesting in their right. At times, it is difficult to make a clear distinction between melody and accompaniment. Nowhere is this more evident than the development section which is reproduced in Example 6.13.

The first eleven bars present the second violin as dominant. Melodic material initially appears in that part; when the two violins join together in the fifth measure, it is the first violin that supports the second by moving in parallel octaves below the "upper voice", in imitation, and again in parallel motion. The lower voices, which have been relegated to simple repeated quarter notes, soon vary their lines. The cello, in the sixth measure and the viola, in the ninth, begin weaving in and out of the violin parts. The increased surface rhythm adds to the already thickening texture to lend definition to the cadence. The first violin's melody, which begins in the twelfth bar is not left unchallenged. The inner voices respond with movement and variety so that the listener is forced to attend to all three parts at the same time. The net result is a phrase which can only truly be appreciated if one considers not only thematic material but the counterlines as well. This is offset by the minimalist nature of the cello part: accompanimental punctuating downbeat quarter notes that reinforce the key of d minor (the relative minor of the movement) followed by five measures of rest. Measure 79 returns the second violin to prominence. The first violin part and to a lesser extent the cello, while supportive, move, not just with repeated patterns but with some variety; the greatest amount of activity occurs when the surface rhythm of the second violin is at its slowest. Conversely, when the melodic line is at its most active (triplets), the others are calmest. Chartrain is careful not to overburden the listener with excessive polyphony. Even when all four parts move as they do with the final three measures of the development, one never has the sense of being overpowered. The increased surface rhythm functions as a means of making the recapitulation the inevitable return to stability.

The debate aspect of the Chartrain example is reinforced by the independence of each line. Despite the fact that melodic material only appears in the two upper voices, all four parts are distinct. A successful reading requires that each performer weave his or her line in and out of the others; a part which moves under the melody can enhance the phrase if the performer knows how to interact with the other voices. Sometimes it is a matter of blending so well with another line that the listener hears but a single one. At other times, a subsidiary voice must

---

[30] See Chapter 5 for a discussion of the last movement of this same quartet.

Example 6.13 Nicolas-Joseph Chartrain, Op. 4, No. 5, Mvt. I, mm 58–89

Example 6.13 concluded

take over momentarily so as to move the line along. If done well, the listener is unaware of these manipulations; he or she simply hears melodic material characterized by varied colors and textures.

Nowhere is this interweaving aspect of debate writing more evident than in the final movement of Mozart's "Hunt" quartet, K.458, one of the six "Haydn" quartets (K.387, K.421, K.428, K.458, K.464, and K.465). The first mention of these works appears in a letter which Mozart wrote to the publisher Sieber on 26 April 1783, noting that he was composing six quartets and would offer them for publication if his price could be met. John Irving suggests that Mozart knew full well Sieber would not agree to his demand and so he would then be free to offer them to Artaria.

The decision to dedicate these works to Haydn came after the aforementioned letter and possibly as a result of the elder composer's favorable reception when he heard three of these works (K.387, K.421, and K.428) at a private performance on 15 January 1785.   The following month, the other three were played by Mozart, his father, and the two Barons Tinti. It was at this event that Haydn made his famous remark, "Before God, and as an honest man I tell you that your son is the greatest composer known to me either in person or by name". Although the decision to dedicate the works to Haydn after such a comment would seem logical, a second reason, suggested by Irving, was also possible. Mozart might well have concluded that the success of Pleyel's Op. 2 set of quartets was due in no small part to that publication's prominently featured reference to Haydn. Mozart's decision may have been influenced by a desire for sales.[31]

Notwithstanding this dedication, much has been written about the musical and stylistic similarities between these six works and Haydn's Op. 33.   Michael Tilmouth's *New Grove* article on the string quartet, for example notes that with the "Haydn" quartets, one finds, for the first time, the assimilation of Haydn's Op. 33.   In doing so, however, Mozart produced greater works than his model.[32] Konold, relying heavily on Finscher's study, points to external factors; he notes that the "Haydn" quartets were, like Op. 33, written after a "long pause" and planned as a self-contained, integrated set.[33] Walter Kreyszig finds a direct link between Mozart's and Haydn's minuet phrase structure.[34]   More general similarities have been noted by Stanley Sadie, who, in his various writings, finds that Mozart's debt to Haydn lies in the way important material is given to the inner parts and in a concentrated style.[35]

Mozart's "Haydn" collection was soon held in high esteem, and together with its predecessor, was regarded as the epitome of the classical string quartet, a position held much to the present day. A notice in the *Pressburger Zeitung* of 4 November 1803, announced that Johann Träg and Son (Art and Music Dealers) would issue these quartets in score form because "these Quartets are unique...they fulfill perfectly all that criticism demands of a quartet: thus they are fit to serve as models for novices in the art of composition".[36]

---

[31]   John Irving, *Mozart: The 'Haydn" Quartets* (Cambridge, UK: Cambridge University Press, 1998), pp. 12–13.
[32]   *New Grove*, s. v., "String Quartet", by Michael Tilmouth, p. 279.
[33]   Konold, *The String Quartet*, p. 80.
[34]   Walter Kurt Kreyszig, "Das Menuett Wolfgang Amadeus Mozarts unter dem Einfluß von Franz Joseph Haydns 'gantz neue besondere art': Zur Phrasenstruktur in den Menuetten der 'Haydn-Quartette'", in *Mozart Jahrbuch 1991: Bericht über den Internationalen Mozart Kongress 1991*, Teilband 2 (ed. by Rudolf Angermüller, Dietrich Beeke, and Wolfgang Rehm; Kassel: Bärenreiter, 1992), pp. 665–63.
[35]   Sadie's comments have been succintly summarized in Irving, *Mozart*, p. 80.
[36]   Pandi and Schmidt, "Music in Haydn's and Beethoven's Time", p. 283.

In focusing specifically on structural similarities and only vaguely on less tangible features such as distribution of material, scholars have perpetuated the "string quartet as structure" model. In failing to assess Mozart's "Haydn" quartets are samples of the chamber medium, they have all but ignored the importance of how Mozart treats his voices. Marianne Danckwardt, for example, suggests that with K.458, Mozart finally learned how to write a quartet, because he began to write in the *new way as first done by Haydn*. Comparing the opening movements of K.458 and Op. 33, No. 1, Danckwardt points out the similarities and simplicity of the motivic/thematic work, the goal-oriented writing, and even motivic similarities between actual melodies. This focus on the theoretical aspects has come at the expense of the genre itself.[37] Rarely does one find references to the treatment of the voices; Orin Moe's work is a nearly isolated example.[38] But it is this very aspect that makes a composition such as K.458 so intriguing.

The final movement of this quartet, a B flat major Allegro assai in sonata form, opens with a homophonic texture and traditional dispensation of parts: melodic first violin, sonority enriching second violin and viola, and when present, foundational cello. Almost immediately afterwards, Mozart chooses to engage all four voices in a section of give-and-take. A small snippet in the lower voices is answered by the upper voices (mm17–21). Not long after, the parts are exchanged and Mozart offers the same passage, but this time with different voicing (mm 25–29). With the conclusion of this interaction, we return to the first violin domination which takes us up to the cadence in measure 46. Slightly more independent writing follows: the second violin and cello, travelling in parallel thirds, respond to a first violin line while the viola sustains a single middle C. This greater individuality of parts is shortlived, however, and yet again the first violin takes center stage. Not until measure 97 do we really see a section of four independent voices. For the next sixteen bars, Mozart provides the listener with a wealth of voices to attend to. While at first it may appear that functions are fixed (the cello parts looks more harmonic than the others, the first violin seems more melodic, etc), halfway through the section, the lines are shuffled. The "more melodic" first violin part is now in the lowest voice; the "foundational" cello part is now assigned to the second violin. The viola has taken over the second violin line, and the first violin has assumed the part previously heard in the viola (Ex. 6.14). The resumption of traditional roles in measure 113 offers a marked change and reminds us that the first violin leadership is the norm. Those portions which allow the other voices to come forward appear in transitory passages; these can be viewed as interjections and interruptions of an otherwise homophonic exposition.

---

[37] Marianne Danckwardt, "Mozarts 'ganz neue besondere Art' zu schreiben: der Kopfsatz aus dem Streichquartett KV 458 (1784)", *Mozart Jahrbuch* (1984–85): 24–31.

[38] Moe, "Texture in the String Quartets of Haydn", p. 352.

Example 6.14 Wolfgang Amadeus Mozart, K.458, Mvt. IV, mm 97–112

It is particularly in the development that Mozart allows all four voices to interact and work as independent participants. Question and answer phrases, imitation, fragmented material, and give-and-take passages fill this section. In such places, the ensemble must have four strong players. Successful execution requires that all members possess similar technical and musical abilities. It is not enough to read one's own line. One must also be aware of how the parts fit together: Whose part imitates whose? Which lines move in parallel motion? Is one snippet a response to another?

The development's initial question and answer passage between upper and lower voices, both in parallel motion, is punctated by homorhythm in all four parts. The movement's opening two bars then serve as the basis for imitation found in all four voices. Once this fragment settles in the viola and cello, the violins proceed in an independent, yet subtly linked fashion. The syncopation in the first violin is reinforced below through the bowing; large leaps in the second violin are countered by similarly large leaps in the upper voice but in the opposite direction. After a fleeting moment of imitation between the violins, the cello presents a single d which seemingly offers a respite to the activity which has preceded it. When the viola enters in measure 167 with the same idea, but up a half step, we realize that Mozart does not intend to return to the homophony of the exposition. The opening idea is yet again used as the inspiration for the next seven bars (mm169–175) leading into a passage of give-and-take involving all four instruments. Pairing the upper and lower voices, first a two-measure snippet, then a single measure is passed back and forth. The violins and viola, moving independently, are grounded by a pedal F in the cello. Not content to sit on the sidelines, the cello rejoins the group for a final question and answer phrase before Mozart concludes the development.

The recapitulation, which begins in measure 199, offers the stability and homophony which was so absent during the development. With this regularity comes the return of a full melody presented by the first violin, supportive cello line, and sonority enriching middle voices. Although one still hears moments of four-voice interaction, the contrast with the development is marked. The equality was achieved not by a rotation of prominence but by the exploration of fragments. Only the first violin is assigned an entire melody and rarely does Mozart reconfigure the function of each instrument. Thus even though we hear four independent parts, each still has a particular role to fulfill and the independence comes at prescribed moments and within certain parameters. While the transition and development passages allow for greater independence and involvement by all, the traditional balance of power is maintained. In this manner, Mozart successfully reconciles the need to provide interesting and satisfying parts to all within a hierarchical framework.

Not all composers relegated active participation to the transition and development sections. Some, such as Karl Ditters von Dittersdorf (1739–99) and Johann Baptist Vanhal approached the debate in a different fashion. These composers found that while the first violin could retain the listener's attention, especially with regard to thematic material, the lower voices could be used to enrich the sonority by letting them weave in and out of the upper line, thereby creating a more active texture and integrated fabric. Although one voice is continuously at the forefront, counterlines also demand our attention. As with previously discussed works, we hear four independent voices, but within the confines of a functional hierarchy. The opening movement of Dittersdorf's fourth quartet from his 1788 collection is a fine illustration.

Published by Artaria, the six three-movement works which make up Dittersdorf's *Sei quartetti*[39] contain a mixture of lectures, debates, conversations, and hybrids. While over half are lectures, Dittersdorf includes a number of fine debate specimens, and it is to a representative of these, the opening Allegro of Quartetto IV, that we turn our attention. In this sonata form movement, all four members of the ensemble are active participants; the first violin line is noticeably and consistently more demanding and prominent. Like so many other debates examined in this chapter, one finds that the composer has written four independent parts but has still managed to impose a hierarchy upon the group. The opening

---

[39] Carlo de Dittersdorf, *Sei quartetti per due Violini, Viola, e Violoncello* (Vienna: Artaria, [1788]). Printed parts are available at Österreich Nationalbibliothek, ms 27174.

melody, found in the first violin, is supported by parallel motion in the second violin and punctuated by the viola; homorhythmic movement in the three upper voices brings the phrase to a close and heralds the cello's entrance in measure 8. During the next twelve bars, Dittersdorf allows the lower voices to come forward while the upper ones transfom from conversants to supporters.   Measure 20 returns the first violin to prominence. Rather than relegating the lower voices to simple sustained notes and repeated patterns, Dittersdorf enriches the texture by introducing imitation, parallel motion, and broken chords in rapid surface rhythms. Although the listener is aware of these other lines, some of which move more quickly than the melody, none detracts from the uppermost one. Instead the composer has created a thicker and more colorful fabric (Ex. 6.15).

Example 6.15   Karl Ditters von Dittersdorf, *Sei Quartetti*, Quartetto IV, Mvt. I, mm 1–46

Example 6.15 continued

Example 6.15 concluded

Measure 47 finds repeated eighth notes in a solo second violin. Such a sudden and dramatic change of texture and line sets the stage for the following section in which the first violin demands our total attention. To ensure our uninterrupted focus, Dittersdorf places the barest of accompaniment below it: repeated eighth notes or broken intervals in all three voices. Not until bar 68 does the composer re-engage the entire ensemble. Parallel motion between the top and at least one of the lower voices occupies the quartet up to the close of the exposition. Such an approach does not create independence, but the activity does give the illusion of separate lines.

The development's beginning is distinguished by its imitative activity. While the lower voices initially answer the upper ones, Dittersdorf soon varies this by rearranging the partnerships. With but one exception, the first violin consistently remains in the forefront. What changes is the type of activity around it and the constant weaving of the other voices. Even the four measures of second violin prominence are offset by the placement of the first violin in a higher register. Parallel motion, punctuating figures, and give-and-take of small snippets lend the development an everchanging array of sounds which take the listener all the way to the fermata in measure 109 (Ex. 6.16). With the return of the opening melody in measure 110, this time in the second violin, we have reached the recapitulation. Intricate punctuating remarks by the first violin ensures that that instrument remains in the forefront; when it takes over as dominant eight measures later, the transition seems natural and expected. The remainder of the recapitulation follows the course laid out in the exposition with minor modifications. The first violinist, insisting that we remember its primary position, plays one final burst of passagework in the coda.

Example 6.16 Karl Ditters von Dittersdorf, *Sei Quartetti*, Quartetto IV, Mvt. I, mm 82–109

Example 6.16 concluded

While both the Dittersdorf and the previously discussed Mozart movements can be categorized as debates, they differ in the type of integration and the placement of it. Mozart prefers to confine the moments of greater independence to transitional and developmental sections. Within these, he places the instruments on a nearly-equal footing and forces the listener to refocus his or her attention many times. In contrast, Dittersdorf establishes the first violin as the bearer of melodic material throughout the movement. Having settled upon this "course of action", he then uses the other three voices as counterparts to enliven and vary what would otherwise be quite similar to a lecture movement. By providing a separate identity for each of the lower three voices, and by writing in such a way as to suggest more than simple accompaniment, Dittersdorf has created lines that are interesting for both the listener and performer.

A similar type of integration can be found in the final movement of the A Major quartet from Vanhal's Op. 13 of 1773.[40] Written shortly after Vanhal's return from Italy, this set includes those features typically found in contemporary Viennese quartets: four movements, emphasis on the first violin, and moderate first movement tempi. The lyricism, however, is a direct result of the Italian sojourn.[41] Like so many of Vanhal's quartets, nearly all the movements are lectures. The inclusion of a debate in the A-Major quartet is all the more significant for it reveals an unexplored aspect of this composer's often ignored output. Preceded by three lecture movements, the finale, a Presto in sonata form, exhibits a greater independence of parts and more give-and-take than is typical for this composer. Although the first violin presents the main melodic material and has a more demanding part, the lower voices are integrated into the texture and have a greater responsibility for the execution of important ideas.

From the very beginning, Vanhal presents us not with a melody plus unobtrusive accompaniment, but a theme supported by inner voices and punctuated by a motive in the cello that will prove to be more than a simple downbeat emphasis. This not-so-straightforward phrase is contrasted with one which does exhibit the expected lecture approach (Ex. 6.17). A repetition of the opening eight bars reinforces the contrast. Measure 17 shows us why the cello figure is significant. The motive, now in the first violin is answered by the viola while the second violin and cello play together in parallel motion. Following a more homophonic phrase, the first violin takes its position as leader to conclude the primary material (Ex. 6.18).

First violin domination is still apparent in measure 31 but the middle voices, which move together in parallel motion, have an interesting counterline. Only in measure 40 do the second violin and viola stop vying for the listener's attention and join with the cello to offer support to the top voice. Up to the close of the exposition, the first violin holds our interest; measures 51–54 and 59–60 offer a respite with a small snippet of cello–viola imitation.

The opening measures of the development immediately establish four independent lines. As the first violin reviews material first heard in the beginning of the movement, the cello and viola engage in give-and-take. Meanwhile, the second violin offers a rhythmic pedal. As the cello moves into the forefront, the upper voices recede into the background with sustained or slow-moving notes.

---

[40] Paris: Huberty, [1773]. This quartet has been reproduced in volume 3 of David Wyn Jones, "The String Quartets of Vanhal" (PhD diss., University of Wales, 1978). Op. 13 was also published as Op. 3 by Hummel, c1776. The latter edition contained numbers in the basso part which, according to Jones, was consistent with the North German practice. Since there was no proof that a basso continuo was needed, this might have been a purely commercial addition. See vol. 1, p. 117 of the above-named dissertation.

[41] See ibid., pp. 115–40, and Hickman, "Six Bohemian Masters", pp. 64–9, for a stylistic discussion of this set.

Example 6.17 Johann Baptist Vanhal, Quartet in A Major (A1), Mvt. IV, mm 1–8

Example 6.18 Johann Baptist Vanhal, Quartet in A Major (A1), Mvt. IV, mm 17–30

Example 6.18 concluded

Measure 80 treats us to the same material, but this time the two outer voices have switched parts. While four-voice interaction is evident in the passage beginning in measure 94, much of the remainder of the development relies on first violin activity to move it along. Only the final ten bars of this section suggest another possibility: here Vanhal sets the cello against the upper three voices in the form of question and answer phrases. A momentary pause signals the recapitulation and from measure 143 to the end, we have an orderly reconstruction of previously heard events.

The movement, noteworthy for the amount of participation seemingly unusual for Vanhal, exhibits those characteristics typical of a debate. The first violin is immediately identifiable as the leader of the group; under no circumstances can one speak of a musical democracy. The lower voices are often rhythmically active and at various moments, may offer snippets of material which are used as the basis for imitation or interaction. What distinguishes the top voice from the bottom ones is its continued presence, and the fact that with a sole exception, one must look to the the first violin in order to hear a complete melody. Elsewhere we will hear only snippets or small references.

Lastly, mention should be made of the various debate hybrids which appear in the eighteenth-century string quartet output. Some works incorporate a more consistent melodic independence among all the voices; such activity might best be described as "approaching" conversation. Elsewhere, the various instruments may be more polite in their interaction; for these we may use the term "debate-polite conversation hybrid". The opening movement of Krommer's Op. 5, No. 1[42] is a fine illustration. Within this Allegro moderato, Krommer mingles elements of the debate – give-and-take, imitation, and independent lines – with those of the polite conversation – marked solos and rotation of emphasis. The first violin is

---

[42] Krommer, *Trois Quatuors*...Opera 5 (Paris: Pleyel, [1796]). Printed parts are available at the Library of Congress, Washington D. C., M451.K9 (case).

the most melodically dominant in the stable areas, but it is often paired with other interesting lines. The contrary motion of the first violin and viola lines at the very beginning offers a marked contrast to what might be heard if the latter mimicked the second violin part (Ex. 6.19). Although measure 9 brings a repetition of the

Example 6.19 Franz Krommer, Op. 5, No. 1, Mvt. I, mm 1–8

opening melody by the cello, variety is achieved through the inclusion of cascading triplets in the uppermost voice. The resumption of first violin prominence is highlighted through purely accompanimental lines. Measure 29 brings a viola solo; politeness on the part of the other voices is evidenced with simple and supportive repeated figures that do not require the listener to divide his or her attention. When the cello enters four bars later with its own melody, this courtesy is not extended. Activity in the middle voices intrudes. Up through measure 62, short, alternating solos in the viola and cello are often paired with at least one other active line in any of the remaining two lower voices. Curiously, it is the first violin that has the most regular and repetitious part (Ex. 6.20). But perhaps this is in anticipation of what happens in measure 62. From here to the end of the exposition, that instrument presents the listener with an abundance of figuration and passagework, and leaves no room for competition from the lower voices. These thirty-two measures could easily be found in any polite conversation. The fact that they occur here, in a movement which has exhibited many characteristics of a debate, provides a curious but satisfactory mix of discourse types.

Example 6.20 Franz Krommer, Op. 5, No. 1, Mvt. I, mm 29–61

Example 6.20 concluded

Far from being a monolithic Viennese phenomenon, the debate is a multi-faceted approach, at home in the hands of composers of many nationalities. While the best-known works remain those by Haydn and Mozart, one should not overlook the many examples by composers such as Beecke, Brunetti, Fodor, Giordani, Jadin, Kammel, Kozeluch, and Vachon. The concept of independence achieved and maintained within set roles and functions is one which can be found in any number of works. What makes each unique is how the composer chooses to achieve this goal.

Chapter 7

The conversation

The conversation presents the listener with four interchangeable lines of similar character and requirements. In this sense, it represents the string quartet in its most democratic form. That so few works consist solely of this approach suggests that composers of the eighteenth century thought of this means of discourse not as the ultimate goal, but as just one option for organizing the voices of the ensemble.[1] While one traditionally thinks of the blossoming of the conversation as a post-1781 (after Haydn's Op. 33) development, in reality, roughly the same number of quartets containing at least one conversation movement appear before that year as after (see Table 4).[2] Chronological distinctions (before or after 1781) are more likely to be based on either an individual composer's stylistic traits or advancements in string playing, than the evolution of the genre itself.

Until the technical development of the cello, and to a lesser extent the viola, approached that of the violin, composers were hampered. Once it diminished, as it did during the last part of the century, composers had fewer restrictions imposed upon them and were free to explore the possibilities offered by four truly equal instruments. Consequently, while conversational movements existed throughout the second half of the century, the style of writing changed owing to a broadening of skills.

Equality of voices is a hallmark of the conversation. This does not mean a perfectly even distribution of melodic material. Rather the listener is presented with four comparable lines; roles and functions are minimized. The same type of thematic material may be found in any of the four voices. Similarly, a supportive line, often considered the province of the lower voices, is equally at home in the first violin. Such is the case with the final movement of Boccherini's Quartet in g minor, G.168 (Op. 8, No. 4) of 1769.

Op. 8 may seem an unusual place to find an example of Boccherini's conversational style. The traditional view holds that while the composer's Op. 2 exhibits a remarkable equality of parts, successive quartets turn away from this

---

[1]   Of the numerous quartets surveyed, only four – less than 1% – consist solely of conversations: Richter's Op. 5, Nos 1, 2, 5, and Pleyel's Quartet in C (Ben 319). In contrast, nearly 20% contain at least one conversation movement.

[2]   The concept of blossoming derives from Finscher's assertion that after Haydn's Op. 33 appeared, there was a virtual explosion in quartet-writing, for composers finally had a model with which to work and imitate. See Finscher, *Studien zur Geschichte des Streichquartetts*, p. 270.

Table 4: A Selected List of Conversations [3]

Year	Composer	Title (Movement[s])
1755–9	J. Haydn	Op. 1, No. 3 (3)
1757	F. X. Richter	Op. 5, No. 1 (1, 2, 3)
	F. X. Richter	Op. 5, No. 2 (1, 2, 3)
	F. X. Richter	Op. 5, No. 3 (1, 2)
	F. X. Richter	Op. 5, No. 4 (1, 2)
	F. X. Richter	Op. 5, No. 5 (1, 2, 3)
	F. X. Richter	Op. 5, No. 6 (1)
1759–66	A.-E.-M. Grétry	Op. 3, No. 2 (2)
	A.-E.-M. Grétry	Op. 3, No. 3 (2)
	A.-E.-M. Grétry	Op. 3, No. 4 (1)
	A.-E.-M. Grétry	Op. 3, No. 6 (1, 3)
1760s	F. Gassmann	H.435 (2)
	F. Gassmann	H.478 (1, 2)
	C. d'Ordonez	Op.1, No. 1 (1)
	C. d'Ordonez	Op.1, No. 2 (4)
	C. d'Ordonez	Op.1, No. 3 (1, 4)
	C. d'Ordonez	Op.1, No. 4 (1, 2, 4)
	C. d'Ordonez	Op.1, No. 5 (1, 2, 4)
	C. d'Ordonez	Op.1, No. 6 (1, 2, 4)
1761	L. Boccherini	G.161 (1)
	L. Boccherini	G.163 (2)
	L. Boccherini	G.164 (1)
1769	L. Boccherini	G.166 (3)
	L. Boccherini	G.168 (3)
	L. Boccherini	G.170 (3)
ca.1770s	A. Zimmerman	Quartetto [in D] (3)
1770s	F. de Giardini	Op. 14, No. 1 (4)
	F. de Giardini	Op. 14, No. 6 (2)
1772	J. Haydn	Op. 20, No. 2 (1, 4)
	J. Haydn	Op. 20, No. 3 (3)
	J. Haydn	Op. 20, No. 5 (4)
	J. Haydn	Op. 20, No. 6 (4)
1772/73	W. A. Mozart	K.158 (2)
1773	W. A. Mozart	K.168 (2, 4)
	W. A. Mozart	K.171 (3)
	W. A. Mozart	K.172 (3)

---

[3] See the bibliography for a full citation of each of the listed compositions.

Table 4 continued

Year	Composer	Title (Movement[s])
1773	J. Schmitt	Op. 5, No. 1 (3)
ca.1777	N.-J. Chartrain	Op. 8, No. 1 (1)
b. 1780	N.-M. Dalayrac	Op. 5, No. 5 (2)
	N.-M. Dalayrac	Op. 5, No. 6 (2)
	N.-M. Dalayrac	Op. 8, No. 1 (2)
	N.-M. Dalayrac	Op. 8, No. 2 (1)
	N.-M. Dalayrac	Op. 8, No. 4 (2)
	N.-M. Dalayrac	Op. 8, No. 5 (2)
ca.1780	J. B. Vanhal	c1 (3)
1780	L. Boccherini	G.206 (2)
	G. M. Cambini	T.45 (2)
	G. M. Cambini	T.46 (2)
	C. Cannabich	Op. 5, No. 2 (1)
1780/81	J. G. Albrechtsberger	Op. 2, No. 1 (2)
	J. G. Albrechtsberger	Op. 2, No. 2 (2)
	J. G. Albrechtsberger	Op. 2, No. 3 (2)
	J. G. Albrechtsberger	Op. 2, No. 4 (2)
	J. G. Albrechtsberger	Op. 2, No. 5 (2)
	J. G. Albrechtsberger	Op. 2, No. 6 (2)
1781	J. Haydn	Op. 33, No. 1 (1)
1781–3	J. G. Albrechtsberger	Op. 7, No. 1 (3)
1782	J. A. Fodor	Book 4, No. 6 (3)
	W. A. Mozart	K.387 (4)
1783	W. A. Mozart	K.428 (1)
1785	W. A. Mozart	K.464 (3, 4)
	J. B. Vanhal	C7 [Op. 33, No. 1] (4)
1786	J. Haydn	Op. 42 (4)
	I. J. Pleyel	Ben 319 (1, 2)
1787	J. Haydn	Op. 50, No. 1 (3, 4)
	J. Haydn	Op. 50, No. 2 (4)
	J. Haydn	Op. 50, No. 4 (4)
1788	L. Boccherini	G.214 (1, 4)
	L. Boccherini	G.215 (2)
	J. Haydn	Op. 54, No. 2 (3)
1789	W. A. Mozart	K.575 (2, 4)
1790	W. A. Mozart	K.589 (1, 2)
	W. A. Mozart	K.590 (2, 4)

Table 4 concluded

Year	Composer	Title (Movement[s])
1792	F. Neubauer	Op. 3, No. 3 (2)
1793	F. Neubauer	Op. 7, No. 2 (1, 3)
	J. Haydn	Op. 71, No. 2 (3, 4)
	J. Haydn	Op. 71, No. 3 (4)
	J. Haydn	Op. 74, No. 1 (4)
	J. Haydn	Op. 74, No. 2 (2)
	J. Haydn	Op. 74, No. 3 (1)
	J. L. Eybler	Op. 1, No. 2 (2)
	J. L. Eybler	Op. 1, No. 3 (1, 2, 4)
1795	L. Boccherini	G.233 (2)
	L. Boccherini	G.235 (3)
1796	F. Krommer	Op. 5, No. 2 (2, 3)
1797	J. Haydn	Op. 76, No. 1 (4)
	J. Haydn	Op. 76, No. 3 (1, 2, 4)
	J. Haydn	Op. 76, No. 4 (1)
	J. Haydn	Op. 76, No. 5 (1)
	J. Haydn	Op. 76, No. 6 (1, 2, 4)
	F. Krommer	Op. 7, No. 3 (2)

approach and rely on a more homophonic/first-violin dominated texture.[4] To a certain extent, this perception is correct. Op. 8, consisting of six three-movement quartets, does require a highly skilled first violinist; the remaining voices can often be executed by amateurs with limited skill. Furthermore, the traditional roles of dominant first violin, texture-enriching second violin and viola, and foundational cello are present much of the time. But the composer does not completely forsake the method so consistently used in his earlier set. Rather he strategically employs this equality of voices at appropriate times to present the listener with an alternative form of instrumental interaction. While Op. 8, No. 1 (G.165) in D Major offers three lecture movements, Op. 8, No. 2 (G.166) in c minor only slightly deviates from this plan by including a conversation between the upper voices in the final movement. The third quartet (G.167) returns us to the lecture format, but the fourth one (G.168) presents a real change. Although the first movement may still be considered a lecture, the lower lines are more

---

[4]   Christian Speck, "On the Changes in the Four-part Writing in Boccherini's String Quartets", in *España en la Música de Occidente*, vol. 2: *Actas del congreso Internacional celebrado en Salamanca 29 de octobre-5 de noviembre de 1985* (ed. by Emilio Casares Rodicio, Ismael Fernández de la Cuesta, and José López-Calo; Madrid: Instituto Nacional de las Artes Escénicas y de la Música, 1987), p. 130.

active and distinct. The second movement, a Grave in common time, is a polite conversation between the outer voices. The third movement, an Allegro non troppo to which we will return, is different still: a conversation. The fifth quartet of the set, G.169, once again contains three lecture movements. The only exception is the trio of the middle movement; the conversational interlude provides a strong contrast to the surrounding homophony. The final work of the collection, G.170, emphasizes the extremes of interaction. From the violin-dominated texture of the first two movements to the four-part equality of the final one, Boccherini once again uses discourse types to provide direction to the work as a whole.

These non-lecture movements are strategically placed to highlight conclusions of compositions and to provide relief from what would otherwise be a series of uniform textures. In his conversations, such as the final movement of G.168,[5] Boccherini forgoes the virtuosity found elsewhere and instead creates four lines of similar character. Rarely does one voice dominate. Musical ideas pass fluidly and seamlessly from one voice to another to fashion a tightly knit ensemble.

The opening of the g minor Allegro non troppo (G.168, iii) immediately calls our attention to the melodic unit formed by the lower voices; the top line provides a rhythmic ornament. Measure 7 introduces a syncopated discussion between the first violin and cello; the inner voices, while supportive, are truly independent. The parts assume both a rhythmic and intervallic autonomy; neither mirrors the other nor the outer ones. The second violin, moving for the most part in disjunct half notes, is offset by the more sustained conjunct motion of the viola. Both these parts contrast with the quicker surface rhythm of the outer voices. Although the first violin and cello move primarily in quarters, the syncopation of the two parts produces a quicker composite rhythm.

Measure 17 introduces the democratic sharing so characteristic of a conversation. A melodic idea is found first in the second violin; before the thought is completed the first violin enters with the same material, followed quickly by the viola and cello (Ex. 7.1). This continuous interaction between the voices produces a texture and timbre which differs from what has been presented earlier and foreshadows the high degree of integration which remains constant up to the close of the first half. Measure 25 reduces the first violin to a sustained pitch while the second violin and cello continue to move. The viola, meanwhile, provides an intermediate level of activity; its half notes recall the surface rhythm and mood of the opening of the movement. Two measures later the violins switchparts. The surface rhythm of the middle voices increases in measure 29; this quicker movement is offset by the cello part, which assumes the role

---

5   Reproduced in modern edition in Luigi Boccherini, *Sei Quartetti per Archi* (ed. by Enrico Polo; Milan: Ricordi, 1928).

Example 7.1 Luigi Boccherini, G.168, Mvt. III, mm 17–24

previously occupied by the viola. The first violin, drawn also from the opening measures, provides an accompaniment.

Measure 33 reveals how easily Boccherini moves material from voice to voice. The line played by the cello is now found in the second violin; the second violin part appears in the viola; and the viola part has moved to the cello. Only the first violin retains its original notes (compare Examples 7.2a and 7.2b).

Example 7.2a Luigi Boccherini, G.168, Mvt. III, mm 29–30

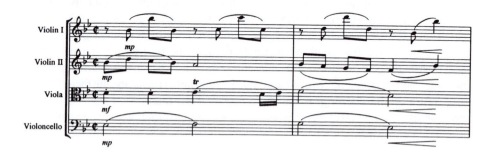

Example 7.2b Luigi Boccherini, G.168, Mvt. III, mm 33–34

The second half of the movement follows a familiar path. After a repetition of the first sixteen measures, with alterations made for the modulation to the relative major, Boccherini produces a sixteen-measure insert based on, but not identical to, measures 17–24. This successful reminder of the previously heard four-part equality means that the listener constantly follows an idea from instrument to instrument. Measure 69 returns us to material we have already heard and from here to the closing of the movement, Boccherini reviews bars 17–36. The same fluidity and interchangeability of parts found in the first half are also present here. The consistent sharing of melodic material ensures that the listener will not focus on a particular instrument for more than a measure or two. Likewise, the lack of uniformity in each of the parts precludes us from assigning a function and role to each part. It is these characteristics which allow the observer to view the movement as a conversation.

These same features are also present in the first movement of Carlo d'Ordonez's Op. 1, No. 1.[6] In this Andante un poco lento, similar material appears in all four parts. No instrument is emphasized over another. For example, within the first six measures, a single figure moves among all the voices; found first in the second violin, it progresses to the first violin, the cello, the viola, and then back to the first violin (Ex. 7.3). This democratic approach is maintained up to the cadence in bar 12. The next phrase brings a disruption and surprise. The figure presented by the first violin, obviously derived from measure 1, is answered in the following bar by the second violin. One naturally assumes that the melodic fragment will next appear in the lower voices. It remains, however, in the second violin for five bars while the lower voices, with one exception, move in whole notes. The first violin sustains a single E to unify the section. This grounding is something one would normally assign to a bass instrument, but in a conversation,

---

[6]   Ordonez, *String Quartets*, pp. 1–5.

Example 7.3 Carlo d'Ordonez, Op. 1, No. 1, Mvt. I, mm 1–6

the individual voices do not assume a particular role. Thus any instrument may take any function at a given moment. Resuming its meandering in measure 19, the motive makes its way to the first violin where it blossoms into several measures of activity. A small question and answer phrase between the outer voices closes the first half of the movement.

Measures 31–46, similar to a development section, remind us of previously heard material. The melodic snippet, so consistently present during the first half, is just as noticeable here. The listener must constantly refocus his or her attention as movement and thematic material appears first in one voice and then another. Measure 45, the only place where all four instruments move homorhythmically, stands out as exceptional and signals a recapitulation. Although Ordonez does not repeat the first half verbatim, the listener is aware that the events which unfold are familiar. Measures 47–52 correspond to bars 1–6; measures 53–59 return us to bars 13–19. This time however, the upper parts have been shuffled. Yet another reorganization of this material occurs in bar 60; here the viola takes over from the first violin while the cello assumes the sustained pitch previously heard in the second violin part. Meanwhile, the violins now play what was earlier rendered by the lower voices. This sharing of lines is typical of a conversation. Parts are interchangeable; roles are not the purview of a particular voice but instead are temporarily assigned to whatever instrument can best serve that function. After a very quiet section filled with suspensions and a dramatically slower surface rhythm, the first violin temporarily assumes dominance. To balance the momentary emphasis on the top voice, Ordonez closes the movement with a moving cello line under sustained pitches. As this was the only voice that had previously been denied the chance to attract our attention for more than a measure or two, Ordonez now provides that opportunity, thereby ensuring that all instruments are treated equally. The cello, with the final word, concludes the conversation.

Similarities of character and technical demands are typical of the conversation, for both ensure that the four parts are treated equally and none is emphasized at the expense of another. Moreover, uniformity of line prevents the creation of a hierarchy. Finding the same material in all the voices is not the only requirement of a conversation. Even more important is the presentation of four independent voices, all of which are integral to the work. Numerous examples appear in Joseph Haydn's Op. 50 of 1787. The entire set consists of six four-movement quartets laid out in the traditional Viennese order of sonata allegro – slow – minuet and trio – sonata allegro.[7] All parts require strong performers of similar technical ability. The fact that this set is dedicated to Friedrich Wilhelm II, the skilled cello-playing King of Prussia, may well account for the equality of demands.[8] The assumption of comparable facility means that the composer can write conversations that truly engage all four participants. This does not necessarily imply that the same material will appear in all four parts; rather one is treated to an interaction between four distinct and independent lines, none of which take precedence over another.

Such is the case with the final movement of Op. 50, No. 2. In this Vivace assai, the listener must constantly shift his or her focus from one part to another. Duets, short question and answer exchanges, and a rapid surface rhythm in all instruments contribute to the overall playful mood. For example, the opening duet between the second violin and viola is periodically interrupted with small fragments in both the first violin and cello. The second phrase is fortified with a

---

[7] The one exception to this pattern is the fugal finale of the fourth quartet. Most musicological literature stresses the monothematic nature of the outer movements, the development of thematic material from a single motivic cell, and the lack of contrasting themes. Although all are important and deserve careful attention, they are not germane to this particular study and will not be considered here.

[8] See my "Chamber Music at the Court of Friedrich Wilhelm II", pp. 370–80 for a discussion of Haydn's decision to dedicate these works to the King. It should be noted that despite the large number of conversation and debate movements, Haydn does not completely overlook other means of organizing his voices. Several of the movements are lectures; see for example, the middle movements of No. 5 and the final two of No. 6. By incorporating all three types of discourse within a single set, the composer offers the listener an interesting mix of textures.

great deal of activity in the cello in the form of rapid string crossings and pedal points. A restatement of the theme (m 23) comes complete with outer voice interjections. This continuous shifting of activity plus simultaneous presentation of interesting ideas permeates the movement. Even when the first violin seems dominant by virtue of its figuration, the lower parts prove important and integral The continuous sixteenth notes of the first violin in measures 30–50 may unify the section, but the real interaction takes place underneath it. Snippets passed back and forth between the second violin, viola, and cello create a dialogue which functions independently of the upper voice (Ex. 7.4).

Example 7.4 Joseph Haydn, Op. 50, No. 2, Mvt. IV, mm 30–50

Example 7.4 concluded

Pairings are constantly shuffled. This reinforces the importance of all four lines. Likewise, the rapid surface rhythms which often attract a listener's attention, are found in all parts. Haydn does not merely provide a token sixteenth-note passage to one of the three lower parts; he guarantees equal opportunity for all. Much of the development follows this path. After the initial phrase, the viola comes forward with twelve measures of continuous sixteenth-note passagework. This is succeeded by thirteen measures highlighting the second violin, which in turn yield to four measures of the first violin. Shorter two-measure segments move between the two violins and cello before the sixteenth notes settle in the viola (four measures) followed by the cello (five measures) (Example 7.5 reproduces this section). Only then does Haydn restrict the continuous movement to the first violin, where it remains almost to the close of the development.

Just as the sixteenth notes move from voice to voice, so too are snippets passed about. Haydn is never content to simply feature one part or another; instead he combines longer lines of quick surface rhythm with dialogues consisting of short snippets, thereby requiring the listener to hear multiple parts simultaneously. Notice for example the single-measure "comments" which appear in the cello, second violin, and first violin as the viola moves along in measures 95–106. These same fragments are then redistributed to the first violin, viola, and cello in measures 107–114 as the second violin assumes the sixteenth-note line. This ability to successfully combine seemingly disparate lines without sacrificing the integrity of the individual provides the listener with a fine example of a conversation.

A similar approach – the creation of equal and distinctive parts – was also found in earlier works such as Franz Xaver Richter's (?1709–89) Op. 5.[9] The dating of his string quartets, has been a matter of some dispute. While

---

9   Op. 5 appears in modern edition in Hugo Riemann, *Denkmäler Deutscher Tonkunst*, vols 27–28, Jg 15: "Streichquartett, Op. 5" (Leipzig: Breitkopf and Härtel, 1915).

Example 7.5 Joseph Haydn, Op. 50, No. 2, Mvt. IV, mm 94–140

Example 7.5 continued

Example 7.5 concluded

Kirkendale suggests they were composed by 1757,[10] Jones hypothesizes an earlier gestation of ca.1747.[11] Publication in 1768 (London) and again ca. 1772 (Paris, Op. 5), offer little assistance in settling the question of the original date of composition. These six three-movement works are often held up as "remarkably advanced for their time, with a balance of the four parts presaging the Classical period".[12] Scholars frequently point out that the lower two voices are assigned "real" parts. For example, Kirdendale writes that in these works, "Richter developed a genuine quartet style, not achieved again until Haydn, with motivic participation by all instruments".[13] These thoughts are echoed by Geiringer who states that Op. 5 is in a "true quartet style with independent parts for viola and cello".[14] Common to these writings as well as so many others, is the notion that Richter's Op. 5 is an isolated example of the early string quartet. In reality, this set is just one of many works which appeared during the third quarter of the century.[15] Of greater interest are the unusually high number of conversations. Only the two lectures in both the third and fourth quartets, and two debates in the final one deviate from this approach. This concentration is seemingly unmatched throughout the rest of the eigthteenth century.

The first quartet contains several good examples of the conversation. In the first movement, an Allegro con brio in C Major, no single instrument dominates the group; melodic material appears in all four voices. While some ideas may be

---

10   Kirdendale, *Fugue and Fugato*, p. 27.
11   Jones, "The String Quartets of Vanhal", p. 28.
12   *The New Grove*, s. v., "Richter, Franz Xaver", by Roland Würtz, pp. 846–7.
13   Kirkendale, *Fugue and Fugato*, p. 27.
14   Karl Geiringer, "The Rise of Chamber Music", in *New Oxford History of Music*, vol. 7: *The Age of Enlightenment, 1745–1790* (London: Oxford University Press, 1973), p. 555.
15   One need only consider the works by Abel, Albrechtsberger, Asplmayr, Baudron, Beecke, Boccherini, Brunetti, Cambini, Camerloher, Davaux, Filtz, Gassmann, Giardini, Graf, Gretry, Haydn, Kammel, d'Ordonez, Schmitt, Starzer, Vachon, Vanhal, and Zach.

shared among the parts, Richter also includes give-and-take passages as well as independently conceived lines. For example, the beginning phrase consists of a melodic first violin, a counterline in the viola, and a supportive bass. Measure six finds the same melodic idea now in the second violin; the lower voices remain as before. When the first violin rejoins the ensemble, it is with new material which is immediately echoed by the second violin an octave below. The viola now functions as support while the cello begins its rise to prominence with four measures of interaction with the first violin; this is succeeded by the cello's complete domination. This is shortlived however, as the first violin comes forward and for four measures, the top voice, like the bottom one before it, moves with a much quicker surface rhythm than the remaining instruments. A second violin-viola duet in parallel motion, also four measures in length, is followed by five measures of give-and-take between the upper three lines. Two homorythmic measures effectively halt the movement's progress. As Richter has avoided this texture until this point, the listener is forced to take notice. This homophony is all the more remarkable when one considers what follows: give-and-take between the upper and lower voices followed by imitation. Only with the eleven bars prior to the double bar do we return to the more traditional melody plus accompaniment texture.

The second half of the movement opens similarly to the first. This time however it is the second violin that enters with the melody which is then echoed by the first. The cello and viola retain their original lines, but by measure 65 the viola's role has been assumed by the second violin. Following a short viola rise to prominence, and an extended cello one, the lower instruments share the spotlight. Not content to sit on the sidelines, the second violin intrudes with its own solo which in turn gives way to interplay between the upper three voices. Only with measure 102 does the first violin receive our undivided attention. Duets, rotation of prominence, and four-part interplay continue up to the close of the movement. While Richter may focus on a single instrument, it is rarely for an extended period of time and he does not favor one voice over another. All four voices are integral to the successful rendering of the movement. Whereas one participant may temporarily assume a role, that same voice is just as likely to take on another one shortly after. Furthermore, the same line may well appear in a different part. Thus one cannot speak of specific functions for each instrument, nor can one identify a single voice as most important. Richter presents us with four independent, yet interconnected parts, all of which will require our attention; none can be dismissed as merely supportive. Any opportunity to focus on a particular voice is usually short-lived. Unlike the extended and unhindered solos of the polite conversation, these are, for the most part, short and migratory; accompaniments are varied.

This movement is by no means unusual for Richter. The remaining ones of the first quartet exhibit similar characteristics. Independence of lines, sharing of the melodic spotlight, duets in various combinations, give-and-take passages, and fluidity of function appear in both the second movement, an Andante poco, as well as the third, a Rincontro presto. This final movement in particular, is noteworthy for the independence of lines. While an occasional moment of homophony may intrude, Richter treats the listener to near-continuous activity in all four parts. One is just as likely to find an interesting idea placed in the cello as the first violin. Likewise, a figure – either melodic or accompanimental – which was first presented in one instrument is just as "at home" in another. These features – functionless voices and independence of parts – are what make Richter's quartet such a good illustration of the conversation.

A similar independence of parts is found in the second movement of Florian Leopold Gassmann's (1729–74) Quartet in g minor, H.478. Most of Gassmann's works come from the 1760s once he had established himself in Vienna. The part-writing is not difficult; awkward leaps, double stops, and other advanced techniques are not required. The violins usually remain in first and third positions, and often travel in parallel motion. In general, Gassmann's works are homophonic with the melody in the top voice supported by the lower ones. This gallant style is sometimes coupled with a more learned one and can be found in those works which include dialogues and contrapuntal writing, especially in the fugal finales. It is this blending that Meyer finds most important.[16]   In contrast, Hickman sees Gassmann's significance as deriving specifically from the divertimenti with fugal finales. He notes that since Joseph II was particularly fond of contrapuntal works, Gassmann's efforts were probably destined for the private concerts which took place three times a week in the ruler's apartments, sometimes with royal participation on the cello part.[17]

While a majority of the movements fit the description given above (either lecture throughout, or lecture with fugal finale), the g minor quartet (H.478)[18] stands out as unusual due to the high degree of individuality and interplay between the lines throughout the entire quartet. The opening Grave, which features a conversation between the violins, also highlights an active cello part. Only the viola remains in the background to provide support throughout the movement. The closing Allegro is fugal. Sandwiched between these movements is a conversational Allegro.

Even a quick persual of this movement reveals four lines of similar character and quality (the first half is reproduced in Example 7.6). No part is rhythmically more active than another. Parallel motion between voices is often followed by

---

[16]   Meyer, "Florian Gassmann", pp. 40–3, 68, 131.
[17]   See Heartz, *Haydn, Mozart, and the Viennese School*, p. 412; and Hickman, "Six Bohemian Masters", pp. 41–3.
[18]   Florian Leopold Gassmann, "[Quartets]", manuscript parts, Library of Congress, Washington D. C., M451L5Q3.

Example 7.6 Florian Leopold Gassmann, H.478, Mvt. II, mm 1–60

Example 7.6 continued

Example 7.6 concluded

contrary movement. This reduces the risk of relegating one instrument to the role of mere supporter. Technical differences between the voices are minimal. Thus in general, one is presented with four lines, none of which stands out as more important than another. What is striking is the amount of interweaving achieved through rhythmic manipulation. Sustained pitches in one part are balanced by a quicker surface rhythm in another. All four voices take part in this rotation of movement. Likewise, voice pairings are varied throughout the movement, thereby reducing the possibility that the listener will hear specific roles and functions for a particular instruments. For example, measure 21 presents parallel movement between the inner parts while the outer ones, although paired, work independently. Four measures later, the violins form a partnership as do the viola and cello. This independence of parts does not require highly skilled performers. Equality is available to both the amateur and professional string quartet player.

This concept is reinforced by the idea that a melodic figure may appear in any part. This sense of fluidity is most obvious in works characterized by interchangeable musical lines and roles. A particularly good example is the

second movement of Mozart's Quartet in F Major, K. 590[19] of 1790, the last of
the three works commonly known as the "Prussian Quartets". Dedicated to
Friedrich Wilhelm II, King of Prussia, these quartets are known for their difficult
cello parts.[20] Often ignored however, is the demanding nature of all the lines.

The second movement, an Andante in compound meter, reveals a fluidity of
line rarely found in late-eighteenth century works. After providing us with a
simple, homophonic presentation of the melody, Mozart places a sixteenth-note
passage in the first violin under which we hear a repetition of the opening theme.
The second violin now bears the responsibility of not only reproducing its own
line, but that formerly rendered by the first violin. Measure 16 finds the
sixteenth-note figure in the cello. The transference of this line to the viola in
measure 18 is achieved seamlessly by placing the two instruments in the same
register and simply allowing the viola to take over what logically would have
continued in the lower voice. This same type of "handing off" occurs between the
viola and second violin in measure 20. The reappearance of the sixteenth-note
line in the first violin in measure 24 is shortlived as the cello interrupts with its
own repetition two measures later. Throughout this section, the slower moving
instruments have not merely supplied support. Reference, either melodically or
rhythmically, is constantly made to the opening lilting theme. Its simplicity
makes it instantly identifiable. Like the sixteenth notes, this material appears in
all voices, but in varying guises. Mozart makes use of both its rhythmic and
intervallic components (Ex. 7.7).

Example 7.7 Wolfgang Amadeus Mozart, K.590, Mvt. II, mm 9–28

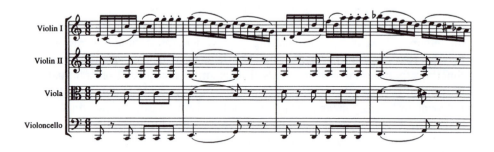

---

[19] The full quartet can be found in Mozart, *Neue Ausgabe Sämtlicher Werke*, vol. 18:
Kammermusik, pp. 535–70.

[20] For an extended discussion of the genesis of these works, see my "Chamber Music at the
Court of Friedrich Wilhelm II", pp. 303–18.

Example 7.7 concluded

This same type of linear fluidity occurs throughout the movement. Measures 48–59 and 78–92 offer both the player and the listener the opportunity to hear again the division of a single line among the four performers. No one instrument dominates these passages. All share common material; a particular line is just as likely to occur in one voice as another. In between these sections, Mozart continues to treat the participants as equals. Small snippets, similar to commentary, may be passed back and forth. Measure 63, for example, reminds us of the opening material. The short Scotch snap in the viola in measure 64 at first seems more like "filler" than something significant. After a modified repetition of these two bars, the viola becomes more insistent that we notice its line. Closer presentations plus a lengthening of the fragment suggest that the listener will have to divide his or her attention among the various parts. Once insinuated into the fabric, the viola commentary is taken over by the cello in alternation with the first violin. It is then the responsibility of the inner voices to maintain the integrity of the lyrical melody (Ex. 7.8). Although the sonority would have been different, Mozart could just as easily have assigned either the melody or commentary lines to any of the instruments. It is this lack of function which makes a conversation distinct from the other modes of discourse.

Haydn also made use of this interchangeability of roles in the trio of his Op. 71, No. 2 of 1793. Opp. 71 and 74, collectively known as the "Salomon" quartets, were written for Haydn's second trip to London and were completed prior to his arrival in that city. They were "the first works of their genre by any of the three Viennese masters – Haydn, Mozart, Beethoven – to have been composed deliberately for the concert hall".[21] Not only were the quartets written with the violinist Peter Salomon's capabilities in mind, but Haydn's compositional decisions seemed to reflect the public arena of the Hanover Square Rooms, the location of the 1794 premiere, rather than the private chamber of Count Apponyi, to whom the quartets were dedicated.[22] In this sense, these works may be regarded as a reflection of London taste and style.

---

[21]   Landon, *Haydn: Chronicle and Works*, vol. 3, p. 458.

[22]   Ibid., pp. 459–61. Much has been made of the public aspect of these works. Landon cites the use of introductions in five of the six quartets, the popular character of the melodies, especially in the minuets, and the emotional concentration in the slow movements as particularly indicative of the public nature of works. Likewise, László Somfai notes the use of the "noise killer" beginnings which effectively alert an audience to a start of a performance. See Somfai, "The London Revision of Haydn's Instrumental Style", *Proceedings of the Royal Musical Association* 100 (1973–4):167. Mary Hunter also points to the sonic qualities adapted to large audiences (audible contrast of melodic material, clear tonal shifts, orchestral sound effects) as significant. See Hunter, "Haydn's London Piano Trios and His Salomon String Quartets: Private vs. Public", in *Haydn and His World* (ed. by Elaine Sisman; Princeton: Princeton University Press, 1997), pp. 103–4.

Example 7.8 Wolfgang Amadeus Mozart, K.590, Mvt. II, mm 63–77

Haydn set out to write works different in tone than his earlier quartets. Although the first violin is often dominant and there are few "solos" for the lower voices, one finds that the string quartet is treated differently – the first violin heads a unified entity.[23] While a majority of the movements are debates and thus support the idea of first violin leadership, there are several fine examples of conversations which give a hint as to how the composer treated this type of discourse within a public forum.[24]

The Trio of Op. 71, No. 2 is a particularly good example (reproduced in Example 7.9). Within a mere twenty measures, Haydn, using the same material in each voice, creates a conversation among equals. No instrument has an assigned role. The same two-note motive, either in quarter or dotted half notes, appears in all four parts. The fact that a melodic idea is not unique to one part but rather shows up in all four lines supports the notion of functionless and interchangeable voices.

The trio begins with dotted half notes in the violins over a quicker moving viola. Because the three parts do not start simultaneously, the listener receives the impression of a viola which weaves in and out of the more sedate violins. Initially, the upward half step movement found in the violins mirrors, in augmentation, the contour of the viola line. The expansion of the violin interval to a leap upward of a fourth in the second half of the phrase adds variety. When the first violin assumes the viola line, it does so with modification. Moving now in descending half steps, it weaves in and out of the lower three voices which produce the more sustained line. The second half of the trio returns the sustained half-step movement to the uppermost line while the lower parts work with the quarter-note version of the motive. The snippet, presented in both ascending and descending form, is passed back and forth between the second violin, viola, and cello. It is only during the last four measures that the first violin takes its turn with the quarter notes; the middle voices, moving in parallel motion descend stepwise. The silence of the cello is a subtle reminder of the Trio's opening.

A similar approach to functionless writing is found in the first movement of Brunetti's A Major Quartet.[25] In the Allegretto Maestoso, each of the four participants takes on a variety of roles and functions. Because melodic material moves from voice to voice, each part shares an equal responsibility for the integrity of the line. Moreover, support and foundation are rendered not just by the traditional bass line, but by all of the four voices. This fluidity can be illustrated with an examination of just one figure, which is first presented in bars

---

[23] McVeigh, *Concert Life in London*, p. 105.
[24] Ibid. The public aspect of the debate is seen with the extroverted exchange of motives, and the many orchestral effects and contrasts.
[25] Manuscript score, Bibliothèque nationale, Paris, Ms 1636, 4.

Example 7.9 Joseph Haydn, Op. 71, No. 2, Trio

30-33. The various components of this short section are subjected to a variety of permutations throughout the movement. Thus the viola and cello sixteenth-note give-and-take passage is initially accompanied by the violins (Ex. 7.10a). When this figure returns in measures 58–62, the upper and lower voices have exchanged parts (Ex. 7.10b). Measures 95–98 again remind us of this previously heard material, but the sixteenth notes are now in the middle voices, while the accompanying eighth notes appear in the outer parts (Ex. 7.10c). Like bars 58–62, measures 115–119 require a rearrangement from the most recent presentation of this passage (Ex. 7.10d). The final appearance of this figure occurs in the recapitulation in bars 145–148; here we are reminded of the second hearing of this figure (Ex. 7.10e). Although Brunetti provides us with the same material many times over, he successfully alters the sonority by varying the voicing. This shuffling of lines is only possible when members of the ensemble are not restricted to either a particular function or role.

If the appearance of the same material in all voices is one of the characterizing features of a conversation, then the fugue represents the purest form of this discourse type.[26] In such movements, each of the four parts shares in the presentation of the subject (and countersubject); one cannot predict the location of the melody at any given moment. In essence, the listener hears four equal participants, each of which vies for his or her attention. The difference between the fugue and the other types of conversations discussed above is that with the

Example 7.10a Gaetano Brunetti, Quartet in A Major, Mvt. I, mm 30–33

---

[26]   For the best discussion of the fugue in chamber music during the second half of the eighteenth century, see Kirkendale, *Fugue and Fugato*.

Example 7.10b Gaetano Brunetti, Quartet in A Major, Mvt. I, mm 58–62

Example 7.10c Gaetano Brunetti, Quartet in A Major, Mvt. I, mm 95–98

Example 7.10d Gaetano Brunetti, Quartet in A Major, Mvt. I, mm 115–119

Example 7.10e Gaetano Brunetti, Quartet in A Major, Mvt. I, mm 145–148

former, one is likely to hear a continuous presentation of the subject but in various forms – i.e., in augmentation or diminution, different registers, stretto, etc. One might liken this to an argument where the bystander hears different versions of the same idea; one's attention must be divided among all four members of the group. Even the words commonly used to discuss a fugue – subject and countersubject – suggest an argumentative nature.

The fugal finales of Haydn's Op. 20, Nos 2, 5, and 6 of 1772, have generated much discussion and often with different conclusions. One camp saw this set as the culmination of Haydn's compositional quartet crisis. Initially discussed by Blume as a highly radical set, Op. 20 came to represent, for Finscher, Haydn's breaking point. In the work of both musicologists, the effort to present a dialogue between the four participants led to a tragic conflict which, if left unresolved, would have produced disorder and disintegration.[27]

In contrast, Kirkendale viewed these particular works not as abortive essays, but rather as a "crowning glory of a repertory legitimized by long tradition". The fact that Haydn's following quartets did not contain fugal finales did not in any way diminish the earlier ones' value or relegate them to experimental status.[28] Rather, they were simply part of a longstanding tradition. A number of composers had chosen this format for the finales of their chamber works; one need only consider those that concluded quartets by Albrechtsberger, Avison, Boccherini, David, Filtz, Gassmann, Gretry, Holzbauer, Krommer, Ordonez, Monn, Mozart, Schuster, Vanhal, and Werner to realize that the use of such a form was a long-standing tradition and certainly not the landmark event suggested by Finscher.[29]

Common to both sides is the concentration on the formal aspect. While Finscher focuses on the fugue as essentially "motivische Arbeit gone astray", Kirkendale looks at the inclusion of the fugue as a compositional choice. Texture and relationship of the voices are usually secondary considerations and remarked upon only in passing. Of interest however are the comments of Moe and Heartz, both of whom describe the voices as independent and equal.[30] Along with Webster,[31] these researchers see the achievement of equality as a result of the

---

[27] See Blume, "Josef Haydns künstlerische Persönlichkeit", pp. 38–9; and Finscher, *Studien zur Geschichte*, pp. 218–20. Finscher's ideas are essentially repeated in Konold, *The String Quartet*, pp. 32, 37.

[28] Kirkendale, *Fugue and Fugato*, pp. 141–2.

[29] For a listing of the composers that used fugal finales during the second half of the eighteenth century, see the chart provided in Kirkendale, *Fugue and Fugato*, pp. 58–9.

[30] Moe, "The Significance of Haydn's Op. 33", p. 446, observes that with equality of voices found in Op. 20, Haydn achieves a true quartet texture for the first time. Heartz, *Haydn, Mozart, and the Viennese School*, p. 346, describes the four voices as "partners [who] discuss all manner of subjects".

[31] Webster, "The Bass Part in Haydn's Early String Quartets", pp. 326–8.

liberation of the cello from the bass line function. By providing that instrument with more mobility, a greater opportunity to participate in thematic work, and the responsibility for melodic material, the original notion of roles and functions for each of the four instruments is altered.

While the fugue may be considered the best representation of egalitarianism in chamber music, there are a number of conversation movements in the eighteenth-century quartet repertoire that incorporate this concept but are not wholly restricted to it. In works such as Boccherini's G.206, Mozart's K.387 and K.590, Haydn's Op. 76, No. 1, and Krommer's Op. 5, No. 2, we find fine illustrations of what happens when the same material appears in some or all of the voices. Perhaps inspired by the potential of true four-part equality, these composers created partnership settings in which identical or near-identical ideas are suitable to any of the four voices. In doing so, they altered the listener's traditional expectations.[32]

This similarity of part-writing appears in the final movement of Krommer's Op. 5, No. 2 of 1796. Even from the very beginning, one realizes that the melodic leadership will not be restricted to the first violin. After an initial presentation of the rondo theme by the first violin with unobtrusive accompaniment, we hear the same material but with different voicing. The melody is presented by the second violin, but now an octave lower. Meanwhile, the line formerly played by the second violin has been assumed by the viola and cello, while the first violin repeats the line previously heard in the cello. In the following sixteen bars, Krommer rearranges the parts yet again: measure 17 finds the thematic material now in the cello; eight measures later, the viola provides us with a final recurrence (Ex. 7.11). Such repetition ensures that no single instrument dominates; furthermore, by using the same line four times over, Krommer prevents a single instrument from emerging as the most technically advanced. Likewise, in the minore section, each instrument is assigned two types of figuration: repeated eighth notes, clearly accompanimental, and stepwise eighths, which form the basis for dialogue, especially between the outer voices. As in the presentation of the rondo theme, the same type of melodic material appears in all voices. Differences are minimal and can be attributed more to the natural register of each instrument rather than compensation for an individual's technical ability.

---

[32]   One reason this is possible is that during the fourth quarter of the eighteenth century, cello technique had begun to catch up with that of the violin. As a result, a composer had greater freedom with regard to the technical requirements imposed on all four voices. For a discussion of the development of cello technique during the last part of the eighteenth century, see my "Chamber Music at the Court of Friedrich Wilhelm II", pp. 122–34.

Example 7.11 Franz Krommer, Op. 5, No. 2, Mvt. III, mm 1–32

Example 7.11 concluded

Mention should be made of those quartet movements which are highly suggestive of a conversation; these works reveal how a composer reconciles his knowledge of the potential of a four-voice partnership with the intent to maintain the more traditional hierarchy and function of the voices. In such works, the first violin will often retain melodic dominance, but the independence of the lower parts is quite marked and consistent throughout the movement. Ignaz von Beecke's (1733–1803), Quartet in C Major (M1) is an excellent case in point.[33]

In general, Beecke's quartets are not difficult, nor are they professional level, public concert type quartets.[34] Gottron's description of these works as "a worthwhile enrichment of the repertory available to domestic music-making" is quite apt.[35] None of the lines calls for an instrumentalist with great skill; even the first violin part, often the one voice requiring the most technical proficiency, can be performed by the average amateur. A majority of these quartets are laid out in four movements, and most are lectures. But even here, within the domestic music-making setting, movement types can be, and are, varied to explore the possibilities inherent in the combination of four voices. With the inclusion of one

[33] A modern edition appears in Fiona Little, *The String Quartet at the Oettingen-Wallerstein Court: Ignaz von Beecke and His Contemporaries*, vol. 2 (New York: Garland Publishing, Inc., 1989), pp. 4–17. Manuscript parts are held by the Staatsbibliothek zu Berlin Preußischer Kulturbesitz, M236.

[34] Of Beecke's quartets, three allow for the replacement of the first violin by either a flute or oboe. These three form part of a set housed at the Staatsbibliothek zu Berlin Preußischer Kulturbesitz, manuscript parts, M225, Nos 1, 3, and 5. They are also catalogued separately as M226, 228, and 230. Twelve of the remaining fifteen have been reproduced in modern edition in volume two of Little's *The String Quartet at the Oettingen-Wallerstein Court: Ignaz von Beecke and His Contemporaries*.

[35] Quoted in *The New Grove*, s. v. "Beecke, (Notger) Ignaz (Franz) von" by Ian Spink, p. 351, from A. Gottron's forward to *Hortus Musicus* (no. 6), vol. 170.

fugal movement, several debates, a handful of lecture hybrids and one near-conversation, Beecke offers textural variety to both the performer and listener.

Although all the works are worthy of study, it is the opening of the String Quartet in C Major which is of primary interest here. This sonata form movement, complete with slow introduction, contains four independent and integrated voices. What distinguishes this movement from a "true" conversation is the fact that the first violin consistently remains in the forefront. If dialogue occurs, it is between the first violin and another instrument. If only one voice executes a melody, it will surely be in the uppermost part. This movement differs from a debate in that not only are the voices independent throughout the movement, but the interplay is not so restricted to particular sections.

The introductory larghetto e maestoso begins with a unison/octave doubling immediately followed by interplay. Throughout this slow beginning, small exchanges between all or some of the voices alternate with passages which emphasize the first violin. This contrast of integration and domination ensures that the listener hears the four lines as part of a hierarchy even before the movement proper begins. Interplay is tempered by the imposition of functions. The Allegro maestoso, which begins in measure 33, reminds us of this hierarchy by presenting a melodic first violin, a repetitive but active second violin, and downbeat punctuation in the lower voices. Once established, Beecke frees the instruments and provides interesting parts for all four lines. The introduction of a dolce melody in bar 36 offers the lower voices a chance to weave in and out of the first violin line. Meanwhile, the second violin continues with its steady sixteenth notes; patterns, however, are varied to add another dimension to the texture (Ex. 7.12). Throughout the exposition, Beecke treats the four parts as independent and equal. The melody remains for the most part in the first violin.

Example 7.12   Ignaz von Beecke, Quartet in C Major (M1), Mvt. I, mm 33–41

Example 7.12 concluded

The remaining voices can be heard engaging in give-and-take either with the first violin or with each other; alternatively, the sixteenth-note pattern first heard in the second violin travels from one part to another. Periodically, the busy texture lapses into short passages of homophony. In these instances, the first violin continues with the thematic material, while the lower ones support with a simple and unobtrusive accompaniment.

The short eleven-measure development (mm 92–102), with its near lecture-like setting, offers a respite from the activity of the exposition. The foundational character of the cello is unmistakable as is the texture-enriching function of the second violin and viola. The first violin, with its rhythmic and melodic variety, naturally draws our attention. The roles of each part are maintained as we enter enter the recapitulation in bar 103 for here, as with the start of the exposition, we are reminded of the previously established hierarchy. The remainder of the recapitulation, which closely follows the path laid out in the exposition, again reveals the conversational aspect of this movement. This movement is a curious mix of conversation, lecture, and even debate. Textures are manipulated to provide direction. The alternation of lecture and conversation in the slow introduction create a musical tension which is resolved only with the four measures of lecture at the start of the exposition. The conversational debate propels the movement forward; only with the first-violin dominated development does the listener have a chance to catch his or her breath. Similarly, the four-voice independence, which dominates the recapitulation, culminates only with the homorhythmic closing of the final measures. The preponderance of passages characterized by active participation by all members of the ensemble allows us to describe the movement as conversational. Conversely, the presence of first-violin dominated phrases, especially at structurally strategic spots requires a modification of discourse category; the term "approaching conversation" reflects this contrast.

A similar "near conversation" appears in the middle movement of Cambini's Quartet in g minor, Op. 11, No. 3 (T.45).[36] In this three-part Adagio set in the work's parallel major of G, the listener is fully aware of the first violin melody in the A sections, and the cello solo in the contrasting B portion. Left unqualified, this description suggests a two-voice polite conversation. The second violin and viola however, do not merely offer unobtrusive support. Especially during the A sections, their lines are very active and compete for our attention. Only with the cello melody and the most elaborate portions of the first violin theme do they recede into the background. Thus, like Beecke, Cambini manipulates texture in order to provide direction and structure in his movement. The conversational outer sections enclose the inner homophonic one. The large amount of interplay, at least between the upper three voices, suggests that the term conversational is a reasonable option. The inconsistency imposed by the appearance of a cello solo in the middle section, reminiscent of the polite conversation, requires that we temper the discourse categorization (Example 7.13 reproduces the entire movement).

---

[36] [Giuseppi] Cambini, *Six Quatuors Concertants Pour Deux Violons, Alto, et Basse*...Oeuvre XI (Paris: Sieber, [1780]). Printed parts are available at the Library of Congress, Washington D. C., M452 C18 T.43–45.

Example 7.13 Giuseppe Maria Cambini, Op. 11, No. 3 (T.45), Mvt. II

Example 7.13 continued

Example 7.13 concluded

In addition, one may mention the many quartets which, although conversational in nature, do not fully incorporate all four voices. In works such as Neubauer's Op. 7, No. 2 of 1793, the outer movements feature a two-voice conversation between the first violin and viola, while the second violin and cello offer support.[37] Karl Friedrich Abel's Op. 8, Nos 5 and 6 of 1769, are three-voice conversations; the foundational cello supports the interplay of the upper instruments.[38]

---

[37]   F[ranz] Neubauer, *Trois Quatuors pour deux violons, alto, et violoncello.* . . Oeuvre 7 (Paris: Offenbach, Andre, [1793]). Printed parts are available at the Sächsische Landesbibliothek, Dresden, Mus 4040 P2. Richard Sjoerdsma has pointed out that the first and third quartets of Op. 7 are revisions of the fourth and first ones respectively of Op. 6. For a discussion of this, see Sjoerdsma, "The Instrumental works of Franz Christoph Neubauer", pp. 109–10.

[38]   [Karl Friedrich] Abel, *Six Quatuor pour deux Violons, Alto et Basse.* . . Op. 8 (Lion: de la Chevardiere, [1769]). Abel (1723–87) was one of the premiere gambists of his day. By 1743, he served as gambist under Hasse in the Dresden court orchestra; the following decade he toured Europe and by 1758, had settled in London. Within five years he became closely allied with Johann Christian Bach; this collaboration led to the famous Bach-Abel concert series which ran from 1765 up to 1781. The following year, Abel left London and traveled to Germany. Returning to the English capitol in 1785, he again became active as a performer,

At times, a composer may manipulate all four lines as part of a single unit. In these instances, the ensemble participants will, instead of functioning as separate and equal, form a unified voice. The goal may be to present a special sonority that can only be achieved by the instrumentation of a string quartet. Alternatively, a composer may be interested in working with a composite set of lines that produce a single idea. In either case, the assignment of roles and functions is avoided. Each part is equally integral to the ensemble; the deletion of even one would severely affect both the texture and quality of sound.

The Trio of Boccherini's Quartettino in F, G.222 of 1792, is an excellent illustration.[39] Here, any sense of a hierarchy is carefully avoided. The opening eight bars are really a sonority study. Instead of the melody plus accompaniment texture previously found in the minuet, we are treated to a series of chords. No one voice can claim either melodic leadership or dominance. If executed properly, the listener will be aware of a single sound which has a thickness and dimension achieved only with the combination of four stringed instruments. In contrast, the second half of the Trio is characterized by a greater distinction of the lines. All four parts are active. A melodic phrase or snippet may appear in any voice; its location, although carefully planned by the composer, is entirely unpredictable to the listener. At times, it is difficult to distinguish thematic from accompanimental material for both exhibit melodic and rhythmic variety. The final result is a single entity comprised of intertwined voices (Example 7.14 reproduces the Trio).

It is this inability to assign a particular function and role to any one instrument that allows us to view the Trio as a conversation. Thus rather than restricting himself to the first-violin dominated approach found in the first movement and minuet, Boccherini explores a texture as far removed as possible – one which focuses on unity rather than stratification. Seen in this light, the trio's conversation is neither a momentary lapse nor respite, but instead the second type of discourse found in this two-movement quartet. That it should occupy such a small portion of the entire work does not alter its significance.

This formation of a composite whole from four independent lines is also evident in the Minuet from Haydn's Quartet in F Minor, Op. 55, No. 2 of 1788. Although the six works of Opp. 54–55, which together make up the "Tost"quartets (so named because of their association with the violinist Johann Tost), are often discussed in relation to the difficult, almost concerto-like first

---

taking part in the Hanover Square Room Concerts and the Grand Professional Concerts.
[39] Luigi Boccherini, "Quartettino per due violini, viola et violoncello obbto [in F, G.222]", manuscript (autograph?) parts, Bibliothèque de l'Opéra, Paris, Rés 507/9.

Example 7.14 Luigi Boccherini, G.222, Trio

Example 7.14 concluded

violin parts, they are, in reality not completely dominated by that instrument.[40] Within each quartet, one finds at least two types of discourse. For example, while the first three movements of Op. 54, No. 3 are lectures, the final one is a debate. In contrast, only the third movement of Op. 55, No. 3 is a lecture; the remaining three are debates. Op. 55, No. 2 has perhaps the most diverse arrangement. An examination of the first movement reveals an interesting mix of lecture and debate; the second and fourth movements are straightforward debates. The third movement includes a conversational minuet and debate trio.

In this last-mentioned minuet, Haydn constructs a unified whole out of two ideas (the entire minuet appears in Example 7.15). Rather than moving a single

---

[40] Johann Tost served as violinist at Esterháza during the years 1783–88. When he left for France, he helped popularize Haydn's works. It was apparently his custom to acquire exclusive rights to the newest chamber music for three years during which time any performance required his presence. John Baron, *Intimate Music*, pp. 218–9, hypothesizes that Haydn, knowing these works would likely be presented throughout Europe in public performances, decided to develop an approach suitable for larger concert settings. The Tost quartets were performed successfully in London's Hanover Square Rooms during the 1789 season. For a generalized discussion of these quartets and their London reception, see Landon, *Haydn: Chronicle and Works*, vol. 2, pp. 635–41. For a typical emphasis placed on the difficulty of the first violin part, see Geiringer, "The Rise of Chamber Music", p. 252.

Example 7.15 Joseph Haydn, Op. 55, No. 2, Minuet

Example 7.15 concluded

melody from voice to voice, thereby creating equality through rotation of prominence, Haydn disperses the material simultaneously in various voicing combinations. Although he begins with two voices, each presenting a distinct idea, Haydn soon expands the ensemble to include all four parts. The "a" motive, first presented by the viola, moves to the first violin, to the cello, and then back to the viola in inverted form within a short span of twenty-four measures. Meanwhile, the "b" motive has traveled from the first violin to the viola, and then to the second violin. Because the surface rhythm of each idea is unique, a combination of the two does not merely produce a chordal sound, but rather a thicker, but unified and composite one. One is aware not so much of separate lines, but of the quality produced when they are heard simultaneously.

The second half of the minuet is no less fluid. Staggered entrances based on "b" lead us from cello to first violin to a brief moment of homophony. Small snippets, derived from both "a" and "b", as well as near complete restatements permeate the remainder of this half. The periodic sustained pitches in the cello line suggest a more foundational function for that instrument, but these are short-lived. That there are relatively few such moments highlights the notable absence of roles within the minuet. Although Haydn could have produced an argument by the simultaneous rendering of a limited number of melodic ideas, he chose instead to mold the four independent parts into a unified voice.

Common to so many of the quartets discussed in this chapter is the lack of role playing. In a conversation, the members of the ensemble share the responsibility for melodic as well as accompanimental material. Assignment of thematic and supportive lines becomes a timbral consideration rather than a functional one. That this occurred throughout the second half of the eighteenth century indicates that composers were interested in exploring the possibilities inherent in a four-voice ensemble. That our familiarity is, for the most part, restricted to works of the 1780s and 1790s and to the output of Viennese composers, reflects a need to reconsider our assessment of the genre.

Chapter 8

The string quartet during the second half of the eighteenth century

At this point it is appropriate to return to the argument presented in the first chapter, namely, that the string quartet of the second half of the eighteenth century is not a single entity which reached its zenith with Haydn's Op. 33 and Mozart's "Haydn" quartets. Rather, it is a chamber genre which received the attention of a variety of composers in a number of different ways, not all of which conform to the practices of the Viennese masters.

Because scholars have either ignored or have had limited access to the vast repertoire of the period, our understanding of the genre is filled with misperceptions. More often than not, the string quartet is presented as a unified medium which undergoes a logical sequence of developmental steps. This is due in large part to the fact that Haydn and Mozart seemed to have arrived at certain approaches within close chronological proximity. A survey of their quartets supports the idea that in the hands of these two composers, the medium progresses from the homophony of the 1760s and early 1770s, to the more integrated works of the 1780s. Their later compositions continue the trend toward even greater interaction and equality. The student is thus presented with fairly convincing evidence that the genre moved smoothly from a first-violin dominated texture to a four-part conversation. Many then transfer these generalizations to the quartets of all eighteenth-century composers.

This view also suffers from an insistence on examining the medium from a structural perspective. Those who see the works of Haydn and Mozart as representing the norm, point not so much to their treatment of the voices, but the regularization of the four-movement sequence, the use of sonata form, and the inclusion of thematic development. These features then become benchmarks with which to compare all other quartets. In the process, those works that do not conform are marginalized. Thus this conception effectively ignores not only the Parisian *quatuor concertant* as a viable form of the genre, but also the myriad of quartets that do not bear these expected characteristics.

While many composers may have indeed moved along a compositional path similar to that Haydn and Mozart, the landmarks (homophony, integration, and conversation) may have been reached during different decades. Others seem not to have followed this line at all. Their compositional progress appears to be "in reverse order", out of sequence, or too dissimilar to compare. All too often, these lesser-knowns have been pushed aside as less significant. One consequence of the traditional emphasis on the works of Haydn and Mozart is that we have lost sight of the many other eighteenth-century composers whose string quartets are worthy of attention; many have been reduced to mere footnotes or parenthetical comments. The result is that our view of the eighteenth-century string quartet is skewed. By creating an artificial set of expectations, we all but guarantee a negative outcome when new works are brought to our attention.

It is time to modify our understanding of the string quartet and to develop a new means of examination that will allow all types to be included and evaluated, not in comparison to Haydn's and Mozart's works, but as unique and independent representatives of the medium. While one should not lose sight of the importance of considering structural components, it is more useful to examine the genre in light of the unique aspect which separates it from others: the relationship of the four string parts. Although the use of sonata form may be important to our understanding of how a movement works, this is not enough, for this structure is found in numerous genres of the period such as the symphony, sonata (both solo and duo), masses, and even some operas. Similarly, thematic development, so often closely connected with sonata form, provides us some insight into a composer's compositional process, but consideration of that aspect alone tells us little about what separates a string quartet movement from one in a symphony. A four-movement sequence, also informative in describing the events of a piece, will not give us further information about the contents of a string quartet. These features are more likely to form the basis for a discussion regarding the classical period.

The danger of past practices is that an examination of the eighteenth-century string quartet has become synonymous with one which details the musical events of that time period. In these instances, one might just as easily substitute the word symphony for string quartet. For those that follow this approach, the non-conforming works are simply discarded as either secondary or of lesser quality. Our insistence upon using the works of Haydn and Mozart as the norm has created a construct that cannot be filled with anything *but* works of those two masters.

If instead, we view the medium as a relationship between four independent voices, we see it in a different light. It becomes a forum within which the members interact in a variety of ways. The lecture highlights a single voice with support provided by the remaining members of the ensemble. Each participant is integral to the successful execution of the work; each is assigned a particular function. A lecture works only when these roles are maintained. The polite conversation expands the role of melodic leadership to more than one voice, but only on a rotational basis which is courteous and respectful. Thus, whereas the texture may be similar to that found in the lecture, the sonority will change with each new speaker. In a debate, the functional aspect is still present, but with variation. While the first violin generally retains leadership throughout a movement, the underlying instruments are more active. Their restlessness expands to full-blown participation in certain sections. As the roles and expectations are temporarily set aside, the instruments are placed on an equal footing. Ideas are tossed back and forth; the listener must constantly refocus his or her attention. That these moments of discussion occur in unstable portions of a movement reinforces the notion that such a section is a deviation from the more regularized surrounding ones. Furthermore, the absence of an intact melody, undisturbed by competing lines, suggests this texture is temporary, especially in light of what the listener has been presented with thus far. Common to these three types of discourse is a reliance on role-playing to provide cohesion. It is the degree of subservience on the part of the accompanying voices that allows us to distinguish one type of quartet from the other. In contrast, the conversation dispenses with assigned roles altogether. While one may temporarily label an instrument as accompanimental, melodic, or participatory, these attributes are temporary. The conversation is unique in that any voice may play any line and/or function at any given moment. The ability to predict what line will be heard in which instrument is gone.

None of these discourse types is restricted to a certain decade or quarter century. All appear in string quartets of the second half of the 1700s. An examination of the output of individual composers does not always yield an obvious line of progression. Rather, composers will mix and match discourse types as needed and as most appropriate to meet the needs of the piece, audience, and expected performers.

What did change was the required level of expertise. From 1750 up to the end of the century, the parts for all four players, along with the technical skills needed for proper execution, became progressively more demanding. While initially, the first violin part was generally more difficult than the others and usually required an able player, by end of century, the viola and cello parts had become harder and were less likely to be satisfactorily rendered by amateurs. This was due not so much to the genre itself as to the fact that idiomatic writing for violins, violas, and cellos was gradually becoming more and more similar. As these unique capabilities developed, composers (in all genres) began to incorporate these new possibilities. Thus performers of Gassmann's conversational H.435 did not need to possess technical facility beyond that of an amateur. Likewise, the lectures of Haydn's Op. 1 could be executed successfully with an accomplished first violinist and amateur second violinist, violist, and cellist.

Things change by the third quarter of the century. While not all parts are equally difficult, more often than not, some instrumentalist other than just the first violinist needs a certain amount of skill to successfully execute its line. For example, Bréval's Op. 1 requires a basso performer who can render both solo and accompanimental lines; throughout, he or she must be able to play in the upper positions, cross strings, and execute a variety of bowings and multiple stops. While its part is certainly not as demanding as that of the first violin, the cello has progressed substantially from the repeated quarters and eighth notes of Jan Zach's *Sinfonie* of ca. 1750. This continued incorporation of greater technical requirements is even more pronounced by the last decade of the century. Mozart's K. 590.can only be performed satisfactorily by four equally skilled players. Rapid and difficult passagework is not restricted to one or two instruments, but instead is evenly dispersed throughout the ensemble. Similarly, performers of Boccherini's G. 237 or Giardini's Op. 29 must possess equivalently high technical expertise in order to produce an adequate reading.

These examples run the gamut of discourse types and span the entire second half of the eighteenth century. The appearance of a specific texture is unpredictable and the idea of enforcing a chronology based on the Haydn and Mozart model is counterproductive. Of greater benefit to the student of eighteenth-century music, however, is the notion that as the end of the eighteenth-century drew near, composers increasingly incorporate more idiomatic and advanced string writing. This insistence on greater facility goes hand in hand with the emergence of the string quartet as a concert medium. Thus as the genre moved from the home to the concert hall, the intention to write professional-level works became more obvious and pronounced. Any evolutionary model should embrace the idea that as the century progressed, works became more technically complicated; this effectively reduced the dilettante – initially the main participant and consumer of the medium – to the role of either listener or home dabbler. By the end of the century, the genre became the province of the professional, a position it has maintained to the present day.

That this progression from amateur to professional string quartets occurs in all types of discourse suggests that we need to rethink the way we have viewed the medium. Rather than seeing the eighteenth-century string quartet as evolving from a homophonic texture to a conversational one, it is more productive to acknowledge that composers approached the medium in a variety of ways. Because scholars have focused on the works of Haydn and Mozart as representative of the period, they have missed the multitude of compositions which did not follow that path. Imposing a set of uniform characteristics and an artificially constructed line of development is ineffective and misleading for it forces us to view the genre as representative of musical classicism. If instead we focus on the genre as a form of discourse, we have effectively created a means with which to examine the string quartet *during* the eighteenth century.

Personalia

Baudron, Antoine Laurent (1742–1834).
French violinist and composer; he received his early training at a Jesuit college in his native Amiens. Baudron moved to Paris where he studied violin with Pierre Gavieniès. By 1763, he had joined the orchestra of the Comédie-Française, and three years later, became the group's leader and conductor. He remained in this position until 1822, when he retired on a pension equal to his full salary.

Beecke, Ignaz von (1733–1803).
German composer and pianist; began his working life as an officer in the Zollern Dragoons of the Bavarian Electorate. Beecke served in battle a number of times during the Seven Years War. During this period, he may have met and studied with Christoph Willibald Gluck. Eventually he arrived in Wallerstein with his military regiment in 1759, and was hired by Count Philipp Karl of Oettingen-Wallerstein as a courtier. He was held in high esteem as a music director (Intendant).[1] As an officer, he was promoted to captain in 1763, and then later major.

Boccherini, Luigi (1743–1805).
Known during his lifetime as both a virtuoso cellist and composer; wrote nearly one hundred string quartets. Arriving in Paris by 1767, Boccherini was taken under the wing of Charles Ernest Bagge (1722–91), a French dilettante, amateur violinist, instrument collector, and himself a composer of quartets.[2] By 1770,

---

[1] The court band, under Beecke's direction, included such fine musicians as F. X. Pokorny, F. A. Rosetti, Joseph Reicha, Anton Janitsch, and Joseph Fiala. For excellent discussions of musical life at the Court of Wallerstein during this time period, see Little, *The String Quartet at the Oettingen-Wallerstein Court*; Sterling Murray, "Antonio Rosetti (1750–1792) and his Symphonies" (PhD diss., University of Michigan, 1973); and Jon R. Piersol, "The Oettingen-Wallerstein Hofkapelle and its Wind Music" (PhD diss., University of Iowa, 1972).

[2] *Six quatuors concertans pour deux violins, alto et basse composées par M. le baron de Bagge chambellan de Sa Majesté le roi de Prusse Œuvre 1ᵉʳ* [1773?]. Bagge also composed two quartets in conjunction with the Italian violinist, violist, and composer Federigo Fiorillo (1755–1823). These works, formerly in Berlin, have been lost.

Boccherini had moved to Spain where he was appointed to the service of the Infante as composer and performer. Following the Infante's death in 1785, Boccherini supported himself through the patronage of Friedrich Wilhelm II of Prussia, the Benavente-Osuna family of Madrid, pensions from Charles III and his successor, and publication of his works. He remained in Spain, his adopted country, until his death.

Bréval, Jean-Baptiste Sébastien (1753–1823).

French cellist, teacher, and composer; published his first composition in 1775. By that time Bréval had already made a name for himself as a performing cellist and instructor. His debut at the *Concert spirituel* three years later marked the first of at least thirty-four different appearances at the prestigious concert series. From this time on and well into the first quarter of the 1800s, the cellist was a member of the *Concert spirituel* orchestra (1781–1791), the Théâtre Feydeau orchestra (1791–1800), and the Paris opera orchestra (1801/04–1813/14). His most important compositions – the quartets, cello concerti, and symphonies concertantes – include "many finely wrought lyrical works of high calibre".[3]

Brunetti, Gaetano (?1744–98).

Italian composer, violinist, and conductor; spent most of his adult career in Spain. Having moved with his family to Madrid in 1762, Brunetti entered the service of Charles III five years later as a violinist in the royal chapel. With the coronation of Charles IV in 1788, the violinist became director of royal chamber music, and assumed the responsibilities of collection and maintenance for the royal library. He remained in this capacity until his death.

Cambini, Giuseppe Maria (?1746–1825).

Italian-born composer and violinist; spent his adult life in Paris.[4] Cambini performed at the *Concert spirituel* in 1773; that same year saw the publication of his Op. 1 set of quartets. By 1800, he had produced close to 600 instrumental works, nearly one-third of which were *quatuors concertants.*[5]

---

[3]   *The New Grove,* s. v., "Bréval, Jean-Baptiste Sébastian", by Barry S. Brook and Richard Viano, p. 267.

[4]   Biographical information about Cambini is scarce and filled with conflicting reports. For two of the better references which discuss the myriad of problems, see Chappell White's article on Cambini in *The New Grove,* and Dieter Lutz Trimpert, *Die Quatuors concertants von Giuseppe Cambini* (Tutzing: Hans Schneider, 1967).

[5]   Of these nearly 200 works, several required a flute instead of one of the violins. Due to instrumentation, those quartets were not included in this study. Many of the quartets were probably written for small, private concerts in the homes of the nobility and rich middle class as a surrogate for orchestral music and solo music accompanied by an orchestra. See Baron, *Intimate Music,* p. 183.

Camerloher, Placidus Cajetan von (1718–82).
German composer and teacher; studied both music and theology. Camerloher served as Kapellmeister at the Court of Freising beginning in 1744, and became prebendary of the monastery of St. Veit in 1748; he took a similar post at St. Andreas in Freising five years later. His travels led him to Bonn, Düsseldorf, Paris, and Liège; by the 1760s, he had ceased touring and had restricted his composition to works primarily for church and school.

Chartrain, Nicolas-Joseph (ca. 1740–93).
Arrived in Paris as a violinist and composer with fellow Low Country musicians François-Joseph Gossec (1734–1829) and André-Ernest-Modeste Grétry (1741–1813). By 1772, Chartrain had joined the Opéra orchestra. During the remainder of the decade, he performed at the *Concert spirituel* thirteen times with great acclaim.

Dalayrac, Nicolas-Marie (1753–1809).
French composer known mainly for his nearly sixty *opéras comiques*. His six sets of string quartets were written and issued prior to 1780; at that point, the composer devoted himself solely to writing works for the stage.

Danzi, Franz (1763–1826).
Began his professional career as a cellist, working first in the Mannheim orchestra, and then eventually succeeding his cello-playing father as first cellist of the orchestra in Munich. Danzi later took positions as Deputy Kapellmeister (Munich, 1798) and as Kapellmeister (Stuttgart, 1807; Karlsruhe, 1812). Although his fame derives primarily from his music for the theater, he is also known as a prolific writer of instrumental music.

Dittersdorf, Karl Ditters von (1739–99).
Spent much of his productive years supporting himself as both a violinist and composer. His considerable skills as a violinist earned him early recognition. It was only in the mid-1760s that he began to support himself in other ways: he served as Kapellmeister for Prince Bishop Adam Patachich in Grosswardein and for Count Schaffgotsch, Prince-Bishop of Breslau, and wrote operas for various theaters including Vienna and Brunswick-Oels. He is best known for his symphonies and singspiels.

Fränzl, Ferdinand (1767–1833).
Earned his reputation as both a violinist and composer. The first part of his career was spent touring Paris, Vienna, Switzerland, and Italy as a virtuoso performer. By 1789, Fränzl had accepted an appointment as leader of the Munich court orchestra; three years later, he took a similar position in Frankfurt am Main. After

a series of concert tours beginning in 1802, the composer assumed the position of music director of the Munich court and later, Kapellmeister, in which capacity he remained until his retirement in 1826.

Gassmann, Florian Leopold (1729–74).
Early life is undocumented and open to speculation.[6] We know of music studies with Johann Woborschil in Brüx (now Most) while Gassmann was a youth, but aside from that, the first datable event in the composer's life is the production of the opera *Merope* at the Teatro S Moisé, Venice during Carnival 1757. Arriving in Vienna by 1763, Gassmann served as ballet composer and successor to Gluck. He later founded the Tonkünstler-Sozietät and became that group's first vice president. After his 1772 appointment as Hofkapellmeister succeeding Georg von Reutter, Gassmann reorganized the court chapel's personnel and library. His death, two years later, was a result of a fall from a carriage.

Giordani, Tommaso (ca. 1733–1806).
Italian composer who spent most of his working life in England and Ireland. His father, an impressario, singer and librettist, took the family opera company on a European tour when Tommaso was but twelve years old. By 1753, Giordani had arrived in England, and made his debut at Covent Garden. From this point until his death, Giordani moved back and forth between London and Dublin, supporting himself primarily through operatic productions.

Gyrowetz, Adalbert (1763–1850).
Bohemian-born composer and conductor; began his musical studies in his native Prague. He arrived in Vienna 1784–5, but left the next year for Italy where he remained until 1789. His first string quartets came from this time. The next four years were marked by traveling; in quick succession, Gyrowetz visited Paris, London, Brussels, Berlin, Dresden, Bohemia, and finally Vienna. It was here that he decided to remain. By 1804, Gyrowetz had assumed the position of composer and conductor of the Vienna Court Theater; he retired in 1831. His popularity began to wane during the 1820s as public musical taste began to change; as a result, his final years were filled with financial hardship.

---

6   For example, Gassmann possibly attended the Jesuit Gymnasium in Komotau (now Chomutov) but this is uncertain. Likewise, the early part of the 1740s was possibly spent in Italy studying with Padre Martini. For biographical information about Gassmann, see Hickman, "Six Bohemian Masters", pp. 9–11; Eve Meyer, "Florian Gassmann and the Viennese Divertimento" (Ph.D. diss., University of Pennsylvania, 1963), esp. chapter 2; and *The New Grove*, s. v., "Gassmann, Florian Leopold", by George R. Hill.

Hoffmeister, Franz Anton (1754–1812).
Austrian composer and publisher; arrived in Vienna ca. 1768 intending to study law. He soon gave up this goal and turned to music instead; by the mid-1780s he had opened a publishing house. His business sense was not always as finely tuned as it should have been, and at times, Hoffmeister's desire to compose prevented him from attending to his publishing obligations.

Jadin, Hyacinthe (1769–1802).
Spent his early years at Versailles where his father, himself a violinist and the younger Jadin's first instructor, was employed. By 1789, Hyacinthe had moved to Paris; he performed at the *Concert spirituel* in April of that year and by 1791, was the second keyboardist at the Théâtre de Monsieur. He joined the faculty of the Conservatoire as a professor of piano in 1795, remaining in this position until his death.

Kammel, Antonín (1730 [baptized]–ca.1787).
Czech violinist and composer; spent much of his professional life in London.[7] He performed publically as well as at court as a chamber violinist and violist. His association with Johann Christian Bach and Karl Friedrich Abel led to performances in their concert series, and to joint publications with them.

Krommer, Franz (1759–1831).
Czech composer; received his early training in his native land. His move to Vienna in 1785 was short-lived for employment opportunities in Hungary soon took him away from the city.[8] It was only in 1798, that Krommer returned to Vienna where he assumed the position of Kapellmeister to Duke Ignaz Fuchs. 1810 found the composer serving as *Ballett-Kapellmeister* at the Imperial Court Theater; five years later he became the *Kammertürhüter* to the emporer. Not only did Krommer lead the private quartet which attended Francis II, he was the last official director of chamber music and composer to the court.

Neubauer, Franz (ca. 1760–95).
Bohemian composer and violinist; received his musical training in Prague. Neubauer traveled to Munich, Zurich, and Vienna where he met Haydn, Mozart,

---

[7]   Kammel was in London at least by 1764, for his name appears in Mozart's diary. See Zdeňka Pilková's biographical discussions in both "Haydn and his Czech Contemporary Antonín Kammel", in *Haydn Studies*, pp. 171–2, and *New Grove*, s.v, "Kammel, Antonín".

[8]   Initially he served as violinist in the orchestra of the Duke of Styrum in Simontornya, Hungary; he was later promoted to musical director. By 1790, Krommer was working as an organist at Pécs Cathedral. Following this he became Kapellmeister to Duke Karolyi and Prince Antal Grassalkovich de Gyarak.

Kozeluch, Georg Joseph Vogler, and Paul Wranitzky. During the 1790s, he served first at the Court of Weilburg and then later in Bückeburg.

Ordonez, Carlo d' (1734–86).
Austrian composer; served as violinist at the Viennese court although he held no salaried chamber music position until 1779, when he replaced Karl Huber. Ordonez's official position was bureaucrat (*Sekretär* or *Registrant*) of the k.k. niederösterreiches Landrecht. A founding member of the Tonkünstler-Societät of Vienna and the Masonic lodge 'Zu den drei Adlern", Ordonez was also active as a performer. Burney's writings chronicled Ordonez's participation in a performance of Haydn quartets in 1773, along with Starzer, Weigl, and Count Brühl. His 1774 performance at Count Thun's residence received notice as well. Ordonez's life after 1780 was less well-documented. His pension, which he began drawing in 1783, was obviously insufficient as his final years were financially difficult.

Pichl, Václav (1741–1805).
Czech composer, violinist, music director and writer; spent much of his early career in his native land working as a violinist and music director.[9] By 1770, Pichl had moved to Vienna where he served as first violinist of the Vienna court theater. Later hired by Archduke Ferdinando d'Este as music director and *Kammerdiener* (valet), Pichl remained with this employer until his death.

Pleyel, Ignace (1757–1831).
Austrian composer, publisher, and piano manufacturer. Pleyel's early years were most likely spent working as Kapellmeister to Count Erdödy (1777). He later took a position at Strasbourg Cathedral, serving first as assistant to F. X. Richter and then as his successor. After a brief sojourn in London in the early 1790s, Pleyel settled in Paris where he opened both a music publishing firm and piano factory. Owing to the problems of piracy, Pleyel simply decided to become his own issuer and manager of his works.[10]

Richter, Franz Xaver (?1709–89).
German composer and singer of Moravian-Bohemian descent. By 1740, he was the vice-Kapellmeister for the Prince-Abbott Anselm von Reichlin-Meldegg in

---

[9]   He held the position of assistant music director for the private orchestra of Bishop Adam Patriachich at Nagyvárad, and later as music director for Count Ludwig Hartig.

[10] This venture began with Pleyel's set of twelve new quartets of 1786, which he described as being in "the same style as my second set, but in a different manner". The similarity to Haydn's own public offering of his Op. 33 should not be overlooked. See Marianne Pandi and Fritz Schmidt, compilers, "Music in Haydn's and Beethoven's Time Reported by the Pressburger Zeitung", *The Haydn Yearbook* 8 (1971): 275

Kempten, Allgäu; seven years later, he established himself in Mannheim, where he worked for the Elector Palatine Carl Theodor. An official appointment as chamber composer came the following year. After concert tours to Oettingen-Wallerstein, France, the Netherlands, and England, Richter assumed the post of Kapellmeister at the Strasbourg Cathedral.

Schmitt, Joseph (baptized 1734–91).
German composer and publisher active in the Netherlands; received his music training with Karl Friedrich Abel. Schmitt took his vows at the Cistercian monastery at Eberbach im Rheingau in 1753; four years later, he was ordained a priest. A venture into music publishing came next, followed by a move to Amsterdam, where in 1788, Schmitt was appointed director of the music section of the Felix Meritis Society of Amsterdam, the most prestigious musical post in that city.

Teyber, Anton (baptized 1756–1822).
Spent most of his productive life in Vienna working as a composer, pianist, organist, and cellist. He briefly held a position as first court organist at Dresden (1787–91).

Vanhal, Johann Baptist (1739–1813).
Bohemian composer of nearly one hundred string quartets.[11] Having first studied music in his native Bohemia, Vanhal arrived in Vienna by 1760 or shortly thereafter where he studied composition with Dittersdorf. The years 1769–71 found the composer in Italy where he suffered what Landon called a "religious mania"; other scholars have made reference to a nervous breakdown. His return to Vienna in 1780, where he became known a composer of salon music,[12] was interrupted by a convalescent period in Hungary and Croatia. Vanhal's Viennese activities have remained obscure. He held no official appointment and earned his living by composing and teaching.

---

[11] Landon, *Haydn: Chronicle and Works*, vol. 2, p. 380, refers to this as a "religious mania".

[12] This turn to salon music is often looked upon in a very negative fashion. Landon, for example, refers to this change of focus as a degeneration. Jones, however, offers a different perspective which is more illuminating. He attributes Vanhal's decision not to compose any more quartets to the fact that the composer realized he could not compete with Haydn and Mozart. Their works were simply on a different intellectual and artistic plane. There were also social and commercial considerations. Since Vanhal did not have a specific patron and was not a businessman like Pleyel and Hoffmeister, he simply had to look elsewhere to support himself. This may in fact be the reason the composer turned to lighter pieces. See Jones, "The String Quartets", pp. 227–38, for an assessment of Vanhal's place in the history of the eighteenth-century string quartet.

Bibliography

Musical scores

Abel, Karl Friedrich. *A Second Sett of Six Quartettos for 2 violins, a tenor and violoncello obligato* . . . Op. 12. London: R. Bremner, [1775].
_____. *Six Quatuor pour deux Violons, Alto et Basse* . . . Op. 8. Lion: de la Chevardiere, [1769].
Albrechtsberger, Johann Georg. "Divertimento Imo a 4tro". Manuscript parts. Unpublished. Országos Széchényi. Könyvtar. Ms mus 2395, no. 39.
_____. "Divertimento [V?] a 4tro". Manuscript parts. Unpublished. Országos Széchényi. Könyvtar. Ms mus 2398.
_____. "Divertimento VIto a 4tro en B". Manuscript parts. Unpublished. Országos Széchényi. Könyvtar. Ms mus 2400.
_____. *Six Quatuors en Fugues a deux Violons, Taille & Basse* . . . Op. 2. Berlin: Hummel, [1780].
Altmann, Wilhelm, ed. *83 String Quartets by Josef Haydn.* 3 vols. London: Eulenberg, nd.
Aspelmayr, Franz. "Quartetto No. VII". Manuscript parts. Unpublished. Gesellschaft der Musikfreunde. Vienna. IX 1116.
Bach, Johann Christian. *Sei Quartetti a due violini, alto e basso* . . . Op. 17. Paris: Chevardiere, [1777?].
Barrière, Etienne-Bernard-Joseph. *Six Quatuors Concertans* . . . Op. 1. Paris: Le Duc, [1776].
Barthélémy, Maurice, ed. *A.-E.-M. Grétry: Six Quatuors Op. III.* Versailles: Éditions du Centre de Musique Baroque de Versailles, 1997.
Baudron, A[ntoine] L[aurent]. *Sei Quartetti per due violini, alto, e violoncello obligati.* Paris: Berault, [1768].
Boccherini, Luigi. "Quartettino [in b, G228]". Manuscript parts. Unpublished. Bibliothèque de l'Opéra. Paris. Réserve 507/14.
_____. "Quartettino [in G, G230]". Manuscript parts. Unpublished. Bibliothèque de l'Opéra. Paris. Réserve 507/17.
_____. "Quartettino per due violini, viola e violoncello obbligato [in A, G216]". Manuscript parts. Unpublished. Staatsbibliothek zu Berlin Preussischer Kulturbesitz. Berlin. M590.
_____. "Quartettino per due violini, viola e violoncello obbligato [in A, G218]". Manuscript parts. Unpublished. Bibliothèque de l'Opéra. Paris. Réserve 507/5.
_____. "Quartettino per due violini, viola e violoncello obbligato [in A, G219]". Manuscript parts. Unpublished. Bibliothèque de l'Opéra. Paris. Réserve 507/6.
_____. "Quartettino per due violini, viola e violoncello obbligato [in A, G227]". Manuscript parts. Unpublished. Bibliothèque de l'Opéra. Paris. Réserve 507/15.

Boccherini, Luigi. "Quartettino per due violini, viola e violoncello obbligato [in Bb, G220]". Manuscript parts. Unpublished. Bibliothèque de l'Opéra. Paris. Réserve 507/7.

_____. "Quartettino per due violini, viola e violoncello obbligato [in C, G217]". Manuscript parts. Unpublished. Staatsbibliothek zu Berlin Preussischer Kulturbesitz. Berlin. M592, 593.

_____. "Quartettino per due violini, viola e violoncello obbligato [in C, G231]". Manuscript parts. Unpublished. Bibliothèque de l'Opéra. Paris. Réserve 507/18.

_____. "Quartettino per due violini, viola e violoncello obbligato [in D, G224]". Manuscript parts. Unpublished. Bibliothèque de l'Opéra. Paris. Réserve 507/11.

_____. "Quartettino per due violini, viola e violoncello obbligato [in D, G237]". Manuscript parts. Unpublished. Staatsbibliothek zu Berlin Preussischer Kulturbesitz. Berlin. M610.

_____. "Quartettino per due violini, viola e violoncello obbligato [in Eb, G225]". Manuscript parts. Unpublished. Bibliothèque de l'Opéra. Paris. Réserve 507/12.

_____. "Quartettino per due violini, viola e violoncello obbligato [in Eb, G229]". Manuscript parts. Unpublished. Bibliothèque de l'Opéra. Paris. Réserve 507/16.

_____. "Quartettino per due violini, viola e violoncello obbligato [in E, G221]". Manuscript parts. Unpublished. Bibliothèque de l'Opéra. Paris. Réserve 507/8.

_____. "Quartettino per due violini, viola e violoncello obbligato [in F, G222]". Manuscript parts. Unpublished. Bibliothèque de l'Opéra. Paris. Réserve 507/9.

_____. "Quartettino per due violini, viola e violoncello obbligato [in F, G226]". Manuscript parts. Unpublished. Bibliothèque de l'Opéra. Paris. Réserve 507/13.

_____. "Quartettino per due violini, viola e violoncello obbligato [in G, G223]". Manuscript parts. Unpublished. Bibliothèque de l'Opéra. Paris. Réserve 507/10.

_____. "Quartetto per due violini, viola e violoncello [in D, G233]". Manuscript parts. Unpublished. Staatsbibliothek zu Berlin Preussischer Kulturbesitz. Berlin. M604.

_____. "Quartetto per due violini, viola e violoncello [in f, G235]". Manuscript parts. Unpublished. Staatsbibliothek zu Berlin Preussischer Kulturbesitz. Berlin. M608.

_____. "Quartetto per due violini, viola e violoncello [in G, G234]". Manuscript parts. Unpublished. Staatsbibliothek zu Berlin Preussischer Kulturbesitz. Berlin. M606.

_____. "Quartetto per due violini, viola e violoncello obbligato [in A, G213]". Manuscript parts. Unpublished. Staatsbibliothek zu Berlin Preussischer Kulturbesitz. Berlin. M587.

_____. "Quartetto per due violini, viola e violoncello obbligato [in c, G214]". Manuscript parts. Unpublished. Staatsbibliothek zu Berlin Preussischer Kulturbesitz. Berlin. M588.

_____. "Quartetto per due violini, viola e violoncello obbligato [in C, G215]". Manuscript parts. Unpublished. Staatsbibliothek zu Berlin Preussischer Kulturbesitz. Berlin. M589.

_____. "Sei Quartettini per due violini, viola e violoncello obbto. . . Op. 33 [G207–212]". Manuscript parts. Unpublished. Bibliothèque de l'Opéra. Paris. Réserve 507 (2).

Bréval, J[ean]-B[aptiste Sébastian]. *Six Quatuors Concertants . . .* Op. 1. Paris: de la Chevardiere, [1775].

Brodsky, Ferenc, ed. *Diletto musicale.* Vol. 288: *Johann Georg Albrechtsberger: Quartetto per due Violini, Viola e Violoncello* [in G]. Budapest: Editio Musica, 1968.

_____. *Diletto musicale.* Vol. 291: *Johann Georg Albrechtsberger: Divertimento per due Violini, Viola e Violoncello.* Budapest: Editio Musica, 1969.

Brown, A. Peter, ed. *Recent Researches in the Music of the Classical Era.* Vol. 10: *Carlo d'Ordonez: String Quartets, Opus 1.* Madison, WI: A–R Editions, 1980.

Brunetti, Gaetano. "[Quartets]". Manuscript scores. Unpublished. Bibliothèque nationale. Paris. 1637, 1–6; 1638, 1–2; 1639.

_____. "Quartets [Opp. 4–5]". Manuscript parts. Unpublished. Library of Congress. Washington D. C. M452.B9 (case).

_____. "[6 quartettos]". Manuscript scores. Unpublished. Bibliothèque nationale. Paris. 1636.

_____. "6 Quatuors [Op. 2]". Manuscript parts. Unpublished. Library of Congress. Washington D. C. M452.B9 (case). Also available as manuscript scores at Bibliothèque nationale. Paris. 1634.

_____. "6 Quatuors [Op. 3]". Manuscript parts. Unpublished. Library of Congress. Washington D. C. M452.B9 (case). Also available as manuscript scores at Bibliothèque nationale. Paris. 1635.

Cambini, Giuseppe. *Quatre Quatuors et deux Quintetto dialogués et concertants. . .* Op. 23. Paris: Michaud, [1781].

_____. *Sei Quartetti per due Violini, Viola, et Violoncello. . .* Op. 1 [No. 1]. Paris: Venier, [1773–74].

_____. *Six Quatuor Concertans . . .* Op. 29. Paris: le Menu and Boyer, [1782].

_____. *Six Quatuor Concertants . . .* Op. 7. Paris: Durieu, [1777–78].

_____. *Six Quatuors Concertants . . .* Op. 10. Paris: Sieber, [1778].

_____. *Six Quatuors Concertants . . .* Op. 11. Paris: Sieber, [1780].

_____. *Six Quatuors Concertants . . .* Op. 16. Paris: Sieber, [ca.1779–82].

Camerloher, Placidus Cajetan von. "Sinfonia [Op. 4, no. 8]". Manuscript parts. Unpublished. Uppsala Universitetsbibliotek. Uppsala. IMHS 12:13.

_____. "Sinfonia a 4tro [Op. 3]". Manuscript parts. Unpublished. Fürstlich Oettingen-Wallerstein'sche Bibliothek Schloß. Harburg. HR III4 1/2 4°425–427.

Chartrain, Nicolas-Joseph. *Six Quatuors Concertant . . .* Oeuvre 8. Paris: Sieber, [1777?].

_____. *Six Quatuors Dialoguées . . .* Oeuvre 4. Paris: Berault, [1778?].

Cooper, Kenneth, ed. *Three Centuries of Music in Score: Facsimiles of Scores Made Under the Works Progress Administration.* Vol. 10: *Chamber Music IV: Classical String Duos and Quartets (1760–c.1850).* New York: Garland Publishing, 1990.

Dalayrac, [Nicolas-Marie]. *Six Quartetto Concertants . . .* Op. 8. Paris: Durieu, [b. 1780].

_____. *Six Quatuor Concertants . . .* Op. 5. Paris: Bouin, [b. 1780].

_____. *Six Quatuors Concertans . . .* Op. 11. Paris: Le Duc, [b. 1780].

Danzi, Franz. "Trois Quatuors pour deux violons, alto et violoncelle [Op. 5]". Manuscript parts. Unpublished. Badische Landesbibliothek. Donaueschinger. Musik ms 302.

_____. "Trois Quatuors pour deux violons, alto et violoncelle [Op. 6]". Unpublished. Manuscript parts. Badische Landesbibliothek. Donaueschinger. Musik ms 303.

Davaux, Jean-Baptiste. *Six Quartettos for two Violins, a Tenor, and Violoncello . . .* Op. 6. London: Forster, [ca. 1785].

_____. *Six Quartettos for two Violins, a Tenor, and Violoncello . . .* Op. 9. London: Napier, [ca.178–].

Distler, [Johann] George. "[7 Quartets]". Manuscript parts. Unpublished. Hrvatski glazbeni Zavod. Zagreb. Sign XXIII B, C, D, E, F, G, H.

_____. *Trois Quatuor pour deux violons [,] alt[o] et violoncelle . . .* II Liavraison. Augsburg: Gombert, [1795].

Dittersdorf, Carl Ditters von. *Sei Quartetti per due Violini, Viola, e Violoncello.* Vienna: Artaria, [1788].

Eybler, Giuseppe. *Tre quartetti a due violini, viola, e violoncello . . .* Op. 1. Printed parts. Library of Congress. Washington D. C. M452E97Op.1.

Feder, Georg, ed. *Joseph Haydn Werke*: Vol. 12, No. 1: *Frühe Streichquartette*. München: G. Henle Verlag, 1973.

_____. *Joseph Haydn Werke*: Vol. 12, No. 2: *Streichquartette "Opus 9" und "Opus 17"*. München: G. Henle Verlag, 1963.

Feder, Georg and Sonja Gerlach, ed. *Joseph Haydn Werke*: Vol. 12, No. 3: *Streichquartette "Opus 20" und "Opus 33"*. München: G. Henle Verlag, 1974.

Feder, Georg and Isidor Saslav. *Joseph Haydn Werke:* Vol. 12, No. 5: *Streichquartette "Opus 64" und "Opus 71/74"*. München: G. Henle Verlag, 1978.

Fiala, Joseph. *Six Quatuors [pour] violino primo, violino secondo, alto viola, violoncello obligatti . . .* oeuvre 1. Paris: Heina, [ca. 1784].

Filtz, Anton. "Quadro in G dur". Manuscript parts. Unpublished. Fürstlich Oettingen-Wallerstein'sche Bibliothek Schloß. Harburg. HR III4 1/2 4°710.

_____. "Quatro in A". Manuscript parts. Unpublished. Universitetsbiblioteket. Lund. Saml. Kraus 324.

_____. "Quatro in Bb". Manuscript parts. Unpublished. Städtische Bibliothek, Musikbibliothek. Leipzig. PM 1618.

_____. "Quatro in F". Manuscript parts. Unpublished. Universitetsbiblioteket. Lund. Saml. Kraus 323.

_____. "Quattro in F". Manuscript parts. Unpublished. Universitäts Bibliothek. Basel. KR IV 87 (ms. 81).

Finscher, Ludwig, ed. *Wolfgang Amadeus Mozart:Neue Ausgabe Sämtlicher Werke*. Vol. 18: *Kammermusik II*. Basel: Bärenreiter, 1991.

Fiorillo, F[ederigo]. *Six Quatuors Concertants . . .* Op. 6. Paris: Sieber, [1788/90?].

Fodor, Joseph. *Six Quatuors Concertans pour deux violons, alto et basse. . .* [Book 4]. Paris: Imbault, [1782?].

_____. *Six Quatuors Concertants pour deux violons, alto, et basse. . .* Op. XI. Paris: Bailleux, [1790?].

Förster, Emanuel Aloys. *Six Quatuors pour deux violons, alto et basse . . .* oeuvre 7me. Paris: Offenbach, Andre, [1794].

Fränzl, Ferdinand. *Six Quatuors pour deux violons, alto, et basse. . .* Op. 1. [Paris]: Offenbach, Andre, 1791–1799.

Gassmann, Florian Leopold. "[Quartets]". Manuscript parts. Unpublished. Library of Congress. Washington D. C. M451 L5Q3.

_____. "Quartett A-dur f. Streichinstr., [H475]". Manuscript score and parts. Unpublished. Universitäts Bibliothek. Basel. KR IV 102, ms 94.

_____. "Quartett B-dur f. Streichinstr., [H480]". Manuscript score and parts. Unpublished. Universitäts Bibliothek. Basel. KR IV 99, ms 91.

_____. "Quartett c-dur f. Streichinstr., [H431]". Manuscript score and parts. Unpublished. Universitäts Bibliothek. Basel. KR IV 95, ms 87.

_____. "Quartett Es dur f. Streichinstr, [H445]". Manuscript score and parts. Unpublished. Universitäts Bibliothek. Basel. KR IV 100, ms 92.

Giardini, Felice de. *Six Quartettos. . .* Op. 23. London: Blandell, [1782].

_____. *Six Quartetts. . .* Op. 29. London: Longman and Broderip, [1790].

_____. *Six Quatuors Concertants. . .* Oeuvre 14. Paris: Bailleux, [ca. 1770s].

Giordani, Tommaso. *Sei Quartetti . . .* Op. 8. London: Napier, [ca. 1775].

Gossec, F. J. "Six quatuor. . . Oeuvre 1[5]". Manuscript parts. Unpublished. Akademiska Kapell. Lunds. Saml. Kraus 452.

Graf, C[hristian] E[rnst]. "Quartetto a F". Manuscript parts. Unpublished. Haags Gemeente Museum. The Hague. MS49D3.

Grosse, Samuel Dietrich. "Six Quatuors Concertans". Manuscript parts. Unpublished. Staatsbibliothek zu Berlin Preussischer Kulturbesitz. Berlin. M1998.

Gyrowetz, Adalbert. *Trois Quatuors concertants*. . . Oeuvre III. Berlin: Hummel, [1790?].

Gyrowetz, Adalbert. "Tre Quartetti per due violini, viola, e basso". Manuscript parts. Unpublished. Helikon Kastélymúzeum. Hungary. 1152 H KE.

_____. *Trois Quatuors*. . . Oeuvre 5, Livre 1. [Paris]: Offenbach, Andre, [1793].

_____. *Trois Quatuors*. . . Oeuvre 5, Livre 2. [Paris]: Offenbach, Andre, [1793].

Hickman, Roger, ed. *Recent Researches in the Music of the Classical Era*. Vol. 42: *Leopold Kozeluch: Six String Quartets, Opus 32 and Opus 33*. Madison: A–R Editions, 1994.

Hoffman-Erbrecht, Lothar, ed. *Organum*. Series 3: *Kammermusik*. Vol. 70: *Johann Georg Albrechtsberger: Quartettfuge A-dur*. Köln: Fr. Kistner and C. F. W. Siegel and Co., 1969.

_____. *Organum*. Series 3: *Kammermusik*. Vol. 71: *Johann Georg Albrechtsberger: Quartettfuge C-dur*. Köln: Fr. Kistner and C. F. W. Siegel and Co., 1969.

Hoffmeister, Franz Anton. "Quartetto I–IV". Manuscript parts. Unpublished. Benediktiner-stift Kremsmünster. Kremsmünster. Fasc. G64, No. 265–270.

_____. *Six Quatuors Concertantes pour 2 violons, alto viole et basse*. . . Oeuvre IX. Vienna: Torricella, [1783].

Horwitz, Karl and Karl Riedel, eds. *Denkmäler der Tonkunst in Österreich*: Jahrg. 15/2, Band 31: *Wiener Instrumentalmusik von und um 1750*. Graz: Akamische Druck - u. Verlagsanstalt, 1959.

Hückner, Walter, ed. *Jean Baptiste Bréval: Quartett, Op. 18, Nr. 1*. Locarno: Heinrichshofen's Verlag, 1963.

_____. *Georg Anton Kreusser: Quartett* [Op. 9, no. 5]. Locarno: Pegasus Edition, 1963.

Jadin, Hyacinthe. *Trois Quatuors pour deux Violons, Alto et Basse*. . . Oeuvre 1. Paris: Hedler, [1795].

James, Dianne, ed. *Franz Anton Hoffmeister: String Quartet in F, Op. 14, No. 1*. Wellington, New Zealand: Artaria Editions, 1998.

_____. *Franz Anton Hoffmeister: String Quartet in Bb, Op. 14, No. 2*. Wellington, New Zealand: Artaria Editions, 1998.

_____. *Franz Anton Hoffmeister: String Quartet in d, Op. 14, No. 3*. Wellington, New Zealand: Artaria Editions, 1998.

Jones, David Wyn, ed. *Vanhal: Six Quartets: An Edition and Commentary*. Cardiff: University College Cardiff Press, 1980.

Kam[m]el, Antonin. "Quartetto a Violino Primo, Violino Secondo, Alto Viola, e Basso". Manuscript parts. Unpublished. Stift Einsiedeln Musik Bibliothek. Einsiedeln. 71/13.

_____. "Quartetto I a Violino Primo, Violino Secondo, Viola, con Violoncello". Manuscript parts. Unpublished. Benediktiner-Stift Kremsmünster. Kremsmünster. 120/41.

_____. "Quartetto III a Violino Primo, Violino Secondo, Viola, con Violoncello". Manuscript parts. Unpublished. Benediktiner-Stift Kremsmünster. Kremsmünster. 120/42.

Kapp, Oskar, ed. *Denkmäler der Tonkunst in Österreich*. Jahrgang 16/2, Band 33: *Johann Georg Albrechtsberger: Instrumentalwerke*. Graz: Akademische Druck - u. Verlagsanstalt, 1959.

Knape, Walter, ed. *Karl Friedrich Abel: Kompositionen*. Band 11-12: *Quartette*. Cuxhaven: Walter Knape, 1964.

Kospoth, Otto Carl Erdmann Freiherr von. *Six Quatuors* . . . Oeuvre 10. Brandenburg: Bossler, [1790].

Krommer, Francois. *Trois Quatuors*. . . Oeuvre 1. Paris: Offenbach, [1793].

_____. *Trois Quatuors*. . . Oeuvre 4. Paris: Offenbach, [1793].

_____. *Trois Quatuors*. . . Opera 5. Paris: Pleyel, [1796].

Krommer, Francois. *Trois Quatuors. . .* Oeuvre 7. Paris: Offenbach, [1797].

Krommer, Franz. *Trois Quatuors pour deux violons, alto et basse. . .* Opera 3. Paris: Pleyel, [1793].

La Laurencie, Lionel de, ed. *Nicolas-Marie Dalayrac: Quatuor III* [Op. 7, No. 3]. Paris: Editions Maurice Senart, 1921.

_____. *Nicolas-Marie Dalayrac: Quatuor V* [Op. 7, No. 5]. Paris: Edition Nationale de Musique Classique, 1921.

Lehmann, Ursula, ed. *Das Erbe deutscher Musik.* Vol. 14: *Ignaz Holzbauer: Instrumentale Kammermusik.* Kassel: Nagels, 1953.

Meyer, Eve R., ed. *Recent Researches in the Music of the Classical Era.* Vol. 16: *Florian Leopold Gassmann: Selected Divertimenti à Tre and à Quattro.* Madison, WI: A–R Editions, 1983.

Monk, Dennis, ed. *Recent Researches in the Music of the Classical Era.* Vol. 56: *Franz Asplymayr: Six Quatuors Concertantes Opus 2.* Madison, WI: A–R Editions, 1999.

Mozart, Wolfgang Amadeus. *Neue Ausgabe Sämtlicher Werke.* Vol. 18: *Kammermusik II.* Basel: Bärenreiter, 1991.

Myslivecék, Josef. "Quartettos". Manuscript parts. Unpublished. Library of Congress. Washington D. C. M451M3.

Neubauer, Francois. *Trois Quatuors Concertans. . .* Oeuvre 3. Paris: Offenbach, Andre, [1792].

_____. *Trois Quatuors pour deux violons, alto et violoncelle . . .* Oeuvre 7. Paris: Offenbach, Andre, [1793].

Ondráček, Stanislav, ed. *Musica Antiqua Bohemica.* Vol. 82: *Pavel Vranický: Quartetti per Archi.* Vol. 1. Praha: Editio Supraphon, 1986.

Pichl, Wenceslas. "Quartetto a due Violini, Violoncello, Viola". Manuscript parts. Unpublished. Stiftsbibliothek. Engelberg. MSA567.

_____. *Tre Quartetti a due Violini, viola et violoncello. . .* Opera XIII. Berlin: Hummel, [1788].

Pleyel, Ignace. *Six Quartettos for Two Violins, a Tenor and a Violoncello . . .* Op. 1. London: Forster, [1782–3].

_____. *Six Quartettos for Two Violins, a Tenor and a Violoncello . . .* Op. 6. London: Forster, [1786].

_____. *Six Quatuors Concertants. . .* Oeuvre III. Paris: Sieber, [1786].

_____. *Trois Quatuors. . .* Oeuvre IX. Berlin: Hummel, [1787].

_____. *Trois Quatuors. . .* Oeuvre X. Berlin: Hummel, [1787].

_____. *Trois Quatuors. . .* Oeuvre XI. Berlin: Hummel, [1787].

_____. *Trois Quatuors. . .* Oeuvre XII. Berlin: Hummel, [1787].

_____. *Trois Quatuors pour deux violons, alto et basse. . .* Oeuvre 13. Paris: Sieber, [1788].

Pleyel, Ignatio. *A Seventh Sett of Six Quartettos for 2 Violins, Tenor and a Violoncello . . .* Op. 20. London: Strand, [1788].

Polo, Enrico, ed. *Luigi Boccherini: Sei Quartetti per Archi.* Milan: Ricordi, 1928.

_____. *Luigi Boccherini: Sei Quartetti per Archi.* Vol. 2. Milan: Ricordi, 1928.

Racek, Jan, ed. *Jan Zach: Cinque Sinfonie d'Archi per due violini, viola e basso.* Prague: Artia, 1960.

Riemann, Hugo, ed. *Denkmäler Deutscher Tonkunst.* Vol. 27–8, Jahrgang 15. Leipzig: Breitkopf and Härtel, 1915.

Ritter, Peter. "Quartetto in A [Op. 1, No. 1]". Manuscript parts. Unpublished. Staatsbibliothek zu Berlin Preussischer Kulturbesitz. Berlin. M4678.

_____. "Quartetto in Bb [Op. 1, No. 2]". Manuscript parts. Unpublished. Staatsbibliothek zu Berlin Preussischer Kulturbesitz. Berlin. M4679.

Ritter, Peter. "Quartetto in Eb [Op. 1, No. 3]". Manuscript parts. Unpublished. Staatsbibliothek zu Berlin Preussischer Kulturbesitz. Berlin. M4680.

_____. "Quartetto in Eb [Op. 1, No. 5]". Manuscript parts. Unpublished. Staatsbibliothek zu Berlin Preussischer Kulturbesitz. Berlin. M4682.

_____. "Quartetto in e [Op. 1, No. 6]". Manuscript parts. Unpublished. Staatsbibliothek zu Berlin Preussischer Kulturbesitz. Berlin. M4683.

_____. "Quartetto in F [Op. 1, No. 4]". Manuscript parts. Unpublished. Staatsbibliothek zu Berlin Preussischer Kulturbesitz. Berlin. M4681.

Schmid [Schmitt], Joseph. "Quartetto a violino po, violino secunda, viola e basso". Manuscript parts. Unpublished. Haags Gemeente Museum. The Hague. VII-4151.

Schmitt, Joseph. "Quartetto [in Bb] a Violino Primo, Violino Secondo, Alto viola e Violoncello". Manuscript parts. Unpublished. Haags Gemeente Museum. The Hague. VII-4149.

_____. "Quartetto [in D] a Violino Primo, Violino Secondo, Alto viola e Violoncello". Manuscript parts. Unpublished. Haags Gemeente Museum. The Hague. VII-4149.

_____. "Quartetto [in F] a Violino Primo, Violino Secondo, Alto viola e Violoncello". Manuscript parts. Unpublished. Haags Gemeente Museum. The Hague. VII-4152.

_____. "Quartro [in A] a Violino 1mo, Violino 2do, Viola et Basso". Manuscript parts. Unpublished. Haags Gemeente Museum. The Hague. VII-4154.

_____. "Quatro f dur a Violino Primo, Violino Secundo, Viola e Basso". Manuscript parts. Unpublished. Haags Gemeente Museum. The Hague. VII-4153.

_____. "Six quatuors... oeuvre Cinquienne". Manuscript parts. Unpublished. Akademiska Kapell. Lunds. Saml. Kraus 399. [Exists in published form: Amsterdam: Hummel, {1773}.]

Sjoerdsma, Richard Dale, ed. *Recent Researches in the Music of the Classical Era.* Vol. 21: *Franz Christoph Neubauer: Chamber Music.* Madison, WI: A–R Editions, 1985.

Speck, Christian, ed. *Luigi Boccherini: Quartett in B dur, Op. 2, Nr. 2 (G160).* Celle: Moeck Verlag, 1994.

_____. *Luigi Boccherini: Quartett in C dur, Op. 2, Nr. 6 (G164).* Celle: Moeck Verlag, 1989.

_____. *Luigi Boccherini: Quartett in D dur, Op. 2, Nr. 3 (G161).* Celle: Moeck Verlag, 1989.

_____. *Luigi Boccherini: Quartett in E dur, Op. 2, Nr. 5 (G163).* Celle: Moeck Verlag, 1994.

_____. *Luigi Boccherini: Quartett in Es dur, Op. 2, Nr. 4 (G162).* Celle: Moeck Verlag, 1994.

Teyber, Anton. "Quartetto I–III [Op. 2]". Manuscript parts. Unpublished. Gesellschaft der Musikfreunde. Vienna. 6287.

_____. "Six Quatuors [Opp. 1, 2]". Manuscript parts. Unpublished. Staatsbibliothek zu Berlin Preussischer Kulturbesitz. Berlin. M5441.

Vachon, Pierre. *Six Quatuors Concertants . . .* Op. XI. Paris: Sieber, [1782–6].

_____. *Six Quatuors pour deux violons, alto et basso. . .* Op. VII. Paris: Venier, [1773].

Zehetmair, Helmut, ed. *Diletto musicale.* Vol. 331: *Michael Haydn: Streichquartett Nr. 1* [MH 308]. Vienna: Ludwig Doblinger, 1971.

_____. *Diletto musicale.* Vol. 332: *Michael Haydn: Streichquartett Nr. 2* [MH 309]. Vienna: Ludwig Doblinger, 1971.

_____. *Diletto musicale.* Vol. 333: *Michael Haydn: Streichquartett Nr. 3* [MH 310]. Vienna: Ludwig Doblinger, 1971.

_____. *Diletto musicale.* Vol. 334: *Michael Haydn: Streichquartett Nr. 4* [MH 311]. Vienna: Ludwig Doblinger, 1971.

_____. *Diletto musicale.* Vol. 335: *Michael Haydn: Streichquartett Nr. 5* [MH 312]. Vienna: Ludwig Doblinger, 1971.

_____. *Diletto musicale.* Vol. 336: *Michael Haydn: Streichquartett Nr. 6* [MH 313]. Vienna: Ludwig Doblinger, 1971.

Zimmerman, [Anton]. "Quartetto VI a Violino Primo, Violino Secondo, Viola con Violoncello". Manuscript parts. Unpublished. Benedikter-Stift Kremsmünster. Kremsmünster. 120/35.

Secondary sources

Agawa, V. Kofi. "The First Movement of Beethoven's Opus 132 and the Classical Style". *College Music Symposium* 27 (1987): 30–45.

Baker, Nancy Kovaleff. "From 'Teil' to 'Tonstuck': The Significance of the 'Versuch einer Anleitung zur Composition' by Heinrich Christoph Koch". PhD dissertation, Yale University, 1975.

Baron, John Herschel. *Intimate Music: A History of the Idea of Chamber Music*. Stuyvesant, New York: Pendragon Press, 1998.

Barrett-Ayres, Reginald. *Joseph Haydn and the String Quartet*. New York: Schirmer Books, 1974.

Belgray, Alice Bunzel. "Gaetano Brunetti: an Exploratory Bio-Bibliograhical Study". PhD dissertation, University of Michigan, 1970.

Benton, Rita. "A la recherche de Pleyel perdu, or Perils, Problems, and Procedures of Pleyel Research". *Fontes artis musicae* 17 (1970): 9–15.

_____. "Bemerkung zu einem Pleyel-Werkverzeichnis". *Die Musikforschung* 29/3 (1976): 280–87.

_____. "Ignace Pleyel, Disputant". *Fontes artis musicae* 13 (1960): 21–4.

Biba, Otto. "Concert Life in Beethoven's Vienna". In *Beethoven, Performers, and Critics: Detroit 1977*. Edited by Robert Winter and Bruce Carr. Detroit: Wayne State University Press, 1980. Pages 77–93.

Blume, Friedrich. "Josef Haydns künstlerische Persönlichkeit in seinen Streichquartetten". In *Jahrbuch der Musikbibliothek Peters* 37 (1932): 24–48.

Bonds, Mark Evan. "Haydn's 'cours complet de la composition' and the *Sturm und Drang*". In *Haydn Studies*. Edited by W. Dean Sutcliffe. United Kingdom: Cambridge University Press, 1998. Pages 152–76.

Botstein, Leon. "The consequences of presumed innocence: the nineteenth-century reception of Joseph Haydn". In *Haydn Studies*. Edited by W. Dean Sutcliffe. United Kingdom: Cambridge University Press, 1998. Pages 1-34.

Brenet, Michel. *Les Concerts en France sous L'ancien Régime*. Paris: Librairie Fischbacher, 1900.

_____. "La librairie musicale en France de 1653 à 1790, d'après les Registres de Privilèges". *Sammelbände der Internationalen Musik-Gesellschaft* 8 (1907): 401–66.

Brook, Barry S. "Piracy and Panacea in the Dissemination of Music in the Late Eighteenth Century". *Proceedings of the Royal Musical Association* 102 (1975–76): 13–36.

_____. *La Symphonie française dans la seconde moitié du XVIIIe siècle*. Paris: Publications de l'Institut de Musicologie de l'Université de Paris, 1962.

Brossard, Sebastian de. *Dictionaire de Musique*. Paris: Ballard, 1705.

Brown, A. Peter. "The Chamber Music with Strings of Carlos d'Ordoñez: a Bibliographic and Stylistic Study". *Acta Musicologica* 46 (1974): 222–72.

_____. "Critical Years for Haydn's Instrumental Music: 1787–90". *The Musical Quarterly* 62 (1976): 374–94.

_____. "An Introduction to the Life and Works of Carlo d'Ordonez". In *Music East and West: Essays in Honor of Walter Kaufmann*. Edited by Thomas Noblitt. New York: Pendragon Press, 1981. Pages 243–59.

Brown, A. Peter. Review of *Joseph Haydn and the String Quartet*, by Reginald Barrett-Ayres. *The Musical Quarterly* 61 (1975): 622–5.

_____. "Structure and Style in the String Quartets of Carlos d'Ordonez". *International Musicological Society: Report of the Congress 1972*. Edited by Henrik Glahn, Søren Sørensen, and Peter Ryom. Copenhagen: Wilhelm Hansen, 1974. Pages 314–24.

Brown, Bruce Alan. "Maria Theresa's Vienna". In *The Classical Era: From the 1740s to the end of the 18th Century*. Edited by Neal Zaslaw. Englewood Cliffs, New Jersey: Prentice Hall, 1989. Pages 99–125.

Bruce, I. M. Review of *Studien zur Geschichte des Streichquartetts. I: Die Entstehung des klassischen Streichquartetts von der Vorformer zur Grundlegung durch Joseph Haydn*, by Ludwig Finscher. *Haydn Yearbook* 11 (1980): 204–208.

Brügge, Joachim. "Joseph Haydn, Op. 20, Nr. 2, Capriccio – eine Vorlagekomposition für W. A. Mozart. KV 171, I". *Neues Musikwissenschaftliches Jahrbuch* 1 (1992): 69–86.

Burney, Charles. *The Present State of Music in Germany, the Netherlands, and United Provinces*. London: 1775. Facsimile edition; New York: Broude Brothers, 1969.

Campardon, Emile. *La cheminée de Madame de la Pouplinière*. Paris: Charavay, [1879].

Carroll, Charles Michael. "A Beneficent Poseur: Charles Ernest, Baron de Bagge". *"Recherches" sur la Musique française classique* 16 (1976): 24–36.

Chamouard, Philippe. "Note sur le quatuor á cordes K.590: le morcellement du style galant". *Ostinato: revue internationale d'âetudes musicales* 1–2 (1993): 139–43.

Clark, Rebecca. "The History of the Viola in Quartet Writing". *Music and Letters* 4 (1923): 6–17.

Cobbett, Walter Willson, ed. *Cobbett's Cyclopedic Survey of Chamber Music*. 2nd edition. 3 volumes. London: Oxford University Press, 1963.

Cole, Malcolm S. "The Development of the Instrumental Rondo Finale from 1750-1800". PhD dissertation, Princeton University, 1964.

Constant, Pierre. *Histoire du Concert Spirituel*. Paris: Heugel, Société française de Musicologie, 1975.

Cucuel, Georges. "Un mélomane au XVIIIᵉ siècle: le Baron de Bagge et son temps (1718–1791)". *L'Année Musicale* 1 (1911): 145–86.

_____. *La Pouplinière et la musique de chambre au XVIIIᵉ siècle*. Paris: Librairie Fischbacher, 1913. Reprint edition, New York: Da Capo Press, 1971.

Cuyler, Louise E. "Tonal Exploitation in the later quartets of Haydn". In *Studies in Eighteenth-Century Music: a Tribute to Karl Geiringer on his Seventieth Birthday*. Edited by H. C. Robbins Landon and Roger E. Chapman. New York: Oxford University Press, 1970. Pages 136–50.

Danckwardt, Marianne. "Mozarts 'ganz neue besondere Art' zu schreiben: der Kopfsatz aus dem Streichquartett KV458 (1784)". *Mozart Jahrbuch* (1984–85): 24–31.

Daverio, John J. "Formal Design and Terminology in the Pre-Corellian 'Sonata' and Related Instrumental Forms in the Printed Sources". PhD dissertation, Boston University, 1983.

Dent, Edward J. "The Earliest String Quartets". *The Monthly Musical Record* 33 (1903): 202–204.

Deutsch, Otto Erich, ed. *Mozart: Die Dokumente seines Lebens*. Kassel: Bärenreiter, 1961.

[Dittersdorf, Karl Ditters von]. *The Autobiography of Karl von Dittersdorf Dictated to his Son*. Translated by A. D. Coleridge. London: Richard Bentley and Son, 1896. Reprint edition, New York: Da Capo Press, 1970.

Drabkin, William. "Corelli's Trio Sonatas and the Viennese String Quartet: Some Points of Contact". In *Studi Corelliani V: atti del quinto Congresso internazionale (Fusignano, 9–11 Settembre 1994)*. Firenze: L. S. Olschki, 1996. Pages 119–41.

Eisen, Cliff, ed. "Introduction". In *Recent Researches in the Music of the Classic Era.* Vol. 53: *Four Viennese String Quintets.* Madison, WI: A–R Editions, 1998.

Emerson, Isabelle. "Of Microcosms and Macrocosms: the String Quartets as Crucible for Mozart's late Style". In *Bericht über den Internationalen Mozart Kongress 1991.* Edited by Rudolf Angermüller, Dietrich Berke, and Wolfgang Rehm. Kassel: Bärenreiter, 1992. Vol. 2, pages 664–70.

Engel, Hans. "Die Quellen des klassischen Stils". In *Report of the Eighth International Musicological Society Conference, New York, 1961.* Kassel: Bärenreiter, 1961. Pages 285–304.

Feder, Georg. "Joseph Haydn: Streichquartett D-Dur, op. 64, nr. 5 ('Lerchenquartett')". In *Werkanalyse in Beispielen.* Edited by Siegmund Helms and Helmuth Hopf. Regensburg: Gustav Bosse Verlag, 1986. Pages 70–81.

Feder, Georg. Review of *Studien zur Geschichte des Streichquartetts. I: Die Entstehung des klassischen Streichquartetts von der Vorformer zur Grundlegung durch Joseph Haydn,* by Ludwig Finscher. *Die Musikforschung* 29 (1976): 106–108.

Finscher, Ludwig. "Corelli, Haydn und die klassischen Gattungen der Kammermusik". In *Gattungen der Musik und ihre Klassiker.* Edited by Hermann Danuser. Laaber: Laaber-Verlag, 1988. Pages 185–95.

_____. "Hausmusik und Kammermusik". *Musica* 22 (1968): 325–9.

_____. "Haydn und das italienische Streichquartett". *Analecta musicologica* 4 (1967): 13–37.

_____. "Mozarts erstes Streichquartett: Lodi, 14. März 1770". *Analecta musicologica* 18 (1978): 246–70.

_____. "Mozarts 'Mailänder' Streichquartette". *Die Musikforschung* 19 (1966): 270–83.

_____. *Studien zur Geschichte des Streichquartetts. I: Die Entstehung des klassischen Streichquartetts von der Vorformer zur Grundlegung durch Joseph Haydn.* Kassel: Bärenreiter, 1974.

_____. "Zum Begriff der Klassik in der Musik". *Deutsches Jahrbuch der Musikwissenschaft* 11 (1966): 9–34.

_____. "Zur Sozialgeschichte des klassischen Streichquartetts". In *Bericht über den Internationalen Musikwissenschaftlichen Kongress Kassel: 1962.* Edited by George Reichert and Martin Just. Kassel: Bärenreiter, 1963. Pages 37–9.

Fischer, Klaus. "Einflüsse Haydns in Streichquartetten Boccherinis". In *Bericht über den Internationalen Musikwissenschaftlichen Kongress Berlin 1974.* Edited by Hellmut Kühn and Peter Nitsche. Kassel: Bärenreiter, 1980. Pages 328–31.

_____. "G. B. Viotti und das Streichquartett des späten 18. Jahrhunderts". In *Atti del XIV Congresso di Società Internazionale di Musicologia, Bologna, 1987: Trasmissione e recezione delle forme di cultura musicale.* Torno: Edizioni di Torino, 1990. Pages 753–67.

_____. "Die Streichquartette Gaetano Brunettis (1744–1798) in der Bibliothèque Nationale in Paris im Zusammenhang mit dem Streichquartett des 18. Jahrhunderts". In *Bericht über den Internationalen Musikwissenschaftlichen Kongress, Bayreuth 1981.* Edited by Christoph-Hellmut Mahling and Sigrid Wiesmann. Kassel: Bärenreiter, 1984. Pages 350–59.

Fleury, Louis. "The Flute and Flutists in the French Art of the 17th and 18th Centuries". *The Musical Quarterly* 9 (1923): 518–37.

Garnier-Betul, Michelle. "Les avatars d'un genre elitiste: Le quatuor a cordes". In *Le tambour et la harpe: oeuvres, pratiques et manisfestations musicales sous la Revolution, 1788–1800.* Paris: Du May, 1991. Pages 189–207.

Geiringer, Karl. "The Rise of Chamber Music". In *New Oxford History of Music*. Vol. 7: *The Age of Enlightenment: 1745–1790*. London: Oxford University Press, 1973. Pages 515–72.

Gratzer, Wolfgang. "Mozart, oder? Der Uniso-Beginn in Streichquartetten der Wiener Klassik: Fragment zu einer Poetik des musikalischen Anfangs". In *Mozart Jahrbuch 1991: Bericht über den Internationalen Mozart-Kongress 1991*. Edited by Rudolf Angermüller, Dietrich Berke, Ulrike Hofmann, and Wolfgang Rehm. Kassel: Bärenreiter, 1992. Vol. 2, pages 641–49.

Grave, Floyd K. Review of *Joseph Haydn and the String Quartet*, by Reginald Barrett-Ayres. *Journal of the American Musicological Society* 29 (1976): 323–6.

Grieg, James, ed. *The Diaries of a Duchess: Extracts from the Diaries of the first Duchess of Northumberland (1716–1776)*. London: Hadder and Stoughton, 1926.

Griffiths, Paul. *The String Quartet*. New York: Thames and Hudson, Inc., 1983.

Gstrein, Rainer. "Musik in der *intimité* der salon: Pariser Salons des früher 19. Jahrhunderts als Stätten privaten Musizierens". In *Musica Privata: Die rolle der Musik im privaten Leben*. Edited by Monika Fink, Raine Gstrein, and Günter Mössmer. Innsbruck: Helbling, 1991. Pages 113–20.

Haimo, Ethan. "Remote Keys and Multi-movement Unity: Haydn in the 1790s". *The Musical Quarterly* 74 (1990): 242–68.

Halton, Rosalind. Review of *The String Quartet at the Oettingen-Wallerstein Court: Ignaz von Beecke and his Contemporaries*, by Fiona Little. *Music and Letters* 72 (1991): 642–3.

Hanning, Barbara. "Conversation and Musical Style in the Late Eighteenth-Century Parisian Salon". *Eighteenth-Century Studies* 22 (1989): 512–28.

Harriss, Ernest C. *Johann Mattheson's "Der volkommene Capellmeister": A Revised Translation with Critical Commentary*. Ann Arbor: UMI Research Press, 1981.

Hausswald, Günter. "Der Divertimento-Begriff bei Georg Christoph Wagenseil". *Archiv für Musikwissenschaft* 9 (1952): 45–50.

Heartz, Daniel. *Haydn, Mozart and the Viennese School: 1740–1780*. New York: W. W. Norton and Co., 1995.

Henrotte, Gayle Allen. "The Ensemble Divertimento in Pre-Classic Vienna". PhD dissertation, University of North Carolina, Chapel Hill, 1967.

Hickman, Roger. "The Flowering of the Viennese String Quartet in the Late Eighteenth Century". *The Music Review* 50 (1989): 157–80.

———. "Haydn and the 'Symphony in Miniature'". *The Music Review* 43 (1982): 15–23.

———. Review of *Joseph Haydn and the String Quartet*, by Reginald Barrett-Ayres. *Notes* 32 (1975): 191–3.

———. "Kozeluch and the Viennese '*Quatuor Concertant*'". *College Music Symposium* 26 (1986): 42–52.

———. "The Nascent Viennese String Quartet". *The Musical Quarterly* 67 (1981): 193–212.

———. "Six Bohemian Masters of the String Quartet in the Late Eighteenth Century". PhD dissertation, University of California, Berkeley, 1979.

———. "Vojtěch Jírovec and the Viennese String Quartet". In *Janáček and Czech Music: Proceedings of the International Conference (Saint Louis, 1988)*. Edited by Michael Beckerman and Glen Bauer. Stuyvesant, New York: Pendragon Press, 1995. Pages 185–90.

Hull, Arthur Eaglefield. "The Earliest Known String Quartet". *The Musical Quarterly* 15 (1929): 72–6.

Hunter, Mary. "Haydn's London Piano Trios and his Salomon String Quartets: Private vs. Public". In *Haydn and His World*. Edited by Elaine Sisman. Princeton: Princeton University Press, 1997. Pages 103–30.

Imeson, Sylvia. "Ridentum dicere verum: Reflexive Aspects of Haydn's Instrumental Style, c. 1768–72". *Canadian University Music Review* 11/1 (1991): 50–67.

Irving, John. *Mozart: The 'Haydn' Quartets*. Cambridge: Cambridge University Press, 1998.

Jans, Hans Jörg. "Italienisch-deutsche Beziehungen in der Instrumentalmusik des 18. Jahrhunderts". *Die Musikforschung* 20 (1967): 193–7.

Johansson, Cari. *French Music Publishers' Catalogues of the Second Half of the Eighteenth Century*. 2 vols. Stockholm: Almqvist and Wiksells, 1955.

Jones, David Wyn. "The String Quartets of Vanhal". 3 vols. PhD dissertation, University of Wales, 1978.

Kaden, Christian. "Sozialer Wandel in der Musikkultur der zweiten Hälfte des 18. Jahrhunderts". In *Zur Entwicklung der Kammermusik in der zweiten Hälfte des 18. Jahrhunderts*. Blankenburg: Michaelstein, 1986. Pages 11–19.

Keller, Hans. Review of *The String Quartet*, by Paul Griffiths. *Tempo* 147 (1983): 32–34.

[Kelly, Michael]. *Reminiscences of Michael Kelly of the King's Theatre and Theatre Royal Drury Lane*. New York: J. and J. Harper, 1826.

King, Alec Hyatt. "The London Tavern: a Forgotten Concert Hall". *Musical Times* 127 (1986): 382–5.

Kirkendale, Warren. *Fugue and Fugato in Rococo and Classical Chamber Music*. 2nd edition. Durham, North Carolina: Duke University Press, 1979.

Klingenbeck, Josef. "Ignaz Pleyel: Sein Streichquartett im Rahmen der Wiener Klassik". *Studien zur Musikwissenschaft* 25 (1962): 276–97.

Koch, Heinrich Christoph. *Introductory Essay on Composition: The Mechanical Rules of Melody Sections 3 and 4*. Translated, with an introduction by Nancy Kovaleff Baker. New Haven and London: Yale University Press, 1983.

_____. *Musikalisches Lexikon*. Frankfurt am Main: August Hermann den Jüngern, 1802. Facsimile edition, Hildesheim: Georg Olms Verlagsbuchhandlung, 1964.

_____. *Versuch einer Anleitung zur Composition III*. Leipzig: Adam Friedrich Böhme, 1793. Facsimile reprint, Hildesheim: Georg Olms Verlag, 1969.

Kolneder, Walter. "Zur Vorgeschichte des Streichquartetts". *HiFi Stereophonie* 13/3 (1974): 266–8.

Konold, Wulf. "Normerfüllung und Norverweigerung beim späten Haydn – am Beispiel des Streichquartetts Op. 76 Nr. 6". In *Joseph Haydn Tradition und Rezeption*. Edited by Georg Feder, Heinrich Hüschen, and Ulrich Tank. Regensburg: Gustav Bosse Verlag, 1985. Pages 54–73.

_____. *The String Quartet, from its Beginnings to Franz Schubert*. Translated by Susan Hellauer. New York: Heinrichshofen, 1983.

Kreyszig, Walter Kurt. "Das Menuett Wolfgang Amadeus Mozarts unter dem Einfluß von Franz Joseph Haydns 'gantz neue besondere art': Zur Phrasenstruktur in den Menuetten der 'Haydn-Quartette'". In *Mozart Jahrbuch 1991: Bericht über den Internationalen Mozart Kongress 1991*. Edited by Rudolf Angermüller, Dietrich Berke, and Wolfgang Rehm. Kassel: Bärenreiter, 1992. Vol. 2, pages 655–63.

La Laurencie, Lionel de. "Les Débuts de la Musique de Chambre en France". *Revue de Musicologie* 15 (1934): 3–34, 86–96, 159–67, 204–231.

_____. *L'École Française de Violon de Lully a Viotti: Études d'Histoire et d'Esthétique*. 3 volumes. Paris: 1922–24. Reprint edition, Geneva: Minkoff Reprints, 1971.

Landon, H. C. Robbins. *Haydn: Chronicle and Works*. 5 vols. Bloomington, Indiana: Indiana University Press, 1976–80.

_____. "On Haydn's Quartets of Opera 1 and 2". *The Music Review* 13 (1952): 181–6.

Lang, Paul Henry. Review of *Studien zur Geschichte des Streichquartetts. I: Die Entstehung des klassischen Streichquartetts von der Vorformer zur Grundlegung durch Joseph Haydn*, by Ludwig Finscher. *The Musical Quarterly* 63 (1977): 133–43.

Larsen, Jens Peter. "Some Observations on the Development of Vienna Classical Instrumental Music". *Studia Musicologica* 9 (1967): 115–39.

_____. "Towards an Understanding of the Development of the Viennese Classical Style". *Report of the 11ᵗʰ IMS Conference, Copenhagen 1972.* Pages 23–33.

Larsen, Jens Peter, Howard Serwer, and James Webster, editors. *Haydn Studies: Proceedings of the International Haydn Conference, Washington D. C. 1975.* New York: W. W. Norton and Co., 1981.

Lehmann, Ursual. *Deutsches und italienisches Wesen in der Vorgeschichte des klassischen Streichquartetts.* Würzburg: Druckerei und Verlag Wissenschaftlicher Werke Konrad Triltsch, 1939.

Levy, Janet Muriel. "Gesture, Form, and Syntax in Haydn's Music". In *Haydn Studies: Proceedings of the International Haydn Conference, Washington D. C. 1975.* Edited by Jens Peter Larsen, Howard Serwer, and James Webster. New York: W. W. Norton and Co., 1981. Pages 355–62.

_____. "The Quatuor Concertant in Paris in the Latter Half of the Eighteenth Century". PhD dissertation, Stanford University, 1971.

Lippmann, Friedrich and Ludwig Finscher. "Die Streichquartett-Manuskripte der bibliothek Doria-Pamphilj in Rom". In *Studien zur Italienisch-Deutschen Musikgeschichte.* Edited by Friedrich Lippmann. Köln: Böhlau Verlag, 1969. Pages 120–44.

Little, Fiona. *The String Quartet at the Oettingen-Wallerstein Court: Ignaz von Beecke and his Contemporaries.* 2 volumes. New York: Garland Publishing Inc., 1989.

Maniates, Maria Rika. "'Sonate, que me veux-tu?': the Enigma of French Musical Aesthetics in the 18th Century". *Current Musicology* 9 (1969): 117–40.

Mattheson, Johann. *Der vollkommene Capellmeister.* Hamburg: 1739. Facsimile reprint, Kassel: Bärenreiter, 1954.

Mazurowicz, Ulrich. *Das Streichduett in Wien von 1760 bis zum Tode Joseph Haydns.* Tutzing: Schneider, 1982.

McVeigh, Simon. *Concert Life in London from Mozart to Haydn.* Cambridge: Cambridge University Press, 1993.

Meyer, Eve. "Florian Gassmann and the Viennese Divertimento". PhD dissertation, University of Pennsylvania, 1963.

_____. "The Viennese Divertimento". *The Music Review* 28 (1967): 165–71.

Milliot, Sylvette. *Que Sais Je? Le quatuor.* Paris: Presses Universitaires de France, 1986.

Moe, Jr., Orin. "The Significance of Haydn's Op. 33". In *Haydn Studies: Proceedings of the International Haydn Conference, Washington D. C. 1975.* Edited by Jens Peter Larsen, Howard Serwer, and James Webster. New York: W. W. Norton and Co., 1981. Pages 445–50.

_____. "Texture in Haydn's Early Quartets". *The Music Review* 35 (1975): 4–22.

_____. "Texture in the String Quartets of Haydn to 1787". PhD dissertation, University of California, Santa Barbara, 1970.

Mongrédien, Jean. "Paris: the End of the Ancien Régime". In *The Classical Era: From the 1740s to the end of the 18th Century.* Edited by Neal Zaslaw. Englewood Cliffs, New Jersey: Prentice Hall, 1989. Pages 61–98.

Morrow, Mary Sue. *Concert Life in Haydn's Vienna: Aspects of a Developing Musical and Social Institution.* Stuyvesant, New York: Pendragon Press, 1989.

Münster, Robert. Review of *Studien zur Geschichte des Streichquartetts. I: Die Entstehung des klassischen Streichquartetts von der Vorformer zur Grundlegung durch Joseph Haydn*, by Ludwig Finscher. *Musica* 29 (1975): 61–2.

New Grove Dictionary of Music and Musicians. 20 volumes. Edited by Stanley Sadie. London: Macmillan Publishers Limited, 1980.

Newman, William S. *The Sonata in the Baroque Era.* 4th edition. New York: W. W. Norton and Co., 1983.

_____. *The Sonata in the Classic Era.* 3rd edition. New York: W. W. Norton and Co., 1983.

Oboussier, Philippe. "The French String Quartet, 1770–1800". In *Music and the French Revolution.* Cambridge: Cambridge University Press, 1992. Pages 74–92.

_____. "Une Révélation Musicale: Les Quatuors de Hyacinthe Jadin". In *Le Tambour et la Harpe: Oeuvres, pratiques et manifestations musicales sous la Révolution.* Edited by Jean-Rémy Julien and Jean Mongrédien. Paris: Éditions du May, 1991. Pages 221–40.

Orr, N. Lee. "The Effect of Scoring on the 'Sonata-Form' in Mozart's Mature Instrumental Ensembles". *College Music Symposium* 23 (1983): 46–83.

Palm, Albert. Review of *The String Quartet: From its Beginnings to Franz Schubert*, by Wulf Konold. *Musikforschung* 39 (1986): 363–4.

Pandi, Marianne and Fritz Schmidt, compilers. "Music in Haydn's and Beethoven's Time Reported by the Pressburger Zeitung". *The Haydn Yearbook* 8 (1971): 267–93.

Papendiek, Charlotte. *Court and Private Life in the Time of Queen Charlotte.* 2 volumes. London: Bentley and Son, 1887.

Parker, Mara. "Friedrich Wilhelm II and the Classical String Quartet". *The Music Review* 54 (1993): 163–82.

_____. "Soloistic Chamber Music at the Court of Friedrich Wilhelm II, 1786–1797". PhD dissertation, University of Indiana, Bloomington, 1995.

Pauly, Reinhard. "The Reforms of Church Music under Joseph II". *The Musical Quarterly* 43 (1957): 372–82.

Pečman, Rudolf. "Alessandro Scarlatti: a predecessor of Joseph Haydn in the genre of the string quartet". In *Haydn Studies: Proceedings of the International Haydn Conference, Washington D. C. 1975.* Edited by Jens Peter Larsen, Howard Serwer, and James Webster. New York: W. W. Norton and Co., 1981. Pages 456–59.

Pilková, Zdeňka. "Haydn and his Czech Contemporary Antonín Kammel". In *Haydn Studies: Proceedings of the International Haydn Conference, Washington D. C. 1975.* Edited by Jens Peter Larsen, Howard Serwer, and James Webster. New York: W. W. Norton and Co., 1981. Pages 171–77.

Pincherle, Marc. "On the Origins of the String Quartet". *The Musical Quarterly* 15 (1929): 77–87.

Pohl, C. F. *Mozart und Haydn in London.* Vienna: Carl Gerold's Sohn, 1867.

Ratner, Leonard G. *Classic Music: Expression, Form, and Style.* New York: Schirmer Books, 1980.

_____. "Eighteenth-Century Theories of Musical Period Structure". *The Musical Quarterly* 42 (1956): 439–54.

_____. "Harmonic Aspects of Classic Form". *Journal of the American Musicological Society* 2 (1949): 159–68.

Rice, John A. "Vienna under Joseph II and Leopold II". In *The Classical Era: From the 1740s to the end of the 18th Century.* Edited by Neal Zaslaw. Englewood Cliffs, New Jersey: Prentice Hall, 1989. Pages 126–65.

Roscoe, Christopher. "Haydn and London in the 1780s". *Music and Letters* 49 (1968): 203–12.

Rosen, Charles. *The Classical Style: Haydn, Mozart, Beethoven.* New York: W. W. Norton and Co., Inc., 1972.

Rosenberg, Wolf. "Vier Spieler, vier Hörer: Zur Rezeptionsgeschichte des Streichquartetts". *HiFi-Stereophonie* 13 (1974): 243–4.

Rothweiler, Hugo. "Zur Entwicklung des Streichquartetts im Rahmen der Kammermusik des 18. Jahrhunderts". PhD dissertation, University of Tübingen, 1934.

Rowen, Ruth Halle. *Early Chamber Music*. Reprint edition, New York: Da Capo Press, 1974.

_____. "Some 18th-Century Classifications of Musical Style". *The Musical Quarterly* 33 (1947): 90–101.

Ruf, Wolfgang. "Die Kammermusik in der Musiklehre des 18. Jahrhunderts". In *Zur Entwicklung der instrumentalen Kammermusik in der 1. Hälfte des 18. Jahrhunderts*. Blankenburg/Harz: Rat des Bezirkes Magdeburg, 1984. Pages 17–22.

Sadie, Stanley. "Concert Life in Eighteenth-Century England". *Proceedings of the Royal Musical Association* 58 (1958–9): 17–30.

Salmen, Walter. *Haus- und Kammermusik: Privates Musizieren im Gesellschaftlichen Wandel zwischen 1600 und 1900*. Leipzig: VEB Deutscher Verlag für Musik, 1982.

Sandberger, Adolf. "Zur Geschichte des Haydnschen Streichquartetts". *Altbayerische Monatsschrift* 2 (1900): 41–64. Expanded in *Ausgewählte Aufsätze zur Musikgeschichte*. Munich: Drei Masken Verlag, 1921. Pages 224–65.

Saslav, Isidor. "The *alla breve* 'March': Its Evolution and Meaning in Haydn's String Quartets". In *Haydn Studies: Proceedings of the International Haydn Conference, Washington D. C. 1975*. Edited by Jens Peter Larsen, Howard Serwer, and James Webster. New York: W. W. Norton and Co., 1981. Pages 308–14.

Schlötterer, Reinhold. "Ein Beispiel zu Mozarts 'Compositions-Wissenschaft' im Streichquartett G-Dur KV 387". In *Mozart Jahrbuch 1991: Bericht über den Internationalen Mozart Kongress 1991*. Edited by Rudolf Angermüller, Dietrich Berke, and Wolfgang Rehm. Kassel: Bärenreiter, 1991. Vol. 2, pages 650–4.

Schwartz, Boris. "Beethovens Opus 18 und Haydns Streichquartette". In *Bericht über den Internationalen Musikwissenschaftlichen Kongress Bonn 1970*. Edited by Carl Dahlhaus, Hans Joachim Marx, Magda Marx-Weber, and Günther Massenkeil. Kassel: Bärenreiter, 1971. Pages 75–9.

Scott, Hugh Arthur. "London Concerts from 1700–1750". *The Musical Quarterly* 24 (1938): 194–209.

Seidel, Wilhelm. "Haydns Streichquartett in B-dur Op. 71 Nr. 1 (Hob. III: 69): Analytische Bemerkungen aus der Sicht Heinrich Christoph Kochs". In *Joseph Haydn Tradition und Rezeption*. Edited by Georg Feder, Heinrich Hüschen, and Ulrich Tank. Regensburg: Gustav Bosse, 1985.

_____. "Sechs musikalische Charaktere zu den Joseph Haydn gewidmeten Streichquartetten von Wolfgang Amadeus Mozart". *Mozart Jahrbuch* (1984/85): 125–30.

Seiffert, Wolf-Dieter. "Vom Streichquartett zum Streichquintett: Satztechnische Bezüge zwischen kammermusikalischen Früh- und Spätwerk bei Mozart". In *Mozart Jahrbuch 1991: Bericht über den Internationalen Mozart Kongress 1991*. Edited by Rudolf Angermüller, Dietrich Berke, and Wolfgang Rehm. Kassel: Bärenreiter, 1991. Vol. 2, pages 671–7.

Siegmund-Schultze, Walther. "Die Entwicklung der Kammermusik in der zweiten Hälfte des 18. Jahrhunderts". In *Zur Entwicklung der Kammermusik in der zweiten Hälfte des 18. Jahrhunderts*. Blankenburg: Michaelstein, 1986. Pages 8–11.

Sisman, Elaine R. *Haydn and the Classical Variation*. Cambridge, Mass.: Harvard University Press, 1993.

Sjoerdsma, Richard Dale. "The Instrumental Works of Franz Christoph Neubauer (1760–1795)". PhD dissertation, Ohio State University, 1970.

Snook-Luther, Susan Cook, translator. *The Musical Dilettante: A Treatise on Composition by J. F. Daube*. Cambridge: Cambridge University Press, 1992.

Somfai, László. "A Bold Enharmonic Modulatory Model in Joseph Haydn's String Quartets". In *Studies in Eighteenth-Century Music: A Tribute to Karl Geiringer on his Seventieth Birthday*. Edited by H. C. Robbins Landon and Roger E. Chapman. New York: Oxford University Press, 1970. Pages 370–81.

_____. "Haydn at the Esterházy Court". In *The Classical Era: From the 1740s to the end of the 18th Century*. Edited by Neal Zaslaw. Englewood Cliffs, New Jersey: Prentice Hall, 1989. Pages 268–92.

_____. "'Ich war nie ein Geschwindschreiber . . .' Joseph Haydns Streichquartetts Hoboken III: 33". In *Festschrift Jens Peter Larsen*. København: Wilhelm Hansen Musik-Forlag, 1992. Pages 275–84.

_____. "'Learned Style' in Two Late String Quartet Movements of Haydn". *Studia musicologica* 28 (1986): 325–49.

Somfai, László. "The London Revision of Haydn's Instrumental Style". *Proceedings of the Royal Musical Association* 100 (1973–4): 159–74.

_____. "Zur Aufführungspraxis der frühen Streichquartett-Divertimenti Haydns". In *Der Junge Haydn: Wandel von Musikauffassung und Musikaufführung in der Österreichischen Musik zwischen Barock und Klassik*. Edited by Vera Schwarz. Graz: Akademische Druck- u. Verlangsanstalt, 1972. Pages 86–97.

Speck, Christian. *Boccherinis Streichquartette: Studien zur Kompositionsweise und zur Gattunggeschichtlichen Stellung*. München: Wilhelm Fink Verlag, 1987.

_____. "Mozart und Boccherini: Zur Frage der Italianita in Mozarts frühen Streichquartetten". In *Internationaler Musikwissenschaftlicher Kongreß zum Mozartjahr 1991 Baden–Wien*. Edited by Ingrid Fuchs. Tutzing: Hans Schneider, 1993. Vol. 2, pages 921–31.

_____. "On the changes in the four-part Writing in Boccherini's String Quartets". In *España en la Música de Occidente*. Vol. 2: *Actas del Congresso Internacional celebrado en Salamanca 29 de octobre – 5 de noviembre de 1985*. Edited by Emilio Casares Rodicio, Ismael Fernández de la Cuesta and José López-Calo. Madrid: Instituto Nacional de las Artes Escénicas y de la Música, 1987. Pages 129–31.

Stegemann, Michael. "Luigi Boccherini: Ein Genie im Abseits der musikalischen Klassik". *Neue Zeitschrift für Musik* 146 (1985): 4–9.

Steinbeck, Wolfram. "Mozarts 'Scherzi' zur Beziehung zwischen Haydns Streichquartetten Op. 33 und Mozarts 'Haydn-quartetten'". In *Joseph Haydn Tradition und Rezeption*. Edited by Georg Feder, Heinrich Hüschen, and Ulrich Tank. Regensburg: Gustav Bosse Verlag, 1985. Pages 14–16.

Temperley, Nicholas, ed. "Preface". In *Recent Researches in the Music of the Classic Era*. Vol. 25: *Tommaso Giordani: Three Quintets for Keyboard and Strings*. Madison, WI: A–R Editions, 1987.

Tilmouth, Michael. Review of *The String Quartet* by Paul Griffiths. *Music and Letters* 65/4 (1984): 410–12.

Trimpert, Dieter Lutz. *Die Quatuors concertants von Giuseppe Cambini*. Tutzing: Hans Schneider, 1967.

Unverricht, Hubert. "Das Divertimento für Streicher". In *Zur Entwicklung des Kammermusik in der zweiten Hälfte des 18. Jahrhunderts*. Blankenburg: Michaelstein, 1986. Pages 66–71.

_____. "Das Generalbassspiel im Streichtrio und Streichquartett der Klassik". In *Generalbassspiel im 17. und 18. Jahrhunderts*. Blankenburg/Harz: Kultur-und Forschungsstatte Michaelstein, 1987. Pages 43–7.

_____. *Die Kammermusik*. Köln: Arno Volk Verlag, 1972.

Unverricht, Hubert. "Privates Quartettspiel in Schlesien von 1780 bis 1850". In *Musica Privata: Die Rolle der Musik im privaten Leben: Festschrift zum 65. Geburtstag von Walter Salmen*. Edited by Monika Fink, Rainer Gstrein, and Günter Mössmer. Innsbruck: Helbling, 1991. Pages 105–12.

Van Oort, Bart. "The English Classical Piano Style and its Influence on Haydn and Beethoven". PhD dissertation, Cornell University, 1993.

Viano, Richard J. "By Invitation Only: Private Concerts in France during the second half of the eighteenth century". *Recherches sur la Musique française classique* 27 (1991–92): 131–62.

_____. "Jean-Baptiste Bréval (1753-1823): Life, Milieu, and Chamber Works with Editions of Ten Compositions and Thematic Catalogue". PhD dissertation, City University of New York, 1983.

Vit, Peter. "Jan Zachs Quartettsinfonien – Kompositionen zwischen Sinfonie und Streichquartett". In *Musikzentren–Konzertschaffen im 18. Jahrhundert*. Blankenburg/Harz: Abt. Kultur, Kultur- und Forschungsstätte Michaelstein, 1984. Pages 58–60.

Von Fischer, Kurt. "Wienerklassik und Musikalische Dramatik: Bemerkungen zu den Letzten Sätzen von Haydns Op. 33, Nr. 5 und Mozarts d-moll Streichquartett KV421 (417b)". In *Evropski Glasbeni Klasicizem in Njegov Odmev na Slovenskem*. Ljubljana: Forschungsgemeinschaft Sloweniens, 1988. Pages 25–9.

Walter, Horst. "Haydn gewidmete Streichquartette". In *Joseph Haydn: Tradition und Rezeption*. Edited by Georg Feder, Heinrich Hüschen, and Ulrich Tank. Regensburg: Gustav Bosse Verlag, 1985. Pages 17–53.

Walter, Rudolf. "Die Autobiographie des Chordirektors von St. Maria auf dem Sande in Breslau Ignatz Lukas (1762–1837)". *Musik des Ostens* 8 (1982): 85–105.

Weber, William. "London: a City of Unrivalled Riches". In *The Classical Era: From the 1740s to the end of the 18th Century*. Edited by Neal Zaslaw. Englewood Cliffs, New Jersey: Prentice Hall, 1989. Pages 292–326.

_____. "The Muddle of the Middle Classes". *19th–Century Music* 3 (1979–80): 175–85.

Webster, Jr, James Carson. "The Bass Part in Haydn's Early String Quartets and in Austrian Chamber Music 1750–1780". PhD dissertation, Princeton University, 1973.

_____. "The Chronology of Haydn's String Quartets". *The Musical Quarterly* 61 (1975): 17–46.

_____. *Haydn's "Farewell" Symphony and the Idea of Classical Style*. Cambridge: Cambridge University Press, 1991.

_____. "Haydn's Symphonies Between *Sturm und Drang* and 'Classical Style': Art and Entertainment". In *Haydn Studies*. Edited by W. Dean Sutcliffe. United Kingdom: Cambridge University Press, 1998. Pages 218–45.

_____. Review of *Studien zur Geschichte des Streichquartetts. I: Die Entstehung des klassischen Streichquartetts von der Vorformer zur Grundlegung durch Joseph Haydn*, by Ludwig Finscher. *Journal of the American Musicological Society* 28 (1975): 543–49.

_____. "The Scoring of Mozart's Chamber Music for Strings". In *Music in the Classic Period: Essays in Honor of Barry S. Brook*. Edited by Allan W. Atlas. New York: Pendragon Press, 1985. Pages 259–97.

_____. "Toward a History of Viennese Chamber Music in the Early Classical Period". *Journal of the American Musicological Society* 17 (1974): 212–47.

_____. "Violoncello and Double Bass in the Chamber Music of Haydn and his Viennese Contemporaries, 1750–1780". *The Musical Quarterly* 29 (1976): 413–38.

Wiesel, Siegfried. "Klangfarbendramaturgie in den Streichquartetten von Joseph Haydn". *Haydn Studien* 5 (1982): 16–22.

Wolff, Christoph, ed. *The String Quartets of Haydn, Mozart and Beethoven: Studies of the Autograph Manuscipts.* Cambridge, Mass.: Harvard University Press, 1980.

Woodham, Ronald. Review of *Studien zur Geschichte des Streichquartetts. I: Die Entstehung des klassischen Streichquartetts von der Vorformer zur Grundlegung durch Joseph Haydn*, by Ludwig Finscher. *Erasmus* 28 (1976): 289–92.

Zaslaw, Neal. "Music and Society in the Classical Era". In *The Classical Era: From the 1740s to the end of the 18th Century.* Edited by Neal Zaslaw. Englewood Cliffs, New Jersey: Prentice Hall, 1989. Pages 1–14.

Index

Abel, Karl Friedrich, 138, 203, 248, 272, 287, 289
Academy of Ancient Music, The, 37, 38
Albrechtsberger, Johann Georg, 206, 248, 263
  Divertimento [in A], 77
  Divertimento V, 76
  Divertimento VI, 76
  Op. 2, 80, 237
  Op. 7, 80, 185, 237
Allegri, Gregorio, 1, 3
amateur, 11, 12, 26, 27, 30, 32, 33, 35, 37, 40, 42, 44–5, 52, 53, 59, 75, 88, 94, 100, 101, 105, 117, 118, 125, 127, 138, 201, 203, 205, 238, 253, 266, 281, 282, 283
Anacreonic Society, 39
Asplmayr, Franz, 248
  Op. 2, 77
Associiierten Cavaliers, 41

Bach, Johann Christian, 2, 138, 272, 287
Bagge, Charles Ernest, Baron de, 34–6, 283
Bambini, Felice, 31
Barrière, Etienne-Bernard-Joseph, 128
Baudron, Antoine Laurent, 34, 52, 248, 283
  Sei Quartetti, 127, 133–5
Beck, Franz, 31
Beecke, Ignaz von, 5, 44, 76, 233, 248, 266–7, 269, 283
  M1, 266, 267–9
  M2, 78
  M3, 82, 186
  M5, 186
  M6, 79, 185
  M9, 185
  M11, 77
  M13, 78

  M14, 80
  M15, 82
  M16, 82
  M17, 78
Benavente-Osuna, 284
Benda, Friedrich
  Quartetto in Eb, 83
  Quartetto in F, 83
Besozzi, Gaetano, 36
Blake, Benjamin, 39
Boccherini, Luigi, 3, 29, 31, 36, 52, 76, 101, 105, 121, 263, 283–4
  G.159, 127
  G.160, 127
  G.161, 77, 127, 236
  G.162, 77
  G.163, 184, 236
  G.164, 184, 236
  G.165, 77, 105, 111–12
  G.166, 77, 236
  G.167, 77
  G.168, 128, 235, 236, 239–41
  G.170, 236, 239
  G.171, 77
  G.174, 77
  G.190, 79, 129
  G.192, 79, 129
  G.206, 80, 237, 264
  G.207, 80
  G.208, 80
  G.209, 80, 130
  G.210, 130
  G.211, 130
  G.212, 130
  G.213, 59–60, 81
  G.214, 237
  G.215, 81, 131, 237
  G.216, 82, 131
  G.217, 82
  G.218, 82

G.219, 82
G.220, 83, 105–10
G.221, 83
G.222, 83, 273–5
G.223, 83, 132
G.224, 83
G.225, 83
G.226, 83
G.227, 83, 133
G.228, 83
G.230, 83
G.231, 83
G.233, 238
G.234, 83, 187
G.235, 187, 238
G.237, 187, 282
Op. 2, 235
Op. 8, 105, 235
Bonnheimer, 42
Borghi, Luigi, 39
Braganza, Duke of, 28, 29
Bréval, Jean-Baptiste Sébastien, 32, 34,
        138, 284
    Op. 1, *Six Quatuors concertantes*, 79,
        138–41, 281
    Op. 18, 143, 146–8
Brühl, Count, 28, 29, 288
Brunetti, Gaetano, 110, 112–13, 233, 248,
        284
    Op. 2, 79, 128, 185
    Op. 3, 79, 128
    Op. 4, 212–14
    Quartet in A Major (F Pn 1636, 4), 82,
        113–16, 258–62
    Quartet in g (F Pn 1637, 5), 82,
        112–16, 132
Bullant, Antoine, 52
Burkhöffer, J. G., 31
Burney, Charles, 17, 28, 29, 30, 35, 40,
        43, 44, 45, 288

Cambini, Giuseppe Maria, 3, 4, 29, 31, 39,
        52, 76, 138, 248, 284
    T.1 [Op. 1, No. 1], 79, 128
    T.13, 128
    T.14, 128
    T.15, 129
    T.16, 129
    T.17, 129
    T.18, 129, 138–9

T.25, 129
T.26, 129
T.27, 129
T.28, 72, 129, 150, 157–61
T.29, 129
T.30, 129
T.37, 129
T.38, 129
T.39, 129
T.40, 129
T.41, 129
T.42, 129
T.43, 80, 130
T.44, 130
T.45, 80, 130, 237, 269–72
T.46, 80, 130, 237
T.47, 80, 130
T.48, 130
T.55, 129
T.56, 129
T.57, 129, 150–56
T.58, 129
T.59, 130
T.60, 130
T.78, 130
T.79, 130
T.80, 130
T.97, 130
T.98, 130
T.99, 130
T.100, 130
T.101, 130
T.102, 130
Camerloher, Placidus Cajetan von, 101,
        285, 248
    Op. 3, 101
    Op. 4, 76, 101
    Sinfonia a 4tro [in C; Op. 3], 76,
        102–04
    Sinfonia a 4tro [in G; Op. 3], 76
Canavas, Joseph-Baptiste, 31
Cannabich, Christian, 2, 49, 52, 138
    Op. 5, 80, 237
Capron, Nicolas, 36
cassatio, 1, 13, 18
Castle-Society of Music, 37
Chabral, Comte, 36
chamber music, 1, 4, 6–13, 14, 15, 16, 17,
        18–23, 26, 28, 29, 30, 31, 33, 35,
        37, 40, 41, 42, 47, 48, 50, 55, 56,

74, 260, 264, 275, 284, 287, 288
Charles III, 284
Charles IV, 284
Charlotte, Queen, 40
Chartrain, Nicolas-Joseph, 148, 285
   Op. 4, *Six Quatuors Dialoguées*, 79,
     129, 148–50, 185, 215–17
   Op. 8, *Six Quatuors Concertant*, 79,
     129, 237
Choral Fund, 38
Concert d'Amis, 32-3
Concert des Amateurs, 32, 33
Concert des Associés, 33
Concert spirituel, 32, 33, 36, 284, 285,
   287
concertante, 22, 27, 53
concerto a quattro, 2, 3
Concerts de la Rue de Cléry, 33
Concerts de la Rue Grenelle, 33
Concerts of Ancient Music, 38
Conti, Prince de, 34, 35
conversation, 4, 20, 21, 22, 23, 34, 35, 50,
     51, 57, 60, 65, 105, 125, 133,
     138, 142, 178, 181, 189, 206,
     209, 221, 229, 235–78, 279, 280,
     281
Corelli, Arcangelo, 9, 10
Corporation of the Sons of the Clergy,
   The, 38
Cramer, Wilhelm, 29, 39, 44
Crown and Anchor Tavern, 37
Crozat, Antoine, 34
Custine, Marquise de, 36

d'Aiguillon, Duke, 35
d'Albaret, Count, 35
d'Arantés, Duchesse, 36
d'Arlincourt, Vicomte, 36
d'Epinay, Madame de, 34
d'Hilheis, Comtesse Baraguay, 36
D'Ogny, Baron, 35
Dalayrac, Nicolas-Marie, 52, 138, 172,
   285
   Op. 5, 130, 237
   Op. 7, 80, 130
   Op. 8, 130, 172–8, 237
   Op. 11, 130
Danzi, Franz, 110, 285
   Opp. 5–6, 82, 118–20

Daube, Johann, 6, 7, 11
Davaux, Jean-Baptiste, 52, 248
   Op. 6, 78, 128
   Op. 9, 129
debate, 34, 57, 60, 65–6,99, 117, 124, 125,
     148, 170, 178, 183–233, 243,
     248, 258, 266, 267, 269, 275, 280
Devienne, François, 36
dialogué, 35, 50, 51, 139, 148
Distler, Johann Georg
   Book II, Quartet No. 5, 57–8, 60, 61
   Opp. 1–2, 83, 133, 187
Dittersdorf, Karl Ditters von, 17, 28, 44,
     120, 206, 221, 285, 289
   Sei Quartetti, 81, 186, 221–6
divertimento, 1, 2, 3, 4, 5, 13–18, 19, 54,
     55, 98, 206
Domanowecz, Nikolaus Zmeskall von, 44
Domnich, Heinrich, 31
Duchess of Northumberland, 40
Duport, Jean-Louis, 36
Durand, August, 36

Elisabeth of Württemberg, Princess, 183
Esterházá Quartet, 29, 39
Esterházy, Prince Paul Anton, 39
Eugen von Württemberg, Duke Friedrich,
   183
Eybler, Joseph Leopold, 83, 187, 238

Feodorovna, Maria, 183
Ferdinand, Prince, 183
Fiala, Joseph, 283
   Op. 1, 81, 131
Filtz, (Johann) Anton, 52, 248, 263
   Quadro in G, 76
   Quatri [in A], 76
   Quatro [in Bb], 76
   Quattro [in F], 76
Fiorillo, Federigo, 283
   Op. 6, 82, 131
Fodor, Josephus Andreas (J. Fodor
     l'Aîne), 52, 233
   Book 4, 80, 130, 131, 185, 237
   Op. 11, 82, 132
Font family, 29, 39
Förster, Emanuel Aloys, 54
Fränzl, Ferdinand, 26, 285
   Op. 1, *Six quatuors*, 82, 83, 132, 150,
     168–70

Friedrich of Saxe-Hildeburghausen, Prince
        Joseph, 42
Friedrich Wilhelm II, 25, 44, 243, 254,
        284
fugue, 21, 23, 206, 260, 263, 264

Gassmann, Florian Leopold, 16, 30, 42,
        206, 248, 250, 263, 286
    H.431, 77
    H.435, 77, 236, 281
    H.461, 77, 184
    H.467, 77
    H.471, 77
    H.475, 77
    H.476, 77
    H.478, 236, 250–53
    H.480, 77, 127, 184
    Merope, 286
Gaviniés, Pierre, 36, 283
Gay, Sophie, 36
Genlis, Madame de, 34, 35, 36
George III, 40
Gesellschaft der Musikfreunde, 41
Giardini, Felice de, 40, 248
    Op. 14, 60, 62–5, 77, 128, 236
    Op. 23, 72, 131
    Op. 29, 132, 186, 282
Giordani, Tommaso, 141, 233, 286
    Op. 2, 141
    Op. 8, 79, 128, 141–2, 185
Giornovichi, Giovanni, 36
Girarden, Emile de, 36
Glee Clubs, 38
Gluck, Christoph Willibald, 31, 286
Gossec, François-Joseph, 36, 52, 138, 285
    Op. 15, 78
Graf, Christian Ernst, 248
    Quartetto a F, 77, 128
Graziani, Carlo, 31, 36
Grétry, André-Ernest-Modeste, 285
    Op. 3, 76, 127, 236
Guéménée, Prince de, 34, 35
Gyrowetz, Adalbert, 26, 39, 52, 53, 56,
        110, 120–21, 286
    Trois Quatuors Concertants (Op. 3),
        82, 83, 121, 132

Hanslick, Eduard, 29
Hausmusik, 11, 26, 30, 47–8, 49, 52, 53,
        105

Haydn, (Franz) Joseph, 1, 2, 3, 4, 5, 14,
        17, 19, 22, 23, 25, 27, 28, 29, 39,
        42, 43, 44, 48, 53, 54, 55, 56, 73,
        75, 76, 88, 94, 100, 101, 105,
        125, 178, 193, 194, 201, 205,
        218, 233, 248, 279, 280, 282,
        287, 288, 289
    Op. 1, 50, 76, 236, 2281
    Op. 2, 76, 184
    Op. 9, 55, 77, 184
    Op. 17, 55, 78, 184
    Op. 20, 55, 78, 183, 184, 236, 263–4
    Op. 33, 1, 2, 3, 4, 6, 17, 44, 55, 80,
        123, 183, 185, 188–92, 235, 237,
        279, 288
    Op. 42, 81, 186, 237
    Op. 50, 81, 183, 186, 237, 243–48
    Opp. 54–55 ("Tost" Quartets), 81,
        123–4, 186, 237, 273, 275–8
    Op. 64, 39, 82, 183, 186
    Opp. 71/74, 83, 187, 238, 256, 258–9
    Op. 76, 56, 84, 187, 238, 264
Haydn, (Johann) Michael , 76
    MH. 308, 79, 185
    MH. 309, 80
    MH. 310, 83
    MH. 311, 81, 131
    MH. 312, 81, 131
    MH. 313, 80, 185
Hindmarsch, 39, 40
Hoffmann, Leopold, 42
Hoffmeister, Franz Anton, 41, 45, 52, 53,
        101, 168, 287, 289
    Op. 9, 72–3, 131, 150, 161–8
    Op. 14, 83, 132, 187, 192–4
Holzbauer, Ignaz, 263
Huber, Karl, 288
Huber, Thaddäus, 188

Jadin, Hyacinthe, 52, 233, 287
    Opp. 1–4, 83, 187, 201–203
Joseph II, Emperor, 41, 43, 206, 250

Kammel, Antonín, 52, 75, 233, 248, 287
    Op. 4, *Six quatuors concertants*, 38,
        75, 77, 84–8, 184
Koch, Heinrich Christoph, 6, 7, 12, 20, 21,
        23, 50, 56, 57
Kozeluch, Leopold, 26, 39, 42, 45, 52,
        233, 288

Opp. 32–33, 82, 187
Kraft, Anton, 43
Kreibich, Franz, 42
Kreusser, Georg Anton, 138
  Op. 9, No. 5, 129
Kreutzer, Rodolphe, 36
Krommer, Franz, 26, 53, 54, 172, 178,
  263, 287
  Op. 1, 83, 132
  Op. 3, 132
  Op. 4, 133, 178–80, 187
  Op. 5, 83, 133, 187, 229–31, 238,
    264–6
  Op. 7, 84, 187, 238
  Op. 19, 56
Krottendorfer, Joseph, 42

L'Augier, M., 28, 29
La Pouplinière, Alexandre-Jean-Joseph le
  Riche, 34, 35, 36
Lancy, Madame de, 36
la Tour de Pin, Madame, 36
lecture, 57–60, 65, 75–125, 127, 139, 142,
  148, 161, 168, 170, 178, 183,
  189, 191, 193, 198, 203, 206,
  209, 221, 226, 227, 238, 239,
  243, 248, 250, 266, 267, 269,
  275, 280, 281
Lichnowsky, Prince, 43, 44
London, 13, 30, 31, 36, 37–40, 41, 49,
  116, 123, 248, 256, 272, 275,
  286, 287, 288
London Tavern, 37
Lukas, Ignatz, 28

Madrigal Society, The, 38
Manfredi, Filippo, 29, 36
Mara, Gertrud, 36, 40
Mary-le-bone Gardens, 37
Mattheson, Johann, 6, 7, 12
Menell, 39, 40
Miroglio, Pierre, 31
Monn, Matthias Georg, 206, 263
Morellet, L'Abbé André, 50–51
  De la conversation, 50
"motivische Arbeit", 1, 2, 188, 263
Mountain, 39
Mozart, Wolfgang Amadeus, 2, 5, 23, 25,
  27, 28, 29, 31, 36, 42, 44, 53, 54,
  56, 73, 75, 76, 94, 100, 101, 125,

183, 205, 226, 233, 256, 263,
  279, 280, 282, 287, 289
"Haydn" Quartets, 55, 98, 183, 217–9,
  279
K.80, 77
K.155, 78, 94, 98–9
K.156, 78, 184
K.157, 78
K.158, 184, 236
K.159, 78, 184
K.160,78, 184
K.168, 78, 184, 236
K.169, 78, 184
K.170, 78
K.171, 78, 184, 236
K.172, 78, 184, 236
K.173, 78, 184
K.387, 185, 237, 264
K.421, 185
K.428, 185, 237
K.458, 100, 185, 217, 219–21
K.464, 185, 237
K.485, 185
K.499,185
K.575, 237
K.589, 186, 237
K.590, 186, 237, 253–57
music functions (eighteenth-century
  conception), 7–9
music printing, 17, 45

Nardini, Pietro, 29
Necker, Madame, 36
Neubauer, Franz Christoph, 75, 94, 138,
  287
  Op. 3, 132, 238
  Op. 7, 83, 94–8, 187, 238, 272
New Musical Fund, 38, 39
Noailles, Maréchal, 35
Noblemen and Gentlemen Catch-Club,
  The, 38
Nodier, Charles, 36
Norden, Countess von, 43
notturno, 1, 13, 18

Oettingen-Wallerstein, 44, 283, 289
Ordonez, Carlo d', 29, 42, 43, 206, 248,
  263, 288
  Op. 1, 77, 127, 184, 206–208, 236,
    241–3

ouverture à quatre, 18

Pantheon Hall, 38
Papendiek, Charlotte, 40
Paris, 30, 31–6, 37, 38, 41, 45, 48, 49, 52,
    116, 283, 284, 285, 286, 287, 288
partita, 3, 13
Patachich, Prince Bishop Adam, 285
Philidor, Anne-Danican, 33
Piccolomini, Princess, 28
Pichl, Václav, 206, 288
    Op. 13, 81, 82, 131, 168, 170–72, 186
Pleyel, Ignace Joseph, 26, 27, 39, 41, 42,
    48, 52, 53, 75, 76, 88, 101, 121,
    141, 218, 288, 289
  Ben 301, 80
  Ben 302, 80, 88–93
  Ben 303, 80
  Ben 304, 80
  Ben 305, 80
  Ben 306, 80
  Ben 313, 81
  Ben 314, 81, 131, 135–7
  Ben 315, 81
  Ben 316, 81, 185
  Ben 317, 81, 131
  Ben 318, 81
  Ben 319, 235, 237
  Ben 320, 131, 186
  Ben 321, 131
  Ben 322, 81
  Ben 323, 131, 186
  Ben 324, 81, 131, 186
  Ben 343, 82, 131, 186
  Ben 344, 186
  Ben 346, 82, 122–3, 186
  Ben 347, 82, 131, 142–5
  Ben 349, 131
polite conversation, 57, 72, 127–81, 183,
    192, 203, 206, 209, 229, 230,
    239, 249, 269, 280
Prince of Wales, 40, 120
Professional Concerts, 38
professional musician, 26, 27, 29, 30, 35,
    48, 52, 53, 125, 188
Proksch, Gaspard, 31
public concert, 25, 30, 36, 37, 38, 39, 41,
    47, 53, 266

quadro, 1, 3, 13, 17, 18, 29

quartet divertimento, 3, 18
quartet parties, 28, 37, 40, 43
quartet symphony, 3, 18
quatuor brillant, 3, 48, 52–3, 54
quatuor concertant, 2, 3, 4, 22, 23, 49–52,
    53, 54, 73, 120, 121, 127, 136,
    148, 172, 194, 279, 284
Quatuors d'airs connues, 48
Quatuors d'airs dialogués, 48
Quatuors en Symphonie, 49
quatuors et simphonies á 4 parties, 49

Rameau, Jean-Philippe, 36
Ranelagh Gardens, 37
Rasumofsky, Prince, 43, 44
Reccamier, Madame de, 36
Reicha, Anton, 51
Reutter, Georg von, 286
Richter, Franz Xaver, 28, 31, 288–9
    Op. 5, 17, 76, 184, 235, 236, 245,
    248–50
Rigel, Henri-Jean, 31
Rigel, Henri-Joseph, 31
Ritter, Georg Wenzel, 31
Ritter, Peter, 25
Rochechouart, M. de, 35
Rode, Pierre. 36
Roeser, Valentin, 31
Rosetti, Antonio, 31, 283
Royal Society of Musicians of Great
    Britain, 38
Ruge, Filippo, 31

Saint-Georges, Joseph-Boulogne de, 52
Salomon, Johann Peter, 39, 40, 256
Sammartini, Giuseppe, 2
Scarlatti, Alessandro, 1, 3
Schaffgotsch, Fürstbischof Philipp
    Gotthard Graf, 28, 285
Schenker, Mademoiselle, 31
Schmitt, Joseph, 32, 248, 289
    Op. 5, *Six quatuors*, 78, 79, 124–5,
    184, 198, 237
    "Quartetto" in G Major, 198–201
Schobert, Johann, 31
Schuppanzigh, Ignaz, 41, 43
Seignelai, Marquis de, 35
serenade, 13, 18
Sharp, William, 40
Sina, Louis, 43

sinfonia, 13, 18
sinfonia a quattro, 206
*Société académique des Enfants
    d'Apollon, 33*
Société de la Loge Olympique, 33
Society of Musicians, The (Musical Fund
    Society), 38
sonata, 8, 9, 10, 11, 13, 14, 21, 31, 38, 39,
    41, 280
sonata a quattro, 3, 13, 18
sonata da camera, 8, 9, 10
sonata da chiesa, 8, 9, 10, 206
Sonnleithner, Christoph, 206
Spiess, Meinrad, 6, 7, 10
Spohr, Ludwig, 29
St. Cecilian Society, 37
Staël, Madame de, 36
Stamitz, Anton, 31, 138
Stamitz, Carl, 31, 52
Stamitz, Johann, 31, 36
Starzer, Joseph , 248, 288
Stich, Johann Wenzel, 31, 36
Stormoht, Lord, 28
Strack, Johann Kilian, 42
Swieten, Baron Gottfried van, 41, 42
symphonie concertante, 49, 284
symphonie en quatuor, 18

Tartini, Giuseppe, 2
Teyber, Anton, 206, 209, 289
    Op. 1, 209
    Op. 2, 82, 132, 186, 209–12
Théâtre de Monsieur, 287
Théâtre Feydeau, 33, 284
Theodor, Carl, 289
Thun, Count and Countess, 29, 288
Todi, Luiza, 36
Tomasini, Luigi, 29, 43, 188
Tonkünstler-Societät, 41, 286, 288
Tost, Johann, 123–4, 273, 275

Umlauff, Ignaz, 42

Vachon, Pierre, 2, 52, 110, 116–7, 194,
    216, 248
    Op. 5, 79, 128, 185, 203–205
    Op. 7, 79, 128, 184, 185
    Op. 11, 80–81, 117–118, 131, 123,
        185, 195–8
Valmoden, General, 28

Vanhal, Johann Baptist, 28, 44, 52, 57–8,
    76, 100–101, 206, 221, 248, 263,
    289
    A1, 78, 185, 227–9
    A4 [Op. 33, No. 2], 81
    Bb10 [Op. 33, No. 6], 81
    c1, 80, 185, 237
    c2 [Op. 1, No. 4], 57–9, 77
    C1 [Op. 13, No. 2], 78
    C7 [Op. 33, No. 1],81, 237
    D3, 77
    Eb11, 81, 185
    E1, 78, 100
    F6, 78
    F11, 77
    g2, 81, 185
    G7 [Op. 24, No. 2], 80
    G8, 80
    Op. 6, 100
Vauxhall Gardens, 33, 37
Vienna, 15, 16, 17, 28, 30, 31, 32, 38,
    41–5, 53, 55, 56, 209, 250, 285,
    286, 287, 288, 289
Viennese quartet, 3, 5, 52, 53–6, 73, 105,
    209, 227
Vigée-Lebrun, Madame, 34, 36
Viotti, Giovanni Battista, 33, 52
Vogler, Georg Joseph, 288

Walter, Johann, 7
Weigl, Joseph, 29, 43, 188, 288
Weiss, Franz, 43
Wendling, Johann Baptist, 31
Woborschil, Johann, 286
Woborzill, Thomas, 42
Wölfl, Josef, 52, 54
Wranitzky, Anton, 53, 54
Wranitzky, Paul, 26, 52, 53, 54, 288
    Op. 10, 82, 186
    Op. 15, 56
    Op. 23, 65–71, 83, 132, 187
    Quartet in A, 186

Zach, Jan, 248, 282
    Sinfonia I, 76
    Sinfonia II, 76
    Sinfonia III, 76
    Sinfonia IV, 76
    Sinfonia V, 76
Zimmermann, Anton, 236